AND IT WAS
BEAUTIFUL

AND IT WAS BEAUTIFUL

Marcelo Bielsa and the Rebirth of Leeds United

PHIL HAY

SEVEN DIALS

First published in Great Britain in 2021 by Seven Dials
an imprint of The Orion Publishing Group Ltd
Carmelite House, 50 Victoria Embankment
London EC4Y 0DZ

An Hachette UK Company

1 3 5 7 9 10 8 6 4 2

A CIP catalogue record for this book is
available from the British Library.

ISBN (Hardback) 978 1 8418 8516 2
ISBN (eBook) 978 1 8418 8518 6

Typeset by Input Data Services Ltd, Somerset

Printed and bound in Great Britain by Clays Ltd, Elcograf S.p.A.

www.orionbooks.co.uk

For my two centre-forwards, Isla and Niamh.

CONTENTS

Foreword by Victor Orta   ix

Introduction   1

 1. September   7
 2. The Appointment   21
 3. October   37
 4. The Revolution   55
 5. November   69
 6. The Demise   85
 7. December   113
 8. Murderball   129
 9. January   145
10. Analysis   157
11. February   177
12. Right-hand Men   189
13. March   205
14. The Hierarchy   217
15. April/May   231
16. Bielsa   247

Acknowledgements   259
Sources   263
Picture Credits   273

FOREWORD
by Victor Orta

In the summer of 1986, while my mother and father were busy with work, I spent most of the holidays with my two brothers. They were older than me, nine or ten years older, and you know how it is when you're 16 or 17 and your little kid brother is always with you. He's annoying, no? In Spain we have a famous card game called Mus and I would go with them when they went to play it with friends. I annoyed them by ruining the game, by doing the wrong things with the cards. We were at this kiosk and the guy who owned it, he saw what was happening and he gave me a box with maybe a hundred packets of football cards in it. I was seven years old and it was the first time I thought about football.

The cards were the faces of the players at World Cup '86. I looked through them all and started to do a bit of a challenge with my brothers. They would pull a card out, say the name on it and I would try to tell them which nation they played for and which club. So Enzo Francescoli, Uruguay and River Plate; Cha Bum-kun, South Korea, Bayer Leverkusen; Alemão, Brazil, who would go on and play at Napoli. I would do this with their friends too. I was good at it. 'You choose a card and I'll tell you this, this and this.' It earned me acceptance from older people and every kid likes that. I thought then that football could be my passion, something to love.

Am I a football romantic? Absolutely. The day I wake up and don't feel passion for football, I'll go home and do something else, like chemistry or something different. I'm still like the young Victor Orta who went to the hotels in Madrid where teams were staying to get their autographs. Lots of us did that when a big team from Europe arrived. It was normal. But sometimes, with smaller teams, I would be the only one there. One day, Racing Santander arrived to play Atlético Madrid. At the hotel, it was just me. Some of the Racing Santander players recognised me (because they'd seen me before) and said, 'Victor, you are always here. Every time we come, we see you. Why?' Because I had an album with a photograph of different footballers with a space for their autograph underneath. I had to fill them all in so I would wait for hours if I had to. It made my day. Sometimes it made my week.

A total passion for football is what many people see in Marcelo Bielsa. I see it too. When I first started to learn about Marcelo, he was a reference for a lot of things that were developing in football. Technical secretaries and scouting departments were not things people spoke about when he was doing those types of jobs at Newell's Old Boys. It seemed like he was first with things. I knew Bielsa didn't have a big career as a player. Yet, he was one of the biggest coaches in the world. He gave me a feeling about the level you could arrive from, the feeling that you could come from nothing. I had a friend, Pablo, who always sent me newspapers from Argentina. He told me once how before Argentina played a friendly against Holland, Bielsa wanted information from the last twenty games Holland had played. I didn't know why but who knows, maybe there was some information he could get from that.

More and more, I started to think about the game in that way.

Then came the meeting at Sevilla. They tried to appoint Marcelo as head coach in 2011. I was working for the club but I wasn't in the meeting. The chairman, José María Del Nido, and director of football Monchi were in there and they've spoken about it before. What happened is not a secret. I prepared a report of perhaps 120 pages, with all the information I could give them. The chairman was able to say to Marcelo: 'This is what I know about you.' Marcelo had prepared a report on Sevilla of one thousand pages. One thousand pages long! 'And this is what I know about you.' The chairman and Monchi talked about him afterwards in this amazing way, like 'wow!' He impressed them both. Really, really impressed them.

I was in football professionally by then but the period that first made me fascinated about Bielsa was the World Cup in 2002. All the games were free on TV in Spain so I watched the whole of the qualifying stage. Argentina were top of their group and had something like a 15-point difference over Brazil. They were incredible. Brazil won the World Cup but for me, I felt it with Argentina. I watched the Olympic Games as a pundit when Argentina won the gold medal in 2004. In one game they beat Serbia and Montenegro 6-0. What energy! More and more the thought in my head was, 'Imagine the level of work of this man in charge – even when you get knocked out in the group stages of a World Cup.'

My opinion was that Marcelo could jump into Europe as a club manager. His football would work here, I thought. But if you ask me why I believed he would be perfect for Leeds United three years ago, my view is that the English environment is really coachable. When you are a coach in England, the players come to you and you can say, 'jump off this bridge.' They will jump and when they are in the cold water, they will ask why you wanted them to jump.

My feeling about Latin football is that you say 'jump off a bridge' and the players stop and ask why first. They don't just jump into the water. Whatever Marcelo asked for, I knew the players here would try. They would have the trust in this incredible coach.

The summer when he came to Leeds was after the first year of Andrea Radrizzani's project here. The project was not bad, in my opinion, but that year taught us something. I said to Andrea that Leeds United did not have the capacity to support a medium-term project because the historic pressure for promotion can't be appeased. We can't be a medium-term project in the Championship. Other teams can be but not us. So either we change the club we are at or we change the project.

At that time, I had an offer to go to a different job in Spain. I had dinner with Andrea where we had lots of conversation and lots of arguments – but arguments in a good way. I thought that to reduce the gap in the league we needed to make a really good investment in a top-class coach. Maybe one who is outside the budget. It was the day after when we were in a car and we had that famous conversation where Andrea asked me to tell him my favourite. The report I made in Sevilla about Marcelo was still on my hard disk so I updated it and presented it to Andrea and our chief executive, Angus Kinnear. 'This is who I am talking about,' I said. 'This is why he could be so amazing.'

The Championship was difficult to offer to Marcelo. I thought Leeds was a good environment for him but my feeling was that he would say no, that he would have something better to consider. That, to me, is why I think he made the challenge for us: to meet him in Buenos Aires. If we were brave enough to travel to Buenos Aires to meet him, we were serious. We had to prove that we were.

I was excited on the flight down there but there was one crazy moment. When we landed I called Marcelo and I didn't get an answer. We had spoken the day before and I was worried that I had said something wrong, something to upset him. The chairman had travelled from Europe for this so I was nervous. At the hotel I asked the guy at reception which meeting room we had hired. I remember the name perfectly: Salon Tilos. I opened the door expecting, well, I don't know what. Honestly, it was like NASA. There were about five computers spread about. There was a big board with all the names of our players. Marcelo was there ready to start. My first thought was 'Help us!'

After a second meeting with Angus and me, I thought it was done. I thought Marcelo would be our head coach. But I knew some people in football would say to Andrea, 'You are crazy, crazy, crazy.' When we landed, I talked to him and told him we had to be brave and have passion. 'Give me this responsibility and I will assume all of it, in a good way and a bad. If it fails, fire me. Fire me and get a new director of football. Put me out as if that was my last chance. But until then, be brave.' Andrea will tell you he had at least twenty messages saying, 'What are you doing?' But before we fail, have passion first. Angus helped me a lot in these discussions.

You don't need me to tell you what a success Marcelo became at Leeds. I'll let that speak for itself. But what we did was change the strategy at the right time. The thing that made me proudest of all about Leeds was the way everyone at the club felt involved and relevant as we tried to win promotion. From Mandy in ticket sales to Patrick Bamford scoring the goals, everyone had the same sense of what we were doing. Everyone made a difference. I have a friend, Alberto García, a goalkeeper at Rayo Vallecano who has won four promotions in his career. I'll never forget something he said to me once: 'The management and the office help win promotion, not just players.' Get it right everywhere in a club and it will work. For sure, we got it right with Marcelo.

Victor Orta
Leeds United Director of Football

INTRODUCTION

Walking in the Rain

I tell the same story whenever anyone asks about Marcelo Bielsa's idiosyncrasies (and because his reputation goes before him, people usually do). Is it fair to portray Bielsa as eccentric? And if it is fair, what form do those eccentricities take?

In 2019 I was working as the *Yorkshire Evening Post*'s chief football writer and up at Leeds United's training ground for Bielsa's regular Thursday press conference. With very rare exceptions, he was bang on time for his chats with the media and there were days when he would leave Thorp Arch as soon as the briefing finished.

On this particular Thursday the rain was hammering down; good Scottish weather, as someone once said. I drove down the driveway leading out to the main road and there was Bielsa, already soaked and walking alone in nothing more than a club tracksuit (he always wore a club tracksuit). I pulled up and wound down the car window. 'Marcelo, can I give you a lift?' My route home went fairly close to his flat in Wetherby, a forty-five-minute walk away. 'No, no, thank you,' he said. 'I like this.' It was not a secret that Bielsa liked to walk. 'You're sure?' A nod, a smile and then he was off, along the pavement up Walton Road and out of sight.

Bielsa was 65 and if it had been my father, I would have told him to grow up and get in the front seat. The mid-May temperature felt bearable but the rain was relentless and the thought popped into my head that if anything happened to Bielsa between here and Wetherby, the police would record that the last person to speak to him was that Scottish reporter from the *YEP* and why on earth did he not insist on driving him home? But then I found myself laughing because Bielsa's odd tendencies were endearing. The exercise did him good and gave him time to think. Every now and again he would talk quite seriously about buying a bike and cycling to work; a multi-million-pound asset pedalling along country lanes where lorries and Range Rovers travelled at breakneck speeds.

We were lucky in Leeds that as journalists we were able to piece together a proper picture of Bielsa – or as clear a picture as you can get of someone who closely guards what privacy he has. At other clubs like Lille, his tenure came crashing down long before any rapport was established with the media or the public; the day before I started writing this introduction, he was on a video link to a court in France arguing over compensation he claimed he was owed by Lille (some £15m-plus).[1] Even at Athletic Bilbao and Marseille – two clubs who felt lasting affection for him – he burned brightly and then he was gone, in a way which generated feelings of regret. But at Leeds, something clicked. In giving Bielsa the right amount of support and deference, Leeds hit the sweet spot with him. To begin with, the club were wary of presuming that Bielsa's first season as head coach would result in a second. By the time this book went to print, they were in the process of finalising a fourth year in charge.

To the uninitiated (and most of us who wrote about Leeds were uninitiated on the subject of Bielsa at first), it was easy to form an image of Bielsa as an incendiary device. Newspaper profiles of him were peppered with details of run-ins and sudden resignations: like the time he accepted the manager's job at Lazio and then quit without boarding his scheduled flight from Buenos Aires to Rome. You read about the brilliance of his football in Bilbao but even that story ended with him reporting himself to the police after a scuffle with a contractor who was working on Athletic's training ground. Leeds had experienced their share of unsuitable managers and most of them had done nothing more than drain the club's diminished pool of hope a little more. When it became clear that Leeds were trying to appoint Bielsa, I spoke to a writer in Argentina about him. 'This could be amazing,' he said, 'or it could be over very soon.' For Leeds it was a big and expensive roll of the dice.

As you educated yourself about his quirks, you naturally questioned if any part of his persona was an act. Or if not an act, whether years of Bielsa being off the wall in comparison to the average coach had accentuated those quirks and led him, perhaps subconsciously, to act up in the way he was expected to. But then you heard the tales of Bielsa moving out of a four-star hotel near Harrogate and asking the logistics staff at Leeds to make enquiries about a bedsit above a newsagents in Boston Spa. You found him settling eventually in Wetherby in a nondescript flat which would not make you look twice as you walked past it. The ferocity of his training sessions was not for show, less still the benefit of anyone peering in. Everything was mapped out, everything was methodical and in so many ways, everything was logical. A French documentary team asked me after Leeds were promoted in 2020 whether Bielsa should be classed as crazy or not (they asked everyone who appeared on the programme the same question). In a footballing sense, not crazy. Not loco in the slightest.

Being Bielsa looks exhausting. Pretending to be Bielsa would probably kill you. The more you see of him and the more you listen to him, the more you learn that a personality like his cannot be manufactured. Slowly you came to understand about some of what was in his head and how intently he fixated on the game. One of his earliest press conferences at Leeds elicited a random apology to Hernán Crespo over a perceived slight which occurred more than fifteen years earlier while Bielsa was coaching Argentina. It stemmed from a question about why Bielsa had only one style and one tactical approach. Why was there no plan B up his sleeve? Because, he said, a footballer has to believe that his coach has faith in his own plan. If you chop and change, you transmit a lack of personal confidence which inevitably infects the players. And then came an eight-minute monologue in which Bielsa explained that he had wronged Crespo by telling him at a young age that he was 'a player of maturity' (a trick designed to nurture the forward's self-assurance). Bielsa was caught in a lie several years later when he forgot that conversation and claimed an older Crespo had benefited from growing up. Crespo took offence and Bielsa regretted it enough to be talking about the slight almost two decades later. 'This is the kind of thing I cannot forgive myself for,' he said. The next morning Crespo responded on Twitter and buried the hatchet by accepting Bielsa's apology. To us it felt like something of nothing but it had evidently been eating away at Bielsa. Covering a club in England's second division, you had the sense of existing in a strange reality as the two famous Argentinian faces made up via the Internet.

Bielsa had his own code when dealing with the press: softly spoken, polite and patient but unwilling to engage personally. On occasions he would walk past you after a game and without looking at you, pat you on the shoulder and then walk on silently; his form of courtesy. His refusal to speak English in public was a bone of contention with some but if you wanted to dig into Bielsa's brain and to grasp his inner thoughts (or to gauge how he actually felt) he had to speak in Spanish. It gave you detail and nuance, even after his comments had passed through a translator. It allowed Bielsa to express himself properly. Covering Bielsa was a wasted opportunity if you got bogged down in standard football chat. Routine questions were dealt with in a few short sentences. The philosophical discussions could go on for ever. And that was where the gold was found.

Football teaches you that every coach is different and every regime is different. No manager at Leeds has ever attacked the job in quite the same way as any other. But very few were as trans-formational as Bielsa. Very few were able to redraw everything at Elland Road in the way that Bielsa did. The speed of the change after his appointment was extraordinary, right from his first game at home to Stoke City. Leeds swarmed all over Stoke, oozing flair and intensity unlike anything Elland Road was used to. Bielsa was still and passive for much of the game, impervious to the crackle around him. Many supporters will say that they felt something stirring on that hot August afternoon. That is easy to say now with hindsight but it is also true; the sensation of a style which seemed too good to fail. An hour or so after full-time I walked through the empty stands and bumped into a steward, Alan, whom I got to know after starting at the *Evening Post*. I looked at him and we laughed. 'Jesus,' he said. Close enough.

In a matter of weeks Bielsa brought sanity to the madhouse. For years, this had been a club where careers came to die. You had to be relatively close to Leeds to fully understand how the club and their inherent ability to implode dragged down managers and players and crushed expectancy. Underachievement was endemic. Bielsa was not without his faults and in no way was he low-maintenance but for Leeds, at that juncture, he was the optimum choice. And Leeds were perfect for him. If and when promotion came, we all wondered how he would react. Now in his sixties, he was no longer the wild-haired man who rode on the shoulders of supporters and swung a shirt around his head after winning his first trophy at Newell's Old Boys in the 1990s. He was older and more restrained, more inclined to take the blame when it went wrong than take the credit when it came good. But the achievement would be incomplete unless Bielsa felt it like the city around him.

The final minutes of *Take Us Home: Leeds United*, the Amazon series covering his reign, drew the emotion from him perfectly. They captured the night in 2020 when his players lifted the Championship trophy and as Bielsa spoke tenderly, a camera drifted over Elland Road and focused on the crowd in the streets below, flares, flags and all. The images are as poignant as they are euphoric; a night frozen in time and one which neither Leeds nor Bielsa will ever experience in the same way again.

'If there is something that makes this profession attractive to me, it's the power to be in contact with the passion of the public,' Bielsa says. 'The supporters, the only thing for them is that they love their club. The only thing they receive in exchange is emotion. This is going to be a lovely moment for all of my life. And it was beautiful.'[2]

1.

SEPTEMBER

Leeds United had pushed all week for Marcelo Bielsa to sign the papers: meetings at Elland Road, meetings at their training ground and repeated discussions about the details of his contract. The club expected the process of renewing his deal to be slow – negotiations with Bielsa generally were – but it is Thursday night and on Saturday evening they are due to start the new Premier League season away at Liverpool. Bielsa will be at Anfield regardless, committed to managing Leeds whether his new contract is finalised or not, but from a PR perspective the club's hierarchy know how this looks: the coach who brought them promotion after sixteen lean years in the EFL stalling on their offer of an extension. On the outside, questions are being asked.

It is not that Bielsa is undecided about his future. At the start of pre-season he and Leeds agreed in principle that he would stay on for a third year as head coach. The relationship is robust and before the club lifted the Championship title in July 2020, Bielsa surprised Leeds by enquiring about the average wage of a manager in that league – a gentle indication that he might consider taking a cut in salary to remain in charge if promotion went begging again. His contract – a huge stack of documents which one official at Elland Road describes as 'War and Peace' – is broadly in place and Leeds have no fear of losing him. It was different twelve months earlier, at the end of Bielsa's first season in the job. The risk of him deciding that one year in England was enough for him prompted Leeds to draw up a shortlist of potential replacements. They were ready to reach out to Slaviša Jokanović and Aitor Karanka, both of whom had won promotion from the Championship before. Bielsa came close to doing the same at the first attempt in 2019 but hit the wall during Leeds' chaotic defeat to Derby County in the play-off semi-finals. A season of promise went up in smoke on one hot, brutal evening at Elland Road. Bielsa's wife, Laura, had flown in from Argentina and was there with him at his lowest ebb. After full-time he went round a despondent dressing room and without saying much, patted his players on the shoulder before picking up his bags and disappearing. For twenty-four hours it felt as if the project was blown. Bielsa believed Leeds would replace him as a result of his failure to win promotion and he did not intend to argue if they chose to let him go. A sombre mood settled on the training ground as his staff began removing equipment and files. His squad met for a drink before heading off for the summer, all of them in the dark about what would come next. Bielsa had left a message on Kalvin Phillips's mobile asking to meet but, for reasons Phillips never discovered, did not follow up the call. It was only when Leeds got in touch and told Bielsa that they wanted to exercise an option to extend his deal for another twelve months that the doubt was removed. The invitation to stay was all Bielsa needed. After witnessing the extent of his impact at Elland Road, Leeds were bemused by the suggestion that their confidence in him might have diminished. Talks ensued with director of football Victor Orta and chief executive Angus Kinnear and the extension was activated within a fortnight.

This time there is no alternative shortlist in play. Bielsa has given a verbal commitment but his latest deal requires non-stop translation from English to Spanish and he fixates on the minutiae in it. These details matter to him as much as the core elements, like his salary and bonus structure. As someone once said to me: 'Pablo Hernández out for six months or work in the training ground car park delayed for a week – in his mind, they're equally big problems. He doesn't differentiate between them.'[1] Bielsa holds off on providing his signature until everything is just-so and set down in print.

The contract itself is unusually complex, containing clauses that most managerial deals do not. His coaching staff are subject to non-disclosure agreements, limiting what they can say in public about Bielsa. He wants Leeds to tighten the terms of the NDAs. The wage package paid to him covers not only his salary but those of his backroom team too and promotion results in pay rises across the board. The entire pot of cash goes to him and he distributes it as he sees fit, paying his assistants directly (and by all accounts, paying them well). Normally, a club of Leeds' size would not agree to an arrangement like that. It runs the risk of financial disputes further down the line. But Bielsa operated like this with other European teams and his system of remuneration is non-negotiable. Leeds are happy to oblige but when it comes to contract renewals, they are not just negotiating with Bielsa. They are negotiating by proxy with the team around him, the iron circle of coaches and analysts who devote themselves to his work.

Among the questions Bielsa has, and one of the things he tries to establish, is how his media commitments will change in the Premier League. For years he has kept journalists at arm's length by establishing firm boundaries with them. He sits willingly in press conferences for as long as anyone wants him to, or for as long as the questions demand, but aside from those he is almost inaccessible. In Argentina they say he was once stung by a bad experience in a one-on-one interview and resolved never to expose himself in that way again. Bielsa's own explanation is that no reporter deserves more time with him than any other and no reporter should have the luxury of exclusive quotes. As he said to Pep Guardiola when they met for the first time in 2006: 'Why am I going to give an interview to a powerful guy and deny it to a small reporter from the provinces? What is my reason for doing such a thing?'[2] When Leeds first appointed Bielsa, he tried to avoid the live pre- and post-match interviews Sky Sports carried out as part of its broadcast contract with the EFL. The threat of sanctions from the EFL persuaded him to play ball but only reluctantly. In the Premier League the media requirements will soar. Bielsa wants to know how much he will be asked to do and what punishment he will face if he declines to fulfil his duties (in the past, the Premier League has fined other managers like Guardiola for skipping interviews). At Anfield, on day one of the 2020–21 season, Bielsa is expected to speak to seven different outlets after full-time. They are lined up along the side of the pitch, waiting for him to step in front of the microphone. Bielsa draws the line at three. And it is not only the external media who are treading on eggshells. Owing to confusion and the summer departure of his assistant and translator, Diego Flores, Bielsa's column in Leeds' matchday programme disappears. It returns suddenly two months later after Bielsa asks why the club are no longer printing it.

On the Friday morning before Liverpool, as his players train for the last time and prepare to take the team bus to Merseyside, Leeds confirm that Bielsa's contract has been signed, another twelve-month extension to the end of the season. 'The worst kept secret in Leeds,' jokes the club's head of communications as he sends the press release through. In a sense it makes no difference to the weekend ahead. Bielsa's previous contract was a rolling deal and the Premier League has already given approval for him to take to the touchline at Anfield either way but negotiations between him and Leeds have gone on for the best part of a month and it suits everyone to bring them to a close. The announcement kills the perception, accurate or otherwise, that Bielsa could walk away.

There is a buzz around him and a buzz around Leeds. It has long been said that the Premier League would be better off with Leeds as one of its twenty clubs but Bielsa's involvement gives the division an additional plot line. By chance the fixture list for 12 September has created the ideal match-up on the opening weekend: Liverpool versus Leeds, Bielsa versus Jürgen Klopp, the Premier League champions versus the winners of the Championship. Klopp is the polar opposite of Bielsa in some respects: outgoing, more playful with the media and far less subdued. Almost hyperactive by comparison. The German has studied Leeds closely and warns his Liverpool squad that playing them will be 'uncomfortable'. An end-to-end match with seven goals in it does not contradict him.

Leeds concede an early penalty which Mo Salah converts but Jack Harrison equalises soon after through a ploy he and Kalvin Phillips have been working on all week. Phillips finds space in a deep area of his own half and hooks the ball down the left. As soon as possession reaches Phillips's feet Harrison bursts forward, takes his pass and finishes sharply from the edge of Liverpool's box. Coffee sloshes out of Bielsa's cup as he jumps up and clenches his fists. The match rages back and forth, caution-free and full of adventure, but Liverpool win it 4-3 after Rodrigo, Leeds' record signing, trips Fabinho inside the box with three minutes to play. Salah scores from the penalty spot again. A point was in the offing but Bielsa thinks Liverpool deserve the victory. 'On the whole, Liverpool were superior,' he says. It is not the end of the world. Klopp looks pleased if a little worn-out by the mayhem and Leeds' performance is widely acclaimed. They have taken on the best Liverpool team in three decades and ruffled their feathers in the most engaging contest of the first weekend. *Match of the Day* places it at the top of its schedule a few hours later. This, though, is how Leeds play and how they have always played under Bielsa. His message throughout the summer was simple: he will change nothing and sacrifice nothing by focusing on dominating possession and prepping his team to attack at will. 'It would be an error to think you should stop doing the things that made you successful,' Bielsa says.

*

The close season has been strange, for Leeds and English football. Covid-19 is restricting everything and having claimed the Championship title in front of empty stadiums, there is no prospect of Leeds welcoming a crowd back to Elland Road soon. Bielsa's players took a fortnight's holiday at the end of the 2019–20 season but have hardly stopped for thirteen months. Even in the weeks of 2020 when football shut down and the Premier League and EFL suspended their schedules, Bielsa insisted on his squad training as vigorously as possible at home: daily fitness routines and strict weight checks via WhatsApp. Leeds sent their players special scales and instructed them to submit photos of the readings every morning. 'We were lucky one week in lockdown when he gave us Sunday and Monday off,' says right-back Luke Ayling.[3] In the main, there is precious little downtime with Bielsa. He has operated this way from the start, right back to his tenure as Newell's Old Boys manager in the 1990s. In his first month of competitive matches as head coach at Leeds, the senior squad were given a single day off.[4]

Some changes have occurred in the backroom staff behind him. Carlos Corberán, the Spaniard who coached Leeds' Under-23s, has left to become manager of Huddersfield Town. Bielsa toys with the idea of using his Chilean assistant, Diego Reyes, to fill in as development-squad boss but changes his mind and promotes Mark Jackson from the Under-18s instead. Diego Flores, another familiar face in Bielsa's dug-out, chooses to leave and draw breath after two years at the coalface in Leeds. Flores doubled as Bielsa's media translator for a while so Bielsa enlists Andrés Clavijo, a Colombian analyst raised in South London, to take on that responsibility. The appearance of the young, fresh-faced Clavijo causes immediate fascination and calls start arriving from journalists in Colombia trying to establish how it was that he came to be part of Bielsa's inner sanctum.

In the transfer market, Leeds land two deals before the season starts. They pay £27m to sign Rodrigo from Valencia, breaking the transfer record set at Elland Road by the £18m purchase of Rio Ferdinand from West Ham United twenty years earlier. Rodrigo, a fully fledged Spain international, is seen as such a key target that Bielsa calls him to discuss the move before it goes through. It is rare for Bielsa to reach out to prospective signings personally but his overtures convince Rodrigo to join. Centre-back Robin Koch arrives from Freiburg for £13m, replacing one of the shining lights of the 2019–20 season, Ben White. Leeds have made attempts to convert White's loan from Brighton into a permanent move but failed with three offers, the highest worth £30m with add-ons. White is off-limits and Brighton refuse to buckle so Leeds give up on him. Koch does not receive any contact from Bielsa himself but in preparation for the transfer, Leeds sent him presentations, video footage and statistical analysis outlining the way Bielsa's side play. August is almost out and neither Koch nor Rodrigo will have much time to get themselves up to speed before the Premier League gets underway.

Bielsa has shown before that he gives no quarter to players who fall short of his physical demands or struggle to grasp the principles of his tactics. In the previous January window, Leeds took striker Jean-Kévin Augustin on loan from RB Leipzig with an obligation to sign him permanently for £18m if they won promotion. Bielsa approved the transfer but Augustin pulled a hamstring before long and played all of 49 minutes. As a result, Bielsa lost faith in him and by the start of the 2020–21 season, Leeds are in dispute with Leipzig. The club have no desire to commit millions to a player Bielsa does not want and whose deal in Germany is worth £90,000 a week. They hope to wriggle out of the transfer on the basis that the clause covering a full-time switch officially expired on 30 June. Covid-19 delayed Leeds' promotion from the Championship until mid-July. Leipzig argue that in good faith, the 30 June date should be taken to mean the end of the season but neither side is willing to compromise. Augustin trains alone in France, estranged from both clubs, until he signs for Nantes as a free agent the day after the transfer window shuts in October. Leipzig submit a complaint to FIFA, asking the world governing body to arbitrate and award them compensation. Leeds signal their intention to fight the claim.

On the pitch, Bielsa limits himself to a few warm-up matches. He talks initially about arranging six or seven friendlies but he loses a clutch of players to international duty in the penultimate week of pre-season, including Kalvin Phillips who has been called up by England for the first time. Bielsa trims the schedule and games against Fleetwood Town and Lincoln City are called off. He uses the spare days to put the remainder of his squad through his infamous murderball sessions. The energy-sapping, 11 versus 11 games are what underpin the fitness levels in Bielsa's dressing room and Leeds' conditioning is exceptional. 'The players just get fitter and fitter,' says first-team sports scientist Tom Robinson.

'Over time, the body adapts.'[5] Bielsa flogs them relentlessly but most are hardened to the routine by now. Liam Cooper, the club's captain, felt the difference when he began training before Bielsa's second season. 'It's not that it's not hard,' Cooper said, 'but we know what to expect and we know what's coming. That makes it a bit easier.'

In the days before the season kicks off, broadcast journalists descend on Leeds' Thorp Arch training ground. Phillips is interviewed by *Soccer AM*. Pablo Hernández is chosen for international media duties. Bielsa does not involve himself in any of it, aside from his standard press conference. It is almost pointless trying to tempt him to do more. His appointment at Elland Road was big enough news for Amazon Prime to follow up its documentary on Manchester City by sending cameras to Leeds for a six-part series covering Bielsa's first year as head coach. Regardless of Amazon's clout, there was no prospect at all of the producers being granted dressing-room access. Bielsa was forever at a distance in the footage and did not speak to the camera directly until, in the last few days of filming, he bowed to repeated requests from chairman Andrea Radrizzani to conduct an interview. Radrizzani's money was funding the documentary and he wanted his head coach to speak. Bielsa did so under duress, allowing no questions and reviewing the season without interruption. He later claimed not to have watched the series but officials at Leeds think that he did, that curiosity must have got the better of him. Despite the impression that he treats the media with indifference, Bielsa's staff translate English articles and cuttings about him every morning, helping him to understand the tone of the coverage. As much as he follows his own mind resolutely, he likes to monitor the daily agenda.

Leeds have been chasing Premier League football for sixteen long years. This is what they craved for so long. But what will Bielsa make of the division, the most commercially powerful football league in the world? The glare of attention is on a different scale and although Bielsa coped with intense scrutiny as Argentina's manager, that period of his career was one of the few that forced him to take a concerted break from the sport. He will tell you that his love of football is an amateur pleasure. In a highly professional industry, the roots of the game are what delight him most. Bielsa marks Phillips's England debut by giving him a shirt he wore as a defender with Newell's Old Boys in Argentina in the 1970s. It is handed over in a plain Nike shoebox and comes with two letters, one written by Bielsa in Spanish and the other a translation in English. In his comments, Bielsa applauds Phillips for acting with professionalism while playing with an amateur ethos. 'He said the [Newell's] shirt represented a time when people didn't play for money,' says Phillips's mother, Lindsay Crosby. 'It represented a time when people played football for feelings and for love.' The Premier League is very different. The Premier League is a goldfish bowl where everything has a price. A few days after Bielsa signs his new contract at Leeds, the governing body strikes a revised broadcast deal in China worth hundreds of millions of pounds.

Bielsa is sceptical about the creep of high-powered business in football. It has been growing for years and Leeds, to an extent, are no different to any other major club. Radrizzani's multi-million-pound fortune was amassed through the sale of TV sports rights and the creation of the company MP & Silva. In the Championship, Leeds were heavily reliant on his personal wealth. Speaking in 2018, Bielsa argued that commercial interests had changed football for the worse by placing too much emphasis on results. It was hard to commit to a thrilling or risky style of play, he said, because clubs will not thank you for it if results fail to match up. On the contrary, most will sack you. And because of this, the entertainment provided by football is destined to suffer as everyone fixates on the scoreline.

'The commercialisation of football when clubs are owned by private people makes the result more important than anything,' Bielsa said. 'But the most attractive thing in football is the beauty of the game. Those who invest in football should be aware of that and take precautions to protect the business they bought. The fact that we are not taking care of the planet, our children will pay the consequence of our acts. And with football it will be the same because we are destroying football. And in the future, we'll see the negative effects of this.' Bielsa commanded large salaries in Europe but to the naked eye his lifestyle was austere. At the time when he made those comments, he was in the process of donating around £2m to Newell's Old Boys for a new training facility in Rosario. His brother Rafael did the legal work on the project and his sister Maria Eugenia produced the architectural designs. It was, in its entirety, an altruistic gesture and back in England, his sparse lodgings in Wetherby were costing him little over £500 a month.

*

Bielsa, in any case, will entertain as best he can. After narrowly losing one seven-goal game at Anfield, Leeds find themselves in the midst of another a week later in their first home game against Fulham at Elland Road. The stadium tells a story about how short the summer has been. Leeds have spent money renovating their media facilities but new floodlights and improved dug-outs – both required to meet Premier League standards – will have to wait. Time has run out and Leeds ask for dispensation to delay the installation of floodlights while parts arrive from China. The club hoped to replace their fibresand pitch too but decided to hold off on that for twelve months. A full reconstruction would take fourteen weeks and they have insufficient time. The surface at Elland Road will become a problem before long but in early September, the sprinklers are on and the sun shines as Leeds and Fulham warm up.

The clubs met here in June as both were edging their way towards promotion (Fulham via the play-offs). It was tight on that occasion until the second half, when Hernández took control and Leeds carved out a healthy 3-0 win. This game looks like going the same way again. Leeds are 2-1 ahead at half-time and Patrick Bamford and Helder Costa score early in the second half. Fulham look beaten. But Bielsa's players make the mistake of easing off, Fulham send on substitutes and Bobby Decordova-Reid and Aleksandar Mitrović bring the scoreline back to 4-3. The closing minutes are twitchy but Leeds have a Premier League win on the board, their first of the season and their first since 2004. Bielsa cuts a relaxed figure beforehand, picking out Fulham substitute Mario Lemina in the stands for a smile and a wave. They know each other from Bielsa's time as head coach of Marseille. But by injury-time he is marching around his technical area, barking at his team incessantly. The football has been worth every penny to watch, a delight for any neutral, but the part which satisfies Bielsa most is the last ten minutes when Leeds reassert themselves in midfield and stifle Fulham's onslaught. He turns over a new leaf by fulfilling all of his required interviews afterwards.

The data shows that over two matches, the established traits of Bielsa's team have flipped on their head. Their expected goals ratio is 1.67 but Leeds have scored seven. It goes against the narrative that followed Bielsa around through his two seasons in the Championship: that Leeds convert too few of their chances and make too little of their slick approach play. In their title-winning term, the club conceded 35 goals in 46 matches but already they have shipped seven. 'We are worried about that,' Bielsa admits and his staff will be busy clipping footage before the usual video analysis session on Monday morning.

By the time Leeds go to Sheffield United the following Sunday, Bielsa has tightened them up at the back. They are more rigid at Bramall Lane and, helped by a brilliant save from goalkeeper Illan Meslier in the first half, they establish proper control. Bielsa respects Chris Wilder, Sheffield United's coach, and is curious about aspects of Wilder's tactics, particularly the novel notion of overlapping centre-backs. He has never seen defenders used like that before and while he and Wilder are at opposite ends of the personality spectrum – Wilder was known for being the life and soul of the party whenever the Yorkshire press corps threw their annual Christmas party – they are both mavericks in their own right. Rodrigo's introduction as a substitute gives Leeds more variation in the second half and two minutes from time, Bamford runs onto Jack Harrison's cross and heads in the only goal. Wilder thinks Sheffield United were unlucky. Bielsa says the result is 'just' but later, after reviewing the match, he concedes that Wilder was right. 'It's a refreshing change to hear a manager say that,' Wilder remarks. 'I've got an awful lot of respect for Marcelo.' Leeds have six points from three games. Pep Guardiola and Manchester City are next.

Not for the first time, Bielsa is making a splash. He and Leeds have found their feet in the Premier League and provided one of the more compelling stories of the opening month. In Argentina, viewing figures for Leeds' defeat at Liverpool exceed expected numbers for Spain's *El Clásico*, the foreign fixture which invariably attracts the biggest television audience there. His previous jobs in club management were relatively short because, it was said, his players ran out of steam eventually. Ricardo Lunari, a retired midfielder whom Bielsa coached at Newell's Old Boys, remembers the intensity of Bielsa's methods taking their toll. 'The wear and tear weakened the relationship,' Lunari says. 'The players no longer wanted to deliver what Marcelo wanted and when he realised that, the end of the cycle began.' But the squad at Leeds are very much with him. Sheffield United away is his 104th game in charge and none of the spark has gone.

Leeds, at the outset, had no idea how long their relationship with Bielsa would last. They admired his brilliance but they were alive to his singularity, the obsessive mind and the uncompromising personality. In certain moments he was a delight to be around. In others he was aloof or difficult to please. In certain moments Leeds would find that a phone call to tell Bielsa that Rodrigo was a done deal for £27m ended with him asking pointed questions about why certain academy players he wanted to keep were being offered out on loan. Life was never easy or at all predictable. And forty-eight hours before the opening fixture of the Premier League season, they would have a draft of his contract extension sat in front of them, still unsigned.

That, in essence, was the nature of the marriage. Take Bielsa as he comes and trust in the best of him. Make him autonomous and make no attempt to restrain him. Paul Heckingbottom, Bielsa's predecessor, had asked for two additions to the coaching team when Leeds recruited him from Barnsley. As part of his own stipulations, Bielsa asked for eight. It was management on his terms and the partnership Leeds were ready for when he stepped off the plane from Argentina with little more than the clothes on his back.

2.

THE APPOINTMENT

Aside from a few personal belongings, Marcelo Bielsa's luggage was filled with tracksuits. He had travelled light and was carrying the bare necessities when Leeds United collected him from the airport. What Bielsa needed for coaching was with him. Everything else he had left in Argentina, including his family. 'He's a simple man,' his brother, Rafael, told me. 'He's complicated in the way he thinks but very simple in the way he lives.' In Argentina they remember how Bielsa took himself off to a convent after exhausting himself as the country's national coach, a tired mind seeking a reclusive home. In England he will gravitate towards a small flat in Wetherby, above the chiropodist's surgery and across the road from a sweet shop. Leeds set him up at first with a room at Rudding Park, a four-star hotel near Harrogate, but Bielsa tired of the surroundings quickly. He was not minded to copy José Mourinho, who lived out of the Lowry Hotel in Salford for the duration of his reign as Manchester United manager. Rudding Park was too plush and too far from Leeds' training ground. Bielsa wanted something modest. Something relatively practical.

In the months that follow, residents of Wetherby get used to regular sightings of him in the street, backpack on, head down and earphones in as he walks in the fresh air. Bielsa liked tango music and Argentinian folk songs in his younger years. He would spend hours listening to lectures on politics and philosophy, given by people whose ideas or opinions interested him. More often than not he would be dressed in Leeds United training gear, his initials on the right side of his chest. Training gear was his usual attire. At the club's centenary dinner in 2019, Bielsa turned up in a tracksuit and white trainers, the sore thumb in a room full of tuxedos. Photos of him appeared in the national press the next day and after seeing them, he wrote to the board at Elland Road, apologising for any offence he had caused. Leeds laughed the letter off, tickled by the notion of Bielsa upsetting them.[1] By then they were well acquainted with his mannerisms.

It was training gear for Bielsa when Leeds unveiled him as their new head coach at a busy press conference. On 25 June 2018: day one of the revolution and ground zero for a club who wanted to extinguish their recent, unproductive history. Leeds had been negotiating with him for more than two months and he was in the building at last, sporting an oversized grey T-shirt and carrying a briefcase packed with notes. His media briefing took place on the fourth floor of Elland Road's East Stand, a level of the stadium which had seen much in its time. It was in the same room that Massimo Cellino, unusually relaxed with sunglasses hanging from his collar, announced the sale of Leeds to a suited-and-booted Andrea Radrizzani in 2017, one Italian businessman selling to another. It was on this floor, a little further down the hall, where Cellino introduced David Hockaday – back in work after his sacking by Forest Green Rovers – as Leeds' new head coach in 2014. Cellino and Hockaday walked out of the upstairs lift and turned right. Bielsa stepped out and turned left, taking everyone in the opposite direction metaphorically and physically. Neither appointment was quite believable but Bielsa's was outlandish for the right reasons; an elite coach taking on English football's impossible job.

Leeds' first phone call to him was made as the 2017–18 Championship season drew to a close. A manager was in place at Elland Road, Yorkshireman Paul Heckingbottom, but confidence in him had dried up after only four months. Heckingbottom hung around after the season finished in May, taking a young squad on a post-season tour of Myanmar, but in the background Leeds were mobilising to replace him. They were looking at a fifteenth straight year outside the Premier League and Radrizzani had come to the conclusion that the route to promotion would be found through the appointment of a stellar manager. If Leeds went big on their head coach, the rest was more likely to fall into place. Raw or unproven choices were delivering mid-table finishes and the club were in a holding pattern. Radrizzani and Victor Orta, Leeds' director of football, spent a car journey together chatting over their next leap of faith. Who would you choose, Radrizzani asked Orta. If money were no object and every coach in the game were available, who would you hire? Orta gave an immediate answer. 'Marcelo Bielsa,' he said. 'But I don't think it's possible.'

Orta knew Bielsa inside out; not personally – very few people know Bielsa well personally – but in a tactical and managerial sense. Bielsa captured his imagination while Orta was employed as a football pundit for Radio Marca in Spain in the build-up to the 2002 World Cup. Argentina blitzed their qualifying campaign and Bielsa's style, as it tended to do, got journalists thinking and talking. Some years later, Orta was technical secretary at Sevilla when they tried and failed to hand Bielsa the head coach's job. He courted Bielsa for a second time in his role as Zenit St Petersburg's head of recruitment, again without success. No top-level coach interested him more but Orta was frank with Radrizzani. The chances were very slim, if not non-existent. Leeds would be offering second division football in England and Bielsa was hard to persuade at the best of times. In his previous job at Lille his contract had been worth around £7m a year. Heckingbottom's salary was well below seven figures. Leeds would be moving to a completely different level of expenditure, if they could afford Bielsa's wage at all.

Orta made the initial call to him, left a message and waited for a few days. The delay was not a surprise. Bielsa always analysed employment opportunities closely and would hold off on responding while he looked for the devil in the detail by picking over a club and their squad. 'I expected he would want to do a pre-evaluation,' Orta said. 'He's a clever man. He does that after the first approach so he doesn't lose time and doesn't waste our time either.'[2] Eventually Orta's mobile rang. Bielsa spoke and thanked him for the approach. Yes, he was interested in the project. And yes, if Leeds sent officials out to Argentina, he would talk to them.

Radrizzani and Orta were first to make the trip along with the club's Under-23s coach, Carlos Corberán. Bielsa sat with them for the best part of a day and laid out his vision. The mood was co-operative and positive, a means of Radrizzani and Bielsa feeling each other out. Before going their separate ways, Orta arranged to return to South America with Leeds' chief executive, Angus Kinnear, in mid-May. The second meeting would take place at the Palacio Duhau in downtown Buenos Aires, a high-end hotel with sweeping gardens and outdoor staircases behind it. It was hot, it was humid but from 10am until 11pm, Orta, Kinnear and Bielsa worked out the basis of an agreement. There were brief interludes for food but no breaks in the conversation and no small talk either. Leeds, on a whim, had explored the possibility of appointing Claudio Ranieiri – unemployed and available after leaving Nantes – but were not convinced that Ranieri knew a single player in their dressing room. (Ranieri, ultimately, had no interest in taking the job. Radrizzani's suggestions of Antonio Conte and Roberto Martínez did not get off the ground either). Orta and Kinnear found Bielsa armed with notes about Leeds' entire squad, the result of him trawling through every one of their league games from the 2017–18 season. He had a list of names he would keep; reassuringly long in the eyes of a club who were about to commit to paying him over £3m a year after tax. He also showed them a list of players who had to leave, no questions asked. Any surplus professionals who stuck around would train at a different time of the day to Bielsa's core squad, creating a line in the sand. (He went a step further the following summer by insisting that some who had no future under him keep fit at external sites, like Askham Bryan College near York.) Orta and Kinnear were struck by his clarity. After false dawns and costly indiscipline in Radrizzani's first season as majority shareholder, they admired Bielsa's uncompromising tone.

Conversations about money were short and straightforward. Leeds understood that they either paid Bielsa what he asked for or they left him in peace. They had a fall-back of sorts: ex-Argentina defender Matías Almeyda who played under Bielsa at international level and had been managing in Mexico, but Bielsa was effectively on a shortlist of one. He wanted three assistants with him: Diego Reyes, Diego Flores and Pablo Quiroga, all of whom would require UK work permits. Gabriel Macaya was his usual fitness coach but Bielsa intended to bring Benoit Delaval to Leeds instead. Delaval, a strict and dedicated Frenchman, had been with him at Lille.

Just as importantly, changes were required at Leeds' Thorp Arch training ground. Orta and Kinnear watched with amusement as Bielsa produced land registry drawings of the complex and began running them through his plans to update it. A running track would be installed around the main pitches. The swimming pool

– dry and derelict since Cellino shut it down to save £250,000 a year in 2014 – was to be reactivated and refilled. Bielsa wanted rooms for his players to sleep in, clearer demarcation between first-team and academy relaxation areas and a new camera system for filming and analysing training. The dorms were needed as soon as possible. In his first pre-season at Leeds, Bielsa ran double and triple training sessions. The days ran on so long that several players chose to stay overnight in a nearby hotel rather than bother with the drive home.

The cost of the renovation work ran to more than £1m, at a training ground which Leeds hoped to vacate for a new facility closer to Elland Road. The logic of investing in an ageing site was questionable but Bielsa expected more than vague commitments. He asked for promises and timelines. Kinnear and Orta told him the improvements could feasibly be finished by Christmas. The list of tasks was passed to Mark Broadley, Leeds' head of IT and facilities and the man responsible for keeping Bielsa happy on the infrastructure front. It was no small undertaking. When Leeds completed the sleeping dorms, Bielsa asked the builders to reposition the plug sockets between each bed. They were off centre and the lack of symmetry bothered him. It would annoy him if it stayed that way.

A few weeks after the second meeting in Buenos Aires, Bielsa's contract was still in draft form. Leeds worked on it, tweaked the parts Bielsa was unsatisfied with and patiently waited for the green light to come. 'It was hard to get him to concentrate on it,' Kinnear said. 'All he wanted to speak about was coaching, the players and the training ground. Getting him to speak about the contract was a challenge. He's already given you his word and he feels like his word is his contract.' The final document took so long to complete that Leeds' application for his work permit only narrowly scraped through before the deadline for the new season. The Football Association approved it even though Bielsa fell short of some of the necessary criteria. With the exception of a few months at Lille, he had not managed in Europe since 2015 but the governing body was persuaded to issue a permit by various submissions, including a letter of support written by Mauricio Pochettino. The process was painstaking but even as they flew home from Argentina, Kinnear and Orta felt certain that Bielsa would follow. They had their end of the bargain to keep up but the deal was on. Somehow they had tempted Bielsa to the Championship. Leeds sacked Heckingbottom on 1 June, holding off past the end of May to limit the severance package owed to him. On 14 June, around 10 p.m. UK time, Bielsa finally picked up his pen in Argentina. One of the people involved on his side of negotiations dropped me a message on WhatsApp. 'Marcelo is heading to sign [the contract],' it said. 'I'm heading to find a revolver.' Or if not a revolver, a very stiff drink.

The following morning Leeds announced that Bielsa had accepted a two-year contract with the option of a third season. In practice it was a twelve-month deal; a season together and then take it from there. Bielsa would throw everything at the task but, no matter the technicalities of their agreement with him, Leeds were in his hands. If Bielsa grew tired of the job he would leave. No contractual clauses were going to change that. They merely entitled Leeds to compensation if Bielsa became manager elsewhere. The club had discovered the reality of his fastidious personality in Buenos Aires and it did not take long to show itself when he arrived at Thorp Arch for the first time, on the morning of 25 June. As he walked around the main building he spotted a mark on a wall, caused by someone leaning their feet against it. 'That mark is a sign of disrespect,' he told Radrizzani. 'The person who did this does not respect the training ground.'

A few hours later, at Elland Road, Bielsa presented himself to the media. The juxtaposition between what was seated in front of you and what you had encountered here previously was striking. The Lord Harewood Suite, to the right of where Bielsa took his seat, was where I first interviewed Cellino four years earlier, a day after his takeover of Leeds. Cellino was in a cloak-and-dagger meeting with his financial adviser, Daniel Arty, and the club's de facto sporting director, Luke Dowling. Dowling had been brought to Elland Road by Leeds' then manager, Brian McDermott, and wore the sheepish look of someone who would rather not have been found in Cellino's company by a journalist. McDermott was nowhere to be seen. Cellino had decided to sack him and was venting about McDermott's unapproved absence from Elland Road (McDermott, with his position in grave doubt and his mother being treated for cancer in Stoke Mandeville hospital, opted to stay away while he waited for Cellino to terminate his contract). Cellino was as annoyed by the cleanliness of the stadium, complaining as he wiped dust off the seats outside the Harewood Suite. 'Where are the cleaners?' he demanded. 'Why does no one here do their job?'[3] It was mid-afternoon and he was halfway through a bottle of Chivas Regal whisky. Life, for him, always started after lunch.

Stranger still was the afternoon when Cellino returned from a meeting in Bahrain with Gulf Finance House, the investment bank which owned Leeds for 14 months in 2012 and 2013. Cellino claimed to have resolved a dispute over loans owed to GFH and GFH, apparently as a mark of its gratitude, sent him off with an Arab headdress and cloak. As I arrived for another interview with him, Cellino was jumping around his office dressed in the outfit and shouting 'Allahu Akbar' in delight. There was only one way in which Cellino and Bielsa were comparable: their minds were incredibly difficult to read. But on every other front they were poles apart; contrasting personalities and men who commanded very different levels of respect. On the day Cellino sold Leeds to Radrizzani in 2017, he had the self-awareness to acknowledge his maddening traits and the volatility that cast him as a madman. 'If you can survive working with me you can survive anything,' he joked. It was a fitting farewell statement.[4]

There were no quips from Bielsa as he sat down with Radrizzani; just a polite, guarded smile beneath a piercing gaze. Introductory managerial press conferences were commonplace at Leeds, a club forever changing tack in the face of perennial mediocrity. Bielsa was their fifteenth permanent boss since relegation from the Premier League in 2004 but he was unlike any of the others, and a source of huge fascination. Journalists made the journey from Europe and South America. The floor in front of him was packed. He had a translator on his staff, a French academic by the name of Salim Lamrani, but Lamrani left the interpreting to Phil Dickinson, an external language expert hired by Leeds. Dickinson gained useful experience of translating for Bielsa while the latter was coach of Argentina and Athletic Bilbao. He had also acted as an interpreter for Diego Maradona when Maradona's Argentina side played Scotland in Glasgow in 2008. Nonetheless, the role at Elland Road came without much warning. 'About five minutes before it started I was told "you'll be doing it",' Dickinson said. 'I'd kept myself ready, which was just as well. Bielsa's the sort of coach who strikes fear into an interpreter. You're trying to pick up the nuance in what he says. He's a really intelligent guy and there's a lot of complexity in his comments. For the first four or five minutes I tried to be literal with my answers.'[5]

Reporters in Argentina told us what to expect. Bielsa would be reserved but considered and if the mood took him, he would talk at great length. He would make little or no eye contact with his audience and would spend most of the press conference staring at the ground or the table in front of him. A socially awkward manner had been his trademark for a long time. Anything that struck him as an interesting question was likely to draw an interesting answer. The rest would be met with a straight bat. Bielsa was not prone to rash predictions and he had very little to say about transfers or the failure of the coaches who came before him at Leeds. Journalists with experience of him said that if you wanted to spark him into life, ask him about coaching or ask him about tactics. Touch on the things he is passionate about.

Bielsa's grasp of English has never been strong. Leeds arranged lessons for him in his first few months in England but Bielsa was unable to find the time to attend. (By his third year at Leeds, the players became aware of a noticeable improvement. 'He's been taking classes and he tries to speak more and more,' said Jack Harrison.)[6] Spanish suited him better. Even though it called for an English translation, he could articulate more clearly what was in his head by speaking in his native language. 'I've got a lot to thank my mother for,' Bielsa said as the press conference unfolded, 'but for one thing in particular. She sent me to English classes for fifteen years as a kid, hoping that today I'd be conducting this in English. I'll try [to learn more] but I said the same at the start in France and I didn't manage it.' Leeds, with hindsight, saw no way in which English lessons would have found much room in Bielsa's diary. When officials at the club asked him how he spent his free time during the Covid-19 lockdown in early 2020, he told them he had devoted almost twenty hours to watching video footage of Alfie McCalmont, a defensive midfielder in the club's academy. McCalmont was in that critical grey area between the Under-23s and the first team and Bielsa wanted to decide if he was good enough to rely on. 'Marcelo's levels of graft and resilience are different to the average level,' Orta said. In the end, McCalmont was sent on loan to Oldham Athletic and League Two.

Radrizzani sat with Bielsa for the opening minutes of the press conference, glowing with satisfaction. 'The weather's great,' Radrizzani quipped. 'Costa Del Yorkshire! The reason behind this appointment is mainly Marcelo and his career which talks for itself but also the desire to change the mentality in the club – to do it in a strong way with a man who can bring innovation and improve the football. We believe his vision reflects our desire to become a winning club.' The point about mentality, and by association professionalism, was pertinent. Leeds had amassed eight red cards in the previous season and lost their way badly after Christmas. Samuel Sáiz, their Spanish midfielder, was banned for six games for spitting during an FA Cup tie at Newport County. The club's end-of-season tour of Myanmar was politically controversial, while an attempt by Radrizzani to change Leeds' club crest had been so badly received that the new design was abandoned within six hours of its unveiling. Leeds lacked a figurehead who inspired confidence and trust. They needed a peg in the dug-out strong enough to hang their hat on; strong enough to carry the weight of a support who, after sixteen years in the EFL, were tired, impatient and malnourished by disappointing football.

Bielsa had a knack of connecting with the public. He was a deity in the eyes of half of Rosario, the city in Argentina where he made his name with Newell's Old Boys. He forged a lasting connection with supporters of Athletic Bilbao and Marseille, two of his previous European clubs. Leeds appealed to him in a similar way. The city had a working-class edge and an underdog feel, a one-club town looking for deliverance. When West Ham United went after Bielsa in 2015, he rejected their offer on the basis of doubts about the credibility of the board who were trying to employ him. But London did not feel entirely right either, a huge expanse in which West Ham were overshadowed by other teams. A source close to him said he saw Leeds as 'a region inhabited by a unique football fervour'. In short, the city loved what he loved and with that common ground they would have a chance of making it together.

Privately, Leeds were plain about what his appointment meant. They had finished 13th in the Championship under Heckingbottom but if Bielsa and his staff were coming at a cost of millions of pounds, qualification for the play-offs was the least they expected from him. Bielsa was not told as much, or not in as many words, but he felt it all the same. It had to work. Even so, he was new to England and new to the Championship. He did not want to sound presumptuous. 'It's imprudent to promise something you cannot be totally certain about,' he said. 'But at the same time, it would be impossible not to dream about promotion happening. What drives you is having the desire, the hope and the belief that you can achieve what everyone wants.' Far easier for him to give was the guarantee of football worth watching. 'I want protagonists on the field,' Bielsa said. 'I want players to take the game by the scruff of the neck and spend time in possession, not to be scared of getting on the ball. You'll see loyalty and faithfulness from them in trying to do what we tell them. I prefer beautiful football to overly pragmatic football. I don't think you can claim that playing badly to win is a means to an end.' While his arrival was pending, the squad at Leeds read up on Bielsa and rapidly deduced that he would take a hard line on diligence, fitness and diet. As a way of pre-empting the boot camp, Liam Cooper and Stuart Dallas decided to cut out alcohol before he landed.

Bielsa's first press conference revealed the traits which would become trademark features of his weekly briefings. Some questions were met with '*bueno*' – 'good' in Spanish but, where Bielsa was concerned, more of an affirmative 'well'. '*Mire*' – 'look' or 'listen' – was a cooler turn of phrase, a response which implied that Bielsa was about to contradict or correct a point which had been made. True to form, his unveiling took almost 80 minutes and as it reached the hour mark, Bielsa turned to Dickinson and asked if he wanted a rest. Dickinson laughed and said no. 'I'm tiring the translator out,' Bielsa said. 'I'm sorry I can't be brief. But I'm very conscious with the spoken or written word of getting my point across.'

That remark begged a question. If Bielsa and his coaches spoke limited English and only a handful of players in the dressing room spoke Spanish, would communication at Leeds be an issue? Was there a risk that the complexity and detail of his tactics would be lost or watered-down in translation? 'There are other ways of getting your point across,' Bielsa said. 'I'm confident enough to believe that my messages will be conveyed. The biggest factor that gets players playing is emotion.'

In all, Bielsa had six weeks to work with; six weeks of pre-season before his first Championship game against title favourites Stoke City. The turnaround seemed tight but Bielsa's CV gave him an edge. As Argentina's coach, and also in his time as manager of Chile, he was in the habit of organising squads quickly. With limited time to drill the players, international management taught Bielsa to make complicated tactics as simple and digestible as possible.

Stoke showed up at Elland Road on 5 August. Following relegation from the Premier League they had invested heavily in transfers and paid £2m to take manager Gary Rowett from Derby County. Bielsa's line-up contained only one new signing, left-back Barry Douglas, but a group of players who finished 13th a few months earlier clicked instantly and wiped the floor with Stoke, winning 3-1. That was what Leeds paid for. That was what Orta was talking about when he and Radrizzani spoke in the back of the car. Bielsa sat in his technical area on a padded blue stool, designed in the shape of an upside-down bucket. It was quirky and strangely iconic and offers to sponsor it began arriving from bookmakers and other companies in a matter of days (the online shopping site Wish eventually got its branding on it). Before long, Leeds were selling replicas in their club shop at £80 a go.

Bielsa's cult appeal took hold in an instant but the club were paying for substance rather than style. It suited them to have both, and Bielsa made light work of delivering both, but mid-table managers were in endless supply and came at a fraction of the price. Leeds had employed several. In the longer term, the partnership with Bielsa was about far more than image. It was, ideally, about more than promotion. Leeds saw in Bielsa not only the ability to regain a place in the Premier League but just as crucially, to stay there and reach a different stratosphere in competitive terms. The club cost Radrizzani £45m when he bought Cellino's shares. Three years later, with promotion secure, Radrizzani tells the *Financial Times* that he envisages the value of the club rising to 'the region of £600m to £1bn'.[7] By then they are a very different animal.

There was always a chance that the gamble would backfire; that Bielsa's ideas would fail and cost Radrizzani dearly. It happened at Lille where Bielsa survived for just six months. But there was quiet confidence that if, hypothetically, Leeds reached the Premier League and started their first season away to reigning champions Liverpool, Bielsa would be in situ and his imaginative football would continue to cause a stir. The journey would not be gentle and neither would he but some things are worth making sacrifices for, like Henry IV converting to Catholicism to prevent his reign in France from crumbling in the 1500s. The monarch's name cropped up randomly as Leeds and Bielsa were trying to nail down the terms of his initial contract. With Marcelo it is never straightforward, one of his closer confidants admitted. In spite of the simplicity of a suitcase filled with tracksuits, there is always one more detail to resolve. 'But Paris is worth a mass.'[8]

3.

OCTOBER

Leeds United's only misstep in the first month of the 2020–21 season comes in round two of the Carabao Cup. Marcelo Bielsa makes eleven changes to his line-up and Leeds lose on penalties at home to Hull City, a club newly relegated to League One. A low-level tie generates some unwanted political fall-out. Bielsa hands the captaincy to Kiko Casilla, the goalkeeper who received an eight-game ban from the Football Association after being found guilty of racially abusing Charlton Athletic winger Jonathan Leko six months earlier. Casilla denied the charge and Leeds defended him resolutely, using character references from his old club Real Madrid and his former manager Rafael Benítez, but the verdict and the written reasons explaining it reflected poorly on him. The FA questioned the credibility of parts of Casilla's evidence and sections of Leeds' support want him gone from Elland Road. Bielsa, though, is determined to keep him as number two keeper behind Illan Meslier and the squad are supportive too. Casilla, despite the damage to his reputation, is happy to stay. 'His team-mates thought he deserved to be captain,' Bielsa insists, explaining why Casilla was given the armband. 'We have to listen to those messages.' There is plenty of criticism of the decision, nonetheless.

The defeat to Hull creates a separate discussion. Despite the glut of changes and the selection of three academy players in the triangle connecting the centre of defence and defensive midfield,

Bielsa expected his team to progress to round three. It was not his intention to drop out of the League Cup early. The disjointed performance is a concern. These players are the back-up options in Bielsa's camp. These are the players he plans to turn to if injuries or suspensions bite. Deep down he likes a small squad. For most of his career he has tried to stick to a policy of having no more than two senior footballers for each position, and fewer if some members of his dressing room are versatile enough to fill multiple roles. 'I like the amount to be sufficient rather than excessive,' Bielsa said in the early stages of his tenure at Leeds. 'This, of course, is risky.' He is aware that other managers prefer to have more players than they strictly need but he is unrepentant about his own approach, even in the face of a result as agonising as Leeds' play-off semi-final defeat to Derby. That night Bielsa had four Under-23s on his bench and found himself turning in desperation to Izzy Brown, a loanee he had hardly been willing to field previously.

Leeds are slightly spooked by defeat to Hull. The result is neither here nor there but the side Bielsa picked have not played well. He and director of football Victor Orta speak at length after full-time. They are a Premier League club now, swimming with much bigger fish. Is the squad as deep and experienced as it should be? Would it not make sense to recruit a little more heavily? At the start of the transfer window, Bielsa wanted only one new centre-back – ideally Ben White but if not him then Robin Koch from Germany. If he found himself short in that position then he would dip into the Under-23s or move Luke Ayling across from right-back (Ayling will make that switch before October is out) but even Bielsa is starting to wonder if makeshift calls are wise. After a short period of reflection, Leeds table a bid for Joško Gvardiol, a Croatian de-fender at Dinamo Zagreb. Gvardiol is only eighteen and would not be first choice at Elland Road immediately but he is ranked among Europe's most highly-rated centre-backs and Leeds are prepared to pay £20m for him. They try hard to court him with the same sort of presentation they sent to Koch but on the night of Leeds' Premier League win over Fulham, Gvardiol agrees to join RB Leipzig instead. Leipzig will allow him to remain in Croatia on loan and Gvardiol thinks a move to the Premier League would be too much too soon for him. 'It was too early to go to England, one of the strongest leagues in the world,' he says. His agent, Andy Bara, says they chose Leipzig because of the quality of the 'sporting project'.[1]

Within days, and a few weeks on from landing Rodrigo, Orta is boarding another flight to Spain. Leeds have changed targets and enquired about Real Sociedad's Diego Llorente, a 27-year-old Spain international. Llorente is more proven than Gvardiol and, as a right-footer, plays on the opposite side of the centre-back pair. The deal is uncomplicated and takes no time to complete. Sociedad are happy to sell him and accept a fee of £18m. Llorente speaks to Pablo Hernández before taking Leeds' offer but says Bielsa is 'an important factor for me to be here'. Rodrigo and Koch made similar comments after joining and Leeds are starting to see the effect of Bielsa's presence when it comes to selling themselves to prospective signings. Footballers want to play for him, even if Bielsa thinks otherwise. 'Players choose clubs rather than the managers they play for,' Bielsa insists. 'When a player comes to Leeds, he comes to Leeds for Leeds.'

Bielsa's specifications for transfers are strict and exact. He wants athletes who tick the right boxes technically and players who reflect his own ethos. Leeds realise that big egos do not sit comfortably in his dressing room. Bielsa and high-maintenance players are a delicate mix. It is well known that he and Fernando Llorente endured an awkward relationship at Athletic Bilbao after the striker tried to force a transfer away from the club in 2012. They argued in public and in front of TV cameras before a UEFA Cup game against Sparta Prague. Bielsa sent Llorente away from that training session, saying his 'behaviour was not as desired'.[2] But Leeds have done a good job of meeting his needs and keeping the peace. In the thirtieth year of his coaching career, they have employed Bielsa for longer than any other club, Newell's Old Boys included. 'He's uniquely challenging,' says chief executive Angus Kinnear, a month into the season. 'The fact that he's left clubs he's worked for within days or weeks, or the fact that we're now his longest employer . . . He's ferociously exacting in terms of his standards and requirements. In the world of football coaching, genius is a word you can't use very often but I think you can apply it to him. When I deal with him I often get imposter syndrome. I've worked in football for twenty years but after an hour with him you realise that you don't understand the game at all.'[3]

The Bielsa factor comes into play again as Leeds try to wrap up a deal for a central midfielder. They have asked about Rodrigo De Paul at Udinese but the Argentina international is valued at £35m and Bielsa is undecided about whether De Paul, a talented and unashamed risk-taker, is the right fit. The club are interested in 22-year-old Ovie Ejaria at Reading but after asking for a series of references, they decide not to pursue him. Orta has an alternative which is ambitious but potentially unrealistic. He and Bielsa carry out analysis of Michaël Cuisance, a 21-year-old Frenchman at Bayern Munich. Cuisance, who has the ability and range of passing to play at number 10 or in a deeper midfield zone, has been at Bayern for just twelve months. In 2019 he forced his way out of Borussia Mönchengladbach and went to the Allianz Arena for £10m. People who watched Cuisance growing up say that from an early age he struggled to accept being a bit-part player. 'He didn't like it if he wasn't playing or was taken off,' says Jean-Robert Faucher, one of his youth-team coaches in France. 'But this is a sign of good character to me.'[4]

Cuisance is playing infrequently at Bayern and in spite of Bayern's status as reigning European champions, he tells the club that he wants to leave for a team who will give him more games. Coach Hansi Flick asks him to reconsider but Hasan Salihamidzic, Bayern's sporting director, relents and tells Cuisance he can go if an acceptable permanent offer arrives. Munich say any deal must include a buy-back clause of close to £50m (something major European clubs look for with increasing regularity). Forty-eight hours before Leeds' 1-0 win over Sheffield United, Orta is up early to travel from Manchester to Bavaria. He meets with Cuisance who says he is ready to take the chance to work with Bielsa and play in the Premier League. Shortly after the victory at Bramall Lane, Orta receives a phone call to tell him that Bayern are ready to thrash out the terms. It takes another two days for the clubs to finalise a £20m fee but the transfer is there to be done.

Leeds go through the process of chartering a jet from Germany and their media team begin preparing an announcement. They request footage of Cuisance's highlights for their social media channels but Bielsa is coy about the transfer at his weekly press conference ahead of a meeting with Manchester City. What will Cuisance bring to the club, he is asked. 'I would prefer to talk about it when it's official,' Bielsa says. 'I don't want a repeat of the Dan James situation.' He is referring to the January 2019 transfer window when Leeds got so close to signing James on loan from Swansea City that the winger had chosen a squad number, been photographed with a home shirt and completed all of his in-house media interviews (none of which saw the light of day). He sat inside Elland Road as the minutes ticked towards FIFA's 11 p.m.

deadline, unaware that Swansea chairman Huw Jenkins planned to pull the plug on the move at the last moment. Bielsa's caution about Cuisance is prescient. Perhaps he already knows what is happening. Not long after he speaks, more news filters through. Cuisance to Leeds is off. The midfielder has failed a medical.

Cuisance, to all intents and purposes, is fit. He played for Bayern two weeks earlier, as a substitute in an 8-0 rout of Schalke, but when Leeds receive the results of routine scans, they spot what they think is evidence of a stress fracture in one of his feet. Cuisance is asymptomatic and aware of no pain but Leeds estimate that the chances of his injury worsening are high. If the bone was to fracture it would need surgery to pin it in place and Cuisance would be looking at a recovery period of three to four months, followed by many more weeks spent regaining his match fitness. Bielsa is a stickler for conditioning, almost without compromise. Leeds have tried in the past to manage injury problems by suggesting he omit certain players from Under-23s fixtures and protect them for first-team games, but his response is always to say that if those players miss Under-23s fixtures, they will not be considered for first-team games either. One usually requires the other and it will be no different with Cuisance. Leeds are not prepared to take the risk. With no end of awkwardness, they tell Cuisance that they are pulling out of the transfer. He flies home to Munich that night.

It is a frantic backdrop to the weekend's match at home to Manchester City, a reunion between Bielsa and Pep Guardiola. Their tender, almost romantic, relationship is well known and every newspaper is writing about it. Both coaches, however, have other things to concentrate on. City are due at Elland Road on 3 October and the international transfer window shuts on the 5th. With the Cuisance signing off the table, Leeds are running out of time to make other deals happen. Guardiola, meanwhile, is licking his wounds from a 5-2 defeat to Leicester City. City controlled more than 70 per cent of possession against Leicester but conceded three penalties and were brought down by a horribly shaky defence. Guardiola has been wrestling with the same weakness for a while, unable to bring his backline to heel, and he does not anticipate an easy night in Leeds. He has a unique sense of admiration for Bielsa, the coach he calls 'the best in the world'. They have not crossed paths too often since Bielsa came to England, getting together for the occasional meal and speaking over the phone, but the professional bond they developed during their first meeting in Argentina in 2006 has never soured or broken. The ambition of Bielsa's football, his devotion to his craft and the intelligence of his management – all of this Guardiola loves. The Spaniard eulogised Bielsa in a column he submitted for *El País* (a favourite newspaper of Bielsa's and one which he has mailed to him in Leeds) before taking over at Barcelona. In an article entitled '*Sentirlo*' ('Feel it'), Guardiola wrote: 'Those of us who love Barça (a lot) and football (a lot more) have long since won the lottery. "I am attracted to victory and I realise that the road which leads closest to it is protagonism. I never think of a game without playing in the opponent's half." Marcelo Bielsa's wonderful phrase is one Barcelona have made their own for more than a decade.'[5] The last time they shared a touchline, in the 2012 Copa del Rey final, Bielsa was in charge of Athletic Bilbao and Guardiola was coaching Barcelona for the very last time. 'Anyone will give you this answer,' Bielsa says as he mulls over Guardiola's talent. 'His Barcelona, they are the best team in history. His teams play like no other team.' Guardiola is so pent up and so wary of Leeds that on Friday, the day before the game at Elland Road, he puts City's squad through a double training session. According to sources at Eastlands, he never does that.[6]

Leeds have pushed themselves hard in the early weeks of the

season. Patrick Bamford's reward for scoring their late winner against Sheffield United was to reach the final whistle with blisters all over his feet, the effect of so much running and chasing. Their tactics are still unmistakably Bielsa's but his side are being forced to adapt slightly. Championship teams were in the habit of sitting deep against Leeds. Managers in the Premier League are using high presses and mid blocks to stop them distributing possession so easily from the back. More than half of Illan Meslier's passes against Fulham were long balls designed to beat the press. Leeds are blending their commitment to Bielsa's system with a touch of pragmatism, refusing to be constrained by dogma if circumstances call for improvisation. Bielsa, for his part, is not opposed to long balls provided they offer more than an aimless hoof upfield but he swore at the outset that he would keep his principles intact: 'In the Premier League, to begin with we will try to play the same way.'

Manchester City start strongly at Elland Road, so strongly that Leeds hardly have the ball long enough for Guardiola's team to think about pressing them. Mateusz Klich trails after Kevin De Bruyne, who hits a post with a free-kick after four minutes, and Kalvin Phillips is in trouble on and off the ball, screened by Riyad Mahrez and unable to put a leash on Phil Foden. Raheem Sterling scores after 16 minutes, shooting into the bottom corner as City wade forward but Leeds, as they have in previous contests, reset, regroup and establish a rhythm. Bielsa out-thinks Guardiola tactically by introducing Ian Poveda, a former Manchester City academy winger, at half-time and providing more pace down the right. Phillips and Klich start to connect and De Bruyne strug-gles to uncover good possession. The Belgian's influence drops rapidly. Rodrigo comes off the bench, equalises in no time and then hits the crossbar twice. Orta is shouting vociferously from his seat in the West Stand and in the absence of a crowd, his Spanish inflection rings around the stadium. Guardiola reacts by turning around, looking straight at him and putting a finger to his lips. There is a late appeal from Sterling for a penalty after Liam Cooper slides in on him but neither referee Mike Dean nor the video assistant referee (VAR) gives Sterling the benefit of the doubt. With the tide turned, Guardiola is forced to shore up a 1-1 draw by adding the combative presence of Fernandinho to City's midfield. 'It was a very intelligent substitution,' Bielsa admits. 'It had a big influence.'

The rain hammers down throughout, not unlike the evening in 2011 when Bielsa and Guardiola first managed against each other. The weather was so torrential during that 2-2 draw between Athletic Bilbao and Barcelona that Athletic's San Mamés stadium was a sea of ponchos in the stands. Both coaches were exhausted by the end of that tussle, one of La Liga's best. Guardiola told Bielsa in admiration that his Bilbao team had played like 'beasts'.[7] As full-time arrives against City at Elland Road, Bielsa crouches down and stares at the ground for a few seconds. 'That was a moment of rest for me before leaving the field,' he says. 'It was a very intense game.' Guardiola shakes Bielsa's hand and embraces him. 'That was very nice,' he tells the Argentinian, 'and the right result.' Bielsa agrees. 'We had to find an immense physical effort to be on terms with City,' he says.

There is no opportunity to dwell on it. Bielsa and Orta have business to deal with. The summer's transfer deadline is closing in and Leeds, as they tangle with City, are on the verge of agreeing a fee for Rennes' Brazilian winger Raphinha. They have chewed over the possibility of submitting a fresh bid for Dan James, now at Manchester United, but despite James struggling at Old Trafford and becoming a lightning rod for frustration over the performance of Manchester United's owners and their manager, Ole Gunnar

Solskjær, there is no sign of Solskjær making him available. Leeds assumed Raphinha – someone Orta and Bielsa tracked independently of each other before discovering their mutual interest in him – would be unavailable too but on the last weekend of the window, Rennes make it known that they will sell him for £17m plus add-ons. Orta jumps on the opportunity immediately. The fee is less than Rennes paid to sign him from Sporting Lisbon a year earlier but the 23-year-old has indicated his desire to find a new club and the Rennes board seem happy to take the cash. Attempts by the club's senior players to talk him round after his final appearance against Reims fail. He flies to England with his agent, the former Portugal international Deco, and signs on a four-year deal half an hour before the summer deadline passes. A fourth new signing completes Leeds' business.

The club have pushed the boat out in terms of investment. Between Raphinha, Llorente, Koch and Rodrigo and permanent deals struck for Meslier and Helder Costa at the end of their loans from Lorient and Wolves, around £100m has been committed to the transfer window. More funds have been spent on a crop of academy recruits. Leeds' first tranche of Premier League broadcast revenue is gone, part of it drained by bonuses due on the back of their promotion from the Championship. The annual wage bill has almost doubled from £50m and they are using a number of different methods to fund their expenditure. They amortise most of the transfer fees, staggering payments across the length of the contracts their new players are signing. This limits the immediate outlay to around £3m per player. They set up a forward funding scheme, borrowing more than £40m through a bank loan and securing it against future television income. Many Premier League sides have similar arrangements in place, as they are a means of securing hard cash. Future shareholder investment is expected, most likely from the San Francisco 49ers, the club's minority shareholder. Leeds are also benefiting from commercial income rocketing overnight. Premier League TV revenue is on a completely different scale to that of the EFL (up from £2m a year to more than £100m). On top of central payments, the club stand to receive an additional £1m for every live game they appear in and by the end of the opening month of the season they have already been chosen for five. A change of shirt sponsor, bringing in foreign bookmaker SBOTOP, is worth £6.5m annually, a massive hike on the £750,000-a-year deal Leeds held with betting firm 32Red in the Championship. Sales of their new Adidas shirts are set to hit 250,000 (and it quickly dawns on the board at Elland Road that they have not ordered enough). In retail terms, Leeds are confident of performing as well as Tottenham Hotspur over the year ahead. What they need as a consequence of Covid-19 and no matchday money is more working capital.

The club are pleased with their window, despite the bid for Cuisance coming to nothing. Bayern Munich dispute Leeds' version of events and claim there is no issue with the midfielder's fitness. 'Our staff have a completely different opinion,' says Flick and Salihamidzic is furious to see details of Cuisance's medical leak out. Cuisance tells the media that there was 'no problem from my side' and he successfully passes a medical with Marseille who step in to sign him on loan. But his form in France proves underwhelming and Leeds are in no doubt that the transfer was too much of a gamble. A philosophical Bielsa accepts their prognosis and lets Cuisance go. He describes himself as 'totally satisfied' with the club's recruitment.

*

The international break that follows the deadline creates headaches for Leeds' medical department. Liam Cooper returns from

Scotland duty with a minor groin strain. Diego Llorente returns from time away with Spain with a similar ailment and is ruled out for three weeks. Leeds threw £18m at Llorente to ensure they were adequately covered at centre-back but when Cooper aggravates his injury in the warm up before their game against Wolverhampton Wanderers on 19 October, Pascal Struijk is the only partner left for Koch. Bielsa is accustomed to coping with absentees. Leeds dealt with so many in his first year that one of their specific aims for his second season was to reduce the number of injuries affecting the squad. In the Premier League Leeds are using a new brand of performance analysis software. Catapult, their supplier of data in the Championship, has been replaced by Statsports, an Irish company which is starting to corner much of the top-flight market. Liverpool and Manchester City are on its list of clients, along with Juventus and Paris Saint-Germain. For the first time Leeds have access to live data as they train and play, using tablets and watches to track the load of individual players. Bielsa does not believe in squad rotation or in the concept of resting players who are fundamentally fit but he pays close attention to the analysis and asks his staff to tailor the intensity of sessions according to the statistics. Leeds are latecomers when it comes to performance technology. As recently as a decade ago they were hiring a handful of GPS vests and sharing them around their squad, unwilling to make a more serious commitment. The results were not quite meaningless but they were not complete either, providing no more than a basic collection of numbers. It took another few years for the club to invest fully in Prozone, the first package of analytical tools the English game embraced. Leeds had dabbled with it in the mid-2000s but financial problems meant the cost of the software was prohibitive in the lower leagues. Tom Robinson, Leeds' sports scientist, has worked at Elland Road for more than ten years. 'GPS has been utilised best since Marcelo's come in,' he says.[8] The players are increasingly obsessional about it.

The match against Wolves, ending in a 1-0 home defeat, transports Leeds and Bielsa back to the Championship. For several weeks they have traded punches with Premier League teams who set out to attack them and allowed Leeds to respond in kind but Wolves and their manager, Nuno Espirito Santo, use cautious tactics. They pack in tightly and push Leeds' attacks out wide by creating congestion in the middle of the pitch. In the EFL, this was how most clubs set up against Bielsa. Very few were able to out-punch his side so the sensible ploy – and the strategy which paid off most often – was to maintain a strict defensive structure. Teams would forgo a large share of possession and trust their discipline to hold Leeds back. If their defence held, they could sucker-punch Bielsa's players by pinching a goal against the run of play. Wolves do exactly that. They are forced to bail water for the whole of the first half but Leeds make nothing of their pressure. Bielsa's players like to hunt for space on the wings but of thirty-seven crosses, only seven are accurate. Bamford spends his time drifting into gaps inside the Wolves box, only to watch deliveries fly beyond him and Wolves start to express themselves more after half-time. They are a Europa League outfit with plenty of class and a volley from Romain Saiss is ruled out for offside by VAR before Raúl Jiménez strikes in the 70th minute, scoring from the edge of the box with the help of a deflection off Kalvin Phillips's head. Bielsa is fairly reticent afterwards, uncharacteristically short of things to say. 'When an offensive team don't take their chances, the opposition reads this,' he says. 'Then they start to grow in confidence.'

Results like this are inevitable – the nights when Bielsa's tactics fall short and established Premier League teams work them out – but the performance was competitive and the scoreline feels harsh. More concerning for Bielsa is the sight of Phillips holding a shoulder after Jiménez bundles him to the ground 10 minutes from time. Phillips plays on but is sore in the morning and Leeds send him for a scan. The results are mixed. The damage to his shoulder ligaments has fallen narrowly below the threshold for surgery but it is bad enough to rule Phillips out for up to six weeks. Leeds have five matches in that period, including a visit to Aston Villa four days after the loss to Wolves.

Villa are in excellent shape. Their first four games have returned 12 points and they hold the Premier League's only perfect record. After avoiding relegation by a whisker at the end of the 2019–20 season, they showed more purpose and intent in the transfer market. Their transfer record was broken by a £28m deal for Ollie Watkins, a striker from Brentford whom Leeds monitored while their pursuit of Rodrigo from Valencia was ongoing. Leeds were dead-set on signing Rodrigo but up until lunchtime on 26 August, when Andrea Radrizzani and Valencia chairman Anil Murthy shook hands on a fee over lunch, they hedged their bets by keeping lines of communication to Watkins open. Much as they had a budget for only one of Rodrigo or Watkins, both players appealed. It was a choice between Spain's number 9 and Brentford's number 11 but Watkins had built a reputation as a natural finisher who scored goals for fun in the Championship. He had a knack of assisting shots for team-mates around him and if Leeds' move for Rodrigo collapsed, Orta knew who he would turn to. As well as signing Watkins, Villa loaned Ross Barkley from Chelsea and spent £17m bringing keeper Emiliano Martínez in from Arsenal. The general consensus is that Villa, like Leeds, enjoyed a good window. Both clubs' initial results back that view up.

Phillips's injury presents Bielsa with a dilemma. The midfielder's position, that of the defensive linchpin, is his alone. For two years Bielsa has survived without like-for-like cover for Phillips, memorably joking in 2018 that 'the best thing for us is if Phillips plays every game.'[9] His hand is already weak without Cooper and Llorente and Struijk is asked to fill in for Phillips at Villa Park. That reshuffle leaves a back four of Stuart Dallas, Luke Ayling, Robin Koch and Gjanni Alioski: a utility player at right-back, a right-back at centre-back, a right-sided centre-back on the left side of the pair and a one-time winger in Alioski at left-back. Leeds look compromised on paper but Bielsa coaches them in a way which pre-empts these crises. He does not hold with the idea of one player being considerably better than another or of anyone being indispensable. He believes in training his squad so they are schooled in the whole range of his methods. If one player drops out, another steps in. All of them should be adaptable, Bielsa would say, or able to improvise. Versatility is one of the traits Bielsa values most. He employs interns, paid for from his own pocket, to carry out research projects for him, fuelling his interest in football's tactical evolution. One of those projects focused on a goalkeeper in Austria's lower leagues who had taken to positioning himself so far up the pitch that he was the equivalent of an extra central defender in possession.[10] Bielsa admired ingenuity like that. Phillips, as an example, never thought of himself as a defensive midfielder before Bielsa took over at Elland Road. In his head he was box-to-box but nothing said more about Bielsa's understanding of ability than Phillips's call-up to the England squad.

It gets more complicated at Villa Park before it gets better. Struijk is booked for an early foul on Jack Grealish and Bielsa substitutes him after 21 minutes. The cut and thrust of the match threatens Struijk with a second yellow card and Bielsa takes him out of harm's way. More reorganisation ensues. Jamie Shackleton is sent on and takes up an advanced midfield position. Klich falls back into the number four zone. Bielsa's line-up grows ever more unfamiliar but after a closely fought first half, Leeds go through the gears spectacularly. Bamford draws first blood in the 55th minute after a counter-attack blitzes Villa down the left. He scores again with a wonderfully casual finish from 20 yards, driven in off the underside of the crossbar. He completes a hat-trick – the first by a Leeds player in the Premier League since Mark Viduka in 2003 – at the end of a classic Bielsa move, woven together by incisive passing and rounded off by Bamford curling a left-footed finish into the far corner. For the last half-hour of a 3-0 loss, Villa are nowhere to be seen in an attacking sense. Watkins is a £28m shadow and Leeds are so relentless that in the 95th minute, with the game already settled, their final attack creates a seven-on-four advantage on the edge of Villa's box. They are driven on through injury-time by Bielsa willing them on from the touchline. Dean Smith, Villa's manager, stands quietly a few yards away, waiting for the whistle to stop the torment.

A certain amount of antipathy exists between Leeds and Villa. When they last met at Villa Park, in the 2018–19 season, Orta caused ructions in the directors' box with his celebrations as Leeds fought back from 2-0 down to win 3-2. In the return game at Elland Road, Bielsa allowed Villa to walk in an equaliser in a 1-1 draw after Klich scored while Jonathan Kodjia was down injured in the centre-circle and Villa's players waited for Leeds to kick the ball out of play. Bielsa's decision diffused a touchline melee (despite objections from one of his own players, Pontus Jansson) and later earned him FIFA's annual fair play award – but some underlying tension remained. Smith, though, is not about to argue with the outcome of their clash in the Premier League. 'They scored the first goal and we got worse,' Smith says. 'They were very good. We probably got away with 3-0 in the end, with the chances they had.'

In that same week, Bielsa's future as head coach at Leeds comes onto the agenda again. It is the subject of remarks made by Radrizzani in an interview with Argentinian newspaper *La Nacion*. Radrizzani admitted he had no idea if Bielsa would see out more than one year in the Premier League. 'I'd like to continue with the cycle but I'm not naive either,' Radrizzani says. 'Marcelo is no longer young. He's 65 years old and his family is often in Argentina. I don't know if he wants to stay.'[11] It is the elephant in the room at Elland Road. How long will this relationship last? How long will Bielsa commit to a job so far from home and his wife and daughters? And more to the point, how would Leeds go about replacing him?

Bielsa was not obviously prone to homesickness. In the summer between his first two seasons in England he spent less than a week with his family in Rosario before travelling to attend football seminars in other parts of South America and turning his attention back to his work. A source who has known him for years describes him as 'a person who doesn't miss anywhere too much, even though he has his affections'. He could return to Argentina and enjoy the seclusion of his home in the countryside for a short time but it never took long for his professional appetite to kick in again. And with Leeds, his appetite has not dissipated. 'I'm very comfortable living and managing in England,' Bielsa says, in response to Radrizzani's comments. 'Annual contracts don't mean I'm not open to staying here longer.' The only thing the board feel certain of is that Leeds will be the only English side he ever manages. Their conversations with him have convinced them that defection is not likely.

Bielsa's fingerprints are all over the club, creating an attachment too strong for anyone to contemplate the idea of breaking it. His coaching has changed their direction completely and his cultural impact is spreading too, turning parts of Leeds into a shrine to him. Murals, tributes and a street named in his honour; this is his city now.

4.

THE REVOLUTION

Hyde Park Corner in Leeds has been Sir Robert Peel's domain for years. His statue at the edge of Woodhouse Moor was erected there in 1852, a bronze likeness of the two-time prime minister, and it kept its place despite an attempt by anti-racism campaigners to remove it in 2020. Peel's father, Robert, was a cotton producer with a history of links to the slave trade. The local council resisted a petition opposing the monument by telling the protesters they were targeting the wrong man.

A few months after that wrangle, paintwork began appearing on the side of an end-terrace building around the corner from Peel's plinth. The property was unremarkable, with a grocery shop on the ground floor and takeaways and tattoo studios around it, but over the course of a few days a mural took shape on its facade. The design was the work of Irek Jasutowicz, a Polish military veteran and street artist known as Tankpetrol (on account of the fact that he once drove tanks in the Polish army). A local property firm had commissioned him to produce a tribute to Leeds United's promotion from the Championship and with careful precision, the face of Marcelo Bielsa was spray-painted on top of a coal-black background, his eyes looking out over the crossroads at Hyde Park. Jasutowicz daubed a quote alongside it, a phrase Bielsa used to sum up his own reputation: 'A man with new ideas is a madman, until his ideas triumph.'

Bielsa is a permanent fixture in that part of Leeds now, in your line of sight as you drive north out of the city. Unlike Peel, he is safe from threats of removal. As uncomfortable as the adulation made him feel, Bielsa was used to seeing himself like this. In Rosario, Argentina, where he has the keys to Newell's Old Boys, graffiti and football street art is rife, an old cultural trend. Many of the designs in Rosario celebrate Newell's history and one remembers the day in 1991 when Bielsa's team routed their rivals Rosario Central 4-0. Central's fans poured out of the stadium in dejection before the thrashing was over. 'With El Loco Bielsa,' the painting reads, 'and at 4-0, your people left.' To quote Buenos Aires-based artist Martin Ron, the public in Argentina have a rare tolerance of graffiti. At its best and most inventive, it is so much more than an act of vandalism.[1]

English football has never caught the street-art bug, or not to the same degree. In Leeds, tributes honouring the biggest icons at Leeds United are relatively few. A statue of Billy Bremner, their feisty, blood-and-guts captain, was built on one corner of Elland Road in 1999 but it took until 2012 for Don Revie, the doyen of Leeds who inspired the club's golden era in the 1960s and '70s, to be honoured in the same way. But Bielsa very quickly changed the face of the city. A few weeks before the mural of him was completed in Hyde Park, another appeared on the side of a pet shop in Wortley, a short walk from Elland Road. It was very different in design – a striking mix of whites, blues and yellows depicting Bielsa as Christ the Redeemer in Rio De Janeiro – but like Jasutowicz's work, it will be there long after Bielsa has gone, a symbol of what happened in Leeds while Bielsa was finding the city's voice. 'You know what it's been like for the club, or what it was like before he came,' says Nicolas Dixon, the artist who designed the image and spent sixty hours completing it. 'There's been so much misery for such a long time but now you've got kids who'll grow up supporting a Premier League club, kids who see Leeds United as it should be. He's done that and if you do that, you deserve something to remember you by.'[2] Bielsa was touched by the acknowledgements. 'It makes me very proud,' he said. 'Of course I won't forget it.'

Leeds, in a footballing sense, are the only show in town, the biggest one-club city in England. But for years their presence in their own backyard was muted or less visible than it should have been. That began to change in 2019 when Andy McVeigh, a local primary school teacher, turned his hand to decorating broadband switch cabinets and other street furniture near his home in the suburb of Burley. It began as a therapeutic release on Christmas Day in 2016 when he painted a Peppa Pig image on a box by Kirkstall Road in memory of his niece, Grace. Grace was born with spinal muscular atrophy and died before her first birthday. McVeigh found peace in the solitude of painting and over time, he turned his hand to Leeds United artwork: some of it depicting shirts of former players, some of it branded with the club's colours and chants. He finished one shortly after Bielsa's first season and dedicated it to both the Argentinian and McVeigh's son, Danny. On the side he inscribed a small but desperate prayer: 'This season Leeds . . .' McVeigh's friends dubbed him 'The Burley Banksy' and the effect of each scrap of art has been to spawn a little more. To mark the Championship title, the Leeds United Supporters Trust arranged for fresh murals to be painted across the city, including a depiction of Pablo Hernández celebrating the goal at Swansea City which all but sealed promotion. It sprang up on the side of the Duck and Drake pub, a shock of green 10 metres high. An image of Kalvin Phillips materialised on The Calls near the River Aire before Christmas and another of Bielsa on a farm building in a field near the village of Menston. Mateusz Klich, a self-confessed graffiti nut, took a backpack filled with paint cans down to Elland Road and sprayed 'Champions' on a wall outside the East Stand. 'I've been into [graffiti] since I was little,' Klich said. 'Painting walls under cover of night was always something I wanted to do.'[3]

Bielsa's influence and the success of his squad brought Leeds to life. The club had rarely been so in touch with their fanbase, or not for the best part of two decades. There was a point in 2016, during Massimo Cellino's three years as owner, where apathy was so high that Leeds were forced to entice supporters to buy season tickets by promising partial refunds if the club failed to make the Championship play-offs (they finished seventh, one place short, and repaid 25 per cent to those who had signed up). In Bielsa's first season sales hit 20,000, the biggest uptake since Leeds' Champions League era. The demand was so high that the club capped season tickets at 23,000 to make sure a ground with 36,000 seats still had some on general sale. The impact of promotion was so great that by the start of the 2020–21 Premier League season, they had sold 23,000 again and created a waiting list with 20,000 names on it (places on the waiting list were sold at £10 a go, to cover administrative costs).

Bielsa aspired to a certain level of entertainment and in Leeds they voted for his football with their feet but the public's focus on his personality, his character and his mind was perplexing for him. The simplicity of his existence and the juxtaposition of a high profile set against a basic lifestyle endeared him to people who thought a coach of his standing would be different. The walking to and from the training ground was unusual (his staff had a car available to them but Bielsa was not inclined to use it much). He did occasionally consider buying a bike and at one point got in touch with officials at Leeds and asked them to think about signing up to the government's Cycle to Work scheme. He was pictured in a club tracksuit pushing a trolley around Morrison's and photographed coming out of the local baker's with bread rolls. The images gained traction on social media but Bielsa was nonplussed. A monologue in one of his press conferences, pondering the celebrity of footballers and the media's mounting obsession with it, ended with him wondering aloud why anyone was bothered about his shopping habits. 'Who cares if I buy my food in one supermarket or another?' he asked. But they did. And the only way of answering that question was to ask when Pep Guardiola or José Mourinho was last seen doing the same.

His aversion to gossip-style publicity did not dissuade him from mingling in everyday settings. Costa Coffee on Wetherby's Market Place became his regular haunt on a Sunday morning, a place for him to go with a tablet for video analysis and written notes. He would share tables with other customers and grant photo requests as they came. If you tried, it was possible to elicit bits of information from him. In the summer of 2019 Bielsa was stopped by a group of supporters in the street and quizzed about his plans for the transfer window. He took a pen and paper and wrote down a long list of players' names; in effect, his squad as he wanted it to be when the window closed a couple of months later. Centre-back Ben White was on there, even before Leeds had signed him on loan from Brighton. And notably, Pontus Jansson was missing.

Jansson's fate during that close season was indicative of Bielsa's management and a demonstration of the red lines Bielsa sticks to. Jansson, a Sweden international, had embedded himself at Leeds over three previous seasons. He was popular with the crowd, a colourful and capable defender, and someone journalists could rely on to say whatever was in his head. No one in the dressing room at Elland Road was more liable to test Bielsa. Their relationship got off on the wrong foot when Jansson took three weeks' holiday after the 2018 World Cup, returning to training six days before the start of the Championship term. Bielsa, who left Jansson to decide on the length of his absence, had hoped to see him rejoin training sooner so put together a defence without him (Jansson would break back in after Gaetano Berardi injured a knee). The following summer, a similar issue arose as Jansson attempted to delay his pre-season start date after another stint of international duty and suggested that other players do the same. Bielsa lost patience over what he saw as a challenge to his authority and told Leeds to sell the centre-back. The demand worried the club's board. Jansson had performed impressively in the main since joining from Torino and the only offer for him had come from Brentford, a Championship team who Leeds expected to compete with them for promotion. Bielsa, though, was adamant. Take £5.5m for Jansson and sign White on loan from Brighton. Before long, the deals were done.

Other players, in other ways, also fell foul of his rigid standards. A few weeks before the January transfer window in 2019, Samuel Sáiz – a skilful and unorthodox number 10 – complained of being homesick and began agitating to leave England for Spain. Though Leeds had fixtures remaining before the turn of the year, Bielsa instructed the club to jettison him immediately. You were in or you were out, and Sáiz was out. Midfielder Izzy Brown signed on loan from Chelsea in the early stages of Bielsa's maiden season but, having come through the latter stages of his recovery from major knee surgery, the midfielder fell short on the intensity scale. Brown's impact in training failed to catch the eye and his involvement in the Championship was so meagre that by the time he appeared as a substitute in the second leg of Leeds' play-off semi-final defeat to Derby, he had touched the ball in competitive fixtures just once (and that touch, a cross which hit him in the face at Queens Park Rangers). 'He lost his self-esteem here,' Bielsa said later, blaming himself for the failure of the transfer. Wherever the fault lay, the handling of Brown was ruthless.

Inside the training ground, most of Bielsa's squad learned to observe the boundaries. His office was private and isolated and players were rarely called in to speak to him there. Some training sessions he watched intently at close range. Others he would leave to his staff, with instructions about how the drills should be structured. Leeds' analytics department soon noticed that the performance data increased markedly whenever Bielsa was pitchside. 'The intensity goes up because the players know he's there,' says sports scientist Tom Robinson.

Bielsa's relationship with them never strayed towards friendship. He was not like Neil Warnock, who has long been in the habit of using pre-season to invite the squad of whichever club he is managing to a barbecue at his home in Cornwall. Some of the players Bielsa has coached in his career found him aloof. Some thought his personality was hard to relate to. 'He always kept his distance,' says Ricardo Lunari, the ex-Newell's midfielder. 'He didn't allow himself to show any feeling or emotions to the players. The relationship wasn't good or bad. It was simply distant.'[4] But many more would say that irrespective of that, they learned from Bielsa and improved. 'I love my players,' Bielsa said during his first year in England, 'but if they were closer to me they would respect me less because they would see how I really am.' It was a professional stance as opposed to a culture of fear. Most clubs implement a system of fines to punish players for specific disciplinary breaches. Chelsea manager Frank Lampard, for example, imposed a £20,000 penalty on anyone who was late for the start of training and a £500-per-minute penalty on anyone who was late for team meetings (two sanctions from a list of more than ten punishable indiscretions). Under Bielsa, there was no fines system at Leeds. He wanted his squad to be disciplined but not because of the threat of financial consequences. 'He doesn't believe in it,' said Patrick Bamford. 'He thinks it's not the best way to get someone to do something. You're allowed a one-off.'[5]

Bielsa's attitude towards the public was deferential by comparison. He cut a shy and retiring figure but his connection with Leeds' support, and the fans of other clubs he has worked for, was relaxed and free of professional limits. Players were paid for their services and paid well, Bielsa would say. So were head coaches. Supporters paid to watch and the distinction mattered to him, as did the disparity in the salaries earned by people in his job and the lower-level staff at a club like Leeds. At the stage where Leeds began bringing employees back from the furlough scheme set up by the UK government during the Covid-19 shutdown, Bielsa insisted that one of the first to start working again was the training ground's long-serving chef, Izzy. In the weeks leading up to his first Christmas in Yorkshire he ran a raffle for the rank and file at Thorp Arch, sending Leeds staff out with his own money to buy prizes: a widescreen television, a mobile phone, a laptop and a Volkswagen Polo. One of the kit men won the car but felt so guilty that he sold it and split the money with his colleagues.[6] Bielsa liked to hand out lollipops to the kids who stood and waited for him and his players to step off the team coach before home matches and to immerse himself in the local psyche. The Leeds fanzine *The Square Ball* pulled out all the stops to publish a 228-page magazine to celebrate the Championship title win. Bielsa came across it, asked for twenty-five copies for his friends and family and repaid the favour by inviting the fanzine's producers to meet him at Thorp Arch.

Every now and again, the bits of generosity were reciprocated. Early in the 2020–21 season, a supporter who had travelled to Argentina on business dropped a carrier bag at Bielsa's flat filled with Yerba *mate* herbal tea and a yellow box of Argentinian Havana chocolates (Bielsa's favourite sweets). Bielsa was upstairs watching Sheffield United play Aston Villa – Leeds were due to meet the Blades that weekend – and one of his old friends from Chile answered the door, telling the fan that Bielsa was otherwise engaged with '*el partido*' (the match). A few days later, the fan received a call from Bielsa. Thank you for the presents, he said. And next time you are in Buenos Aires, I will arrange for you to have a tour of the city. I will also arrange for you to be driven north to see Rosario too. Some who meet Bielsa and chat to him randomly in the street are given invites to watch Leeds train. At the height of the coronavirus, with Bielsa's family unable to fly over from Argentina, a woman in Wetherby took to leaving homemade soup on his doorstep every week. In all it was a story of improbable and unconditional friendships between people who barely knew each other.

Bielsa felt the same love in Rosario, or in half of it. But the divided opinion about him there matches his reputation in Argentina as a whole. Some of the population see Bielsa as a forward-thinking genius, the coach's coach. Some treat him with unyielding respect. At one of his first pre-season friendlies, away at York City, he was engaged in conversation by Sebastian Casiro, an agricultural specialist who had moved from Buenos Aires to England. They spoke at length, chatting and joking in Spanish. I got in touch with Casiro to ask about his perception of Bielsa and what they had talked about. Casiro replied politely and said that he would rather not say. 'It's a personal memory I want to keep to myself,' he said. 'I want those memories to be just mine.' Almost as if they were too valuable to share.

Others in Argentina think Bielsa is a myth, an overrated manager whose reputation and prestige has been manufactured, concocted or built on weak ground. Former Argentina coach Alfio Basile is scathing about the credit given to him. 'He is surrounded by marketing like I've never seen in my life,' Basile said in an interview in 2018. 'He never takes on a big team who are obligated to win [trophies].'[7] Much of the antipathy towards Bielsa stemmed from the 2002 World Cup in Korea and Japan which Argentina entered with so much promise. They dropped out of the competition after failing to qualify from their group. Before the tournament, Bielsa was under pressure from the media to pair Hernán Crespo with Gabriel Batistuta up front but resisted on the grounds that his system was not designed to accommodate a front two. Even Batistuta, confused by Bielsa's thinking, could not talk him round.[8] Bielsa's football, which had strong European influences behind it, lacked the fantasy element many in Argentina craved. He tried to point out that as the sport became more defensively savvy, tactical precision was more essential and more important to a coach than individual brilliance. 'There are no more Maradonas,' he said pointedly as the World Cup drew near but the blame for his squad's poor performance at that tournament was laid at his door and although Argentina went on to win the gold medal at the Olympic Games in 2004, Bielsa was a spent force and resigned that same year. 'Except for very few occasions, the breaks Marcelo needs from football are brief,' says a source close to him. 'But one of them was after winning the gold medal in Athens.'

Bielsa's adventure in England garnered plenty of attention in his home country. Interest grew steadily and ESPN, for the first time, televised live Championship matches. Normally, Argentina's viewing audience had next to no interest in England's lower leagues. It took the Premier League or something like El Clásico to make broadcasters find space in their schedules. 'It's a fact that before Bielsa arrived in Leeds, almost nobody watched the

Championship,' said journalist Ariel Senosiain.[9] As a cult following developed, people took to hunting down illegal online streams for games which ESPN chose not to show. In Rosario they saw the same levels of intrigue. 'I almost think that Leeds is the club where the Bielsa connection has had the biggest impact for us,' said Newell's Old Boys media officer Juan Mattos. 'There was never so much talk about the English second division here.' When promotion was sealed in 2020, the board of directors at Newell's wrote to Leeds and Bielsa, congratulating them on the achievement. Vice-president Cristian D'Amico said it 'filled our hearts with joy to see an icon of our house prevail'.

Basile and people like him could not comprehend why Argentine television was devoting so much time to non-Premier League fixtures. To them, it felt like fawning coverage. But Bielsa's magnetism was most apparent on 17 July 2020, the evening when Leeds were officially promoted. His team were not even playing that night. He was at home in Wetherby and most of his players gathered together in a hospitality suite at Elland Road, watching Huddersfield Town play West Bromwich Albion. The permutation was simple. If West Brom dropped points, Leeds were up; they lost 2-1, conceding the decisive goal four minutes from time. Champagne went everywhere as Leeds' squad erupted. Bielsa, normally subdued and reserved, was tempted down to Elland Road to join in.

Seven thousand miles away, Argentinian eyes were on the result at Huddersfield too. Leeds had developed a pocket of enthusiasts in South America but there was no denying that ESPN carrying a live feed of Huddersfield against West Brom was remarkable. 'They would never have considered showing a game like that,' Senosiain said but the audience justified the broadcast. Author Andrea D'Emilio, who compiled a book on Bielsa entitled *Los Locos del Loco* ('The Madmen of the Madman'), said she was persuaded to write about him by 'the affection aroused for an English team in Argentina'. Her nephews have taken to supporting Leeds and wearing Leeds colours. The club, as a result of Bielsa's presence, have generated a fanbase in a country that took next to no interest in them before.

At *El Ciudadano*, a daily newspaper in Rosario, they cleared the front page on the day Bielsa's squad went up. At the time, Argentina was as consumed as England by reports about the coronavirus. Media coverage was glued to the pandemic and *El Ciudadano*'s splashes focused on little else. Compared to that, Bielsa's Leeds were a feel-good story and the paper knew the appetite for reading about it was there. Their website already had a section devoted to him. Even among supporters of Rosario Central, there was a degree of curiosity about the waves Bielsa was making abroad. 'Everything he does at Leeds has great repercussions,' said José Odisio, one of *El Ciudadano*'s journalists. 'We were in the midst of negative covers [front pages] so Leeds and Bielsa was an unmissable opportunity to shift the axis and the agenda.'

The following morning *El Ciudadano* ran with Leeds' promotion as its splash.[10] The main image was of fans gathered outside Elland Road, waving flags and carrying flares. Above it was the headline '*Su Reino Unido*' ('His United Kingdom') and the paper talked about the 'Locovirus' – an outbreak of affection for Bielsa – infecting English football. But not everyone was impressed. To certain pundits in Argentina, the Championship was a second-rate title and in a debate about Bielsa's credentials as an elite coach, in a career where trophies had been sparse, they considered it to be meaningless. What that opinion lacked was the context of where Leeds had been, how long their exile in the EFL had lasted and how impossible his job had seemingly become before he took it on. 'I try to explain to people that it's the equivalent of a big Argentine team like Racing Club or San Lorenzo being relegated and not coming back up for sixteen years,' said Nicholas Bloj, a video blogger and supporter of Newell's. 'Then they start to understand the significance of the achievement.'

In England the significance spoke for itself. Guardiola invited Bielsa to Manchester for a special dinner.[11] Within days of promotion, a street by Leeds' Trinity shopping centre had been named after him. The euphoria was enough to crack Bielsa's facade. 'Love is what every human being wants in life,' he said as he reflected on the title win and the reaction to it. 'You have two kinds of love – that which comes from your closest people, your family, and that which comes from situations like this, the feeling when you provoke happiness in a lot of people. It is a great feeling, the greatest feeling this job offers us I think.'

There is video footage of Bielsa emerging from his flat an hour or so after West Brom's defeat at Huddersfield, stepping outside to find a small crowd gathered around his driveway. Bielsa smiles modestly and waves to them, grateful that they have made the effort. He apologises for his inability to speak English but they are there to see him rather than hear from him. 'You are God,' one supporter tells him. Bielsa fails to catch the comment. 'You are God,' the fan shouts again. Bielsa grins for a second but then stops and looks back, wagging his finger and replying with one word. 'No.'

5.

NOVEMBER

As 2020 wears on, Bielsa's spontaneous encounters with supporters dwindle. There are no crowds at Elland Road and as the government's approach to tackling Covid-19 swings between local and national lockdowns, there is no prospect of crowds returning to the stadium before Christmas either. Bielsa sympathises with the fans who are looking on from a distance. Passion and escapism are two of his ideals and two of the things this spectator-less version of football are missing. A sanitised game is almost an image of what Bielsa worries about: football detaching itself from the public and losing touch with its roots completely. It was because of that concern that in the early weeks of his tenure he made his players at Leeds collect litter for three hours around the pitches at their training ground. Three hours of manual labour was, give or take, what it took to earn enough money to buy a ticket to a game at Elland Road. Bielsa saw litter-collecting as a way of reminding his squad what a normal job was like.[1] 'Football's not the same without the fans,' he says. 'It becomes less attractive. Football's a party and it's very difficult to have a party with everything that's going on in the world.'

The outlook for football in England is stark. Covid-19 infection rates are rising nationally and beginning to cause postponements. The pandemic is depriving every club of typical revenue streams and in the lower leagues, many teams are badly starved of cash.

Rescue packages are discussed with the government and the Premier League and midway through October, the EFL's chairman, Rick Parry, colludes with a handful of the top-flight's most powerful sides – Liverpool and Manchester United predominantly – to bring forward 'Project Big Picture', a proposal designed to reshape the English game. The ideas listed in it are wide in scope and controversial, including a reduction in the size of the Premier League from twenty to eighteens teams, a move to scrap the League Cup and a change in the weighting of top-flight voting rights. In return for its implementation, hundreds of millions of pounds from the Premier League would be filtered down the domestic pyramid. The first Leeds learn of Project Big Picture is when one of their directors reads about it in the *Daily Telegraph* on the morning of Sunday, 11 October.[2] Like most clubs, they have not been briefed about the plan or even made aware of its existence and as a newly promoted side, the prospect of a slimline Premier League does not appeal to them at all. Their immediate assumption is that Liverpool, Manchester United and other clubs of that size would use a smaller domestic schedule to play more, and earn more money, in European tournaments. Other top-flight executives share that view. Project Big Picture is roundly savaged and rapidly shelved after a tense meeting involving all twenty Premier League clubs. Everton CEO Denise Barrett-Baxendale asks for apologies from Liverpool and Manchester United over what she sees as a brazen attempt to hand more control to the teams who already hold most power.[3] Bielsa sides with the plan's critics, convinced that the Premier League is already strong enough. 'A humble opinion of mine is that the tip of the iceberg has a responsibility to the rest of the iceberg,' he says. He has warmed to England's lower leagues and likes to watch League One and League Two fixtures, just for a change of scenery.

To Leeds and Andrea Radrizzani, any consolidation of the established top six is a direct threat to their own ambition. On Radrizzani's watch the club's commercial performance has been growing consistently. Like almost every Championship team, they made multi-million pound losses in the EFL – losses Radrizzani was happy to finance through loans and equity exchanges – but by the end of his third year as majority shareholder, Leeds' annual turnover has jumped from £34m to around £54m, the highest income of any team outside the Premier League. Operations at Elland Road were re-organised and modernised (there were times under Massimo Cellino where they survived without a full-time chief executive) and Bielsa's football meant tickets were incredibly easy to sell. But conversely, full houses pose a problem. Leeds have maximised their matchday revenue and a capacity crowd of around 36,000 will not help them be competitive in the longer term. They have major plans to redevelop Elland Road and the area around it, including a project which will see them leave their Thorp Arch training complex for a new site in Holbeck, a mile or so from the stadium. There are two reasons for seeking to quit Thorp Arch: firstly, to make the academy more accessible for inner-city children. Thorp Arch is twenty miles out of town and awkward to reach by bus. As one person at the club put it, the number of Range Rovers driving in and out does not speak to a diverse social reach. The second reason is to vacate a facility which the club do not own and is costing an annual rent not far short of £1m. At Elland Road, Leeds envisage rebuilding the West Stand and increasing the stadium's capacity to 50,000 and by the end of 2020, they are starting to wonder if 50,000 will be enough. Additional work on the North Stand behind one goal would provide more seats and allow for crowds of 55,000. The club feel increasingly confident that the demand for tickets will be high enough if their Premier League status remains intact.

In proposing to upgrade their ground, Leeds have a useful partner in the boardroom. In 2018, a month before Bielsa's appointment, Radrizzani secured a £10m cash injection from 49ers Enterprises, the investment arm of NFL franchise the San Francisco 49ers. The Americans took on a minority stake of just over 10 per cent and appointed Paraag Marathe, the president of 49ers Enterprises, as a Leeds director. From 2014 onwards, the 49ers had occupied a new state-of-the-art home, the Levi's Stadium, in Santa Clara. As venues go, it was a leader in technological innovation, with a mobile app allowing for contactless payment and systems set up to deliver food, drink and merchandise to fans in their seats. Some who supported the 49ers the venue was devoid of soul and personality (it was also based fifty miles south of the San Francisco Bay area) but Leeds liked the thought of tapping into that experience. On the back of promotion, the 49ers began weighing up a deal to increase their stake at Elland Road. Midway through November, a new venture capital fund – 49ers Enterprises Leeds II SPV – is registered by Marathe with the United States Securities and Exchange Commission, indicating that more investment is on the way. The 49ers' clout is huge and their involvement with Leeds is one of several reasons why Radrizzani and his board are opposed to Project Big Picture. Among other things, the project proposes a framework whereby a small cabal of clubs can veto any takeover of a rival Premier League side. As Leeds see it, they are one of the teams below the top six with scope to grow exponentially. They are the sort of club whose ambition Project Big Picture threatens to contain.

Despite promotion, Leeds are not immune from the pressures created by Covid-19. Radrizzani estimates that the cost to the club of the pandemic will be £40m but they have avoided redundancies among their full-time employees and at an all-staff meeting in early November, chief executive Angus Kinnear offers further assurances that cuts will not be coming. Preventing redundancies was one of the commitments made by Leeds' hierarchy when their squad accepted wage deferrals during the early stages of the pandemic. The players agreed that anyone earning more than £6,000 a week would drop down to that figure and defer the rest of their salaries (Kiko Casilla, their highest earner at the time, was pulling in more than £30,000 a week). Full pay among the squad was reinstated after Leeds won the Championship title but in the interim, the spare funds helped to protect jobs. Bielsa and his coaches were also part of the deferral, one of the first put in place by a major English club after Covid-19 forced the suspension of the 2019–20 season.

On the pitch, Leeds' start to the Premier League campaign has been so good that on 2 November, the night of Leicester City's visit to Elland Road, they have the chance to move into third place. The table is in its infancy but the impetus is there, even if Bielsa's full resources are not. Rodrigo's wife tests positive for Covid-19 before the game and the forward is forced to self-isolate. He tests positive himself the following day. Raphinha is absent with a minor ankle injury but Bielsa is able to start Pablo Hernández, fully fit again after a groin strain. The main worry is the weather and stodgy underfoot conditions which are unlikely to suit Hernández or Bielsa's fluent style. It rains heavily for two hours before kick-off and water starts to settle on the pitch. The drainage system – originally installed around Euro 96 and largely past its sell-by date 24 years on – is archaic and the surface is deteriorating. By November, though, belated progress is being made with Leeds' new floodlights. Better illumination of the pitch is necessary to meet the standards expected by the Premier League's multiple broadcast partners. Leicester take a sensible approach and employ a low block and a disciplined defensive shape, designed to punish errors in transition and exploit the pace of players like Jamie Vardy. Robin Koch's poor back-pass leads to a tap-in for Harvey Barnes after three minutes. Youri Tielemans scores from close range on the rebound from Vardy's header 18 minutes later. Stuart Dallas pulls a goal back early in the second half with a cross which bounces in without a touch from anybody and Hernández shakes Leicester's crossbar at 2-1 but that pivotal moment aside, it feels like Leicester's evening. Vardy strikes 14 minutes from the end and Tielemans converts an injury-time penalty, by which point the contest is already over. Bielsa holds his hands up to a 4-1 defeat and blames himself for failing to organise his team in a way that would allow them to recover possession effectively. 'It was difficult to win the ball back and this caused us to defend poorly,' he says.

There is an additional consequence of the defeat too. Shortly after hitting the bar, Hernández is substituted by Bielsa. Leeds' players are wearing black armbands to mark the anniversary of the Armistice and the death a few days earlier of former Manchester United midfielder Nobby Stiles. As he leaves the pitch, a TV camera catches the Spaniard throwing his armband into the stands. He walks back to the dug-out and kicks out at a water bottle, visibly annoyed by either his performance or the decision to replace him while the game is in the balance. Hernández can be prone to occasional flashes of temper. Seconds before the end of Leeds' 1-0 win over Barnsley in July – a result which meant promotion was virtually assured – he disappeared down the tunnel after being taken off. His body language was frustrated. But in general, he is a model professional and one of the players who coped best with the changes in diet and fitness instigated by Bielsa, prehabbing and managing his body sensibly. Bielsa was once asked whether he thought he could make Hernández (by then well into his thirties) a better player. 'I think he can make me a better coach,' Bielsa replied and for two years, Hernández has been turning in big performances at the right times, a talisman given the nickname *El Mago* (The Magician).

Bielsa is not immediately aware of the show of petulance against Leicester. Hernández is on the opposite side of the field when he tosses his armband, too far away for Bielsa to see. Bielsa has his back to him when Hernández gives the water bottle a whack with his boot. When the incident is raised in the post-match press conference, Bielsa is unapologetic about the substitution. 'I thought Tyler Roberts would be more influential in the final part of the field,' he says. And what about Hernández's dissent? 'If the reaction he had after I made my decision was to kick a bottle, what can I do?'

Bielsa insists that he has no need to address the issue with Hernández directly. And for the next few days, he says next to nothing about it. There is little in the way of conversations between them and little warning for Hernández, or any of Leeds' other senior players, about what is coming. Bielsa is not in the habit of telegraphing his decisions or running them past anyone else. Radrizzani, Kinnear and Victor Orta all accept that managing the squad is Bielsa's responsibility alone, free from any interference (Orta says he learned years ago not to stick his nose into a coach's selection policy).[4] When the travelling party for Leeds' next fixture at Crystal Palace is chosen three days later, Hernández's name is missing from it. He is fit and available but he will be left behind, without much of an explanation. Bielsa's party includes Jack Jenkins, an eighteen-year-old academy midfielder who has never

75

made the bench previously. It goes without saying that questions will be asked, particularly if Leeds lose in London.

The visit to Selhurst Park brings about another 4-1 loss, Leeds' second in five days. A contentious offside decision against Patrick Bamford and a big deflection for Palace's third goal go against Bielsa but the man-marking is looser than usual and their creativity dips. Leeds' expected goals ratio for the season is holding at almost two a game but at Palace the figure drops to 0.97. Palace are not as dominant as the scoreline suggests – an 'exaggerated' result, Bielsa calls it – but they deserve to win. Afterwards, the conversation turns quickly to Hernández. He was ready to play but not in the squad, Bielsa confirms. Why not? 'I evaluate all the players for the upcoming game and I didn't pick him for this game,' he replies. 'The decision may seem strange but I chose the eighteen players who I felt were most apt for the game. You can qualify my decision as the wrong one.' Was the decision linked to Hernández's reaction to his substitution against Leicester? That is the obvious conclusion to draw and people within the club are drawing it. 'I have already explained the decision,' Bielsa replies. 'There is no point in you insisting on more.' He leaves us to read between the lines of what is being said. The following afternoon, on Remembrance Sunday, Hernández uses his Instagram account to apologise for throwing his black armband away. 'It was a reaction that [doesn't] describe my way of being or my way of thinking,' he writes and in the international break that follows there are talks between him and Bielsa which help to smooth the waters. But the chances of Hernández making amends rapidly are then hindered by a muscle strain, sidelining him for three weeks.

Kalvin Phillips, though, is making good progress from the shoulder injury he sustained against Wolves. Bielsa has the final say on his players' fitness but the club's medical team estimated that Arsenal at home on 22 November would be the first game Phillips could make. Having missed international duty with England, the midfielder trains at full tilt in the lead-up to the clash with Arsenal and returns to the starting line-up. The season's first international break brought nothing more than selection concerns for Bielsa but on this occasion he has happy players returning from abroad. Liam Cooper has qualified for the European Championships with Scotland. Gjanni Alioski has qualified for the same tournament with North Macedonia, the country's first appearance at a major finals. The North Macedonian government pays each of the players responsible, Alioski included, 10,000 Euros, a token of the gratitude felt there. At the same time, Leeds open talks with Alioski over a new contract. His deal is up in the summer of 2021 but Bielsa likes him and values his versatility on the left, where Alioski can play as a full-back or a winger.[5] Alioski has worked hard for his career. Seven years earlier, he spent part of the summer of 2013 claiming unemployment benefits after being released by Young Boys in Switzerland. At the insistence of his father, he kept fit and he kept training, hoping for a break which materialised when second-division FC Schaffhausen made him an offer and signed him on a free transfer. His agent, Dino Lamberti, says a subsequent move to Lugano gave him the 'final polish' and honed him for England and the Premier League but Alioski, who is regarded as one of the jokers in Bielsa's dressing room, will take his time before committing himself to Leeds again. 'Don't be fooled by the moments of extroversion,' Lamberti says. 'He's a quiet, serious, down-to-earth guy.'

Bielsa has a stronger hand to play against Arsenal than he did against Leicester or Palace. Rodrigo is free of Covid-19 and although his match fitness suffered slightly because of it, Bielsa names him on the bench. Leeds' head coach decides to let Raphinha loose, starting the Brazilian for the first time on the right wing. There is plenty of chatter around Raphinha, particularly inside the recruitment department at Elland Road. At £17m, they think they have landed a bargain. Had Raphinha stayed with Rennes, he would have been in the midst of the Champions League's group stages by now. Two days after Leeds' meeting with Arsenal, his former team-mates in France are hosting Chelsea. But Bielsa's project was sold to him convincingly and Raphinha tells ESPN in Brazil that he felt 'undervalued' when he learned that Rennes were ready to part with him for less than they paid to buy him from Sporting Lisbon a year earlier. 'They told me they would not want to sell me for less than 60m Euros,' he says. 'That made it clear to me that I was not part of the plans of the club or the coach.'[6] Sources in France saw the situation differently, claiming Raphinha had been purposely pushing Rennes to consider any offers for him. He had spoken just a few weeks before his move to England of his desire to play in the Premier League, describing it as 'the strongest league in the world'.[7] Whoever was pushing it, the transfer went through at a price which Leeds were very happy with (and a price which would seem increasingly bizarre as his form took off). His raw pace and natural flair gave Bielsa something a little different to work with. 'I sincerely think I can add very little to his game,' Bielsa would say a few months later. 'The best thing you can do with players so spontaneous is let them be themselves.'

Imagination is something Arsenal are lacking. They had appointed Mikel Arteta as their manager in December 2019 (one of Arteta's first games in charge was against Bielsa's Leeds in the FA Cup) but despite his experience of working as Pep Guardiola's assistant at Manchester City, Arteta's transitional period at the Emirates Stadium is proving to be slow. There is talent in Arteta's squad and the club spent £45m signing midfielder Thomas Partey from Atlético Madrid before the 2020 transfer deadline but their football is restrained and short of attacking flair. There is a feeling that Arteta is too tactically controlling and too reluctant to let the handbrake off by allowing Arsenal to play freely. At Elland Road his team are barely able to breathe, even before Nicolas Pépé is sent off for a needless headbutt on Alioski early in the second half. Pépé and Alioski have been niggling at each other for a couple of minutes but not enough to justify the Ivorian's reaction. 'It's unacceptable,' Arteta says afterwards, clearly furious but trying his best not to flay Pépé in public. If that moment changes the game, it is only in making Leeds more dominant than they have been already. They press Arsenal with precision and produce 25 shots on goal, hitting the crossbar and the same post twice. Bernd Leno keeps the contest goalless with a brilliant, one-handed save from Stuart Dallas. Raphinha is lively, roaming into central areas, and Arsenal's total entries into the final third are their second lowest of the season, after their defeat to champions Liverpool at Anfield. Everything is there for Bielsa, except a winning goal. 'Offensively we did enough to deserve a lead,' Bielsa says.

That topic of conversation is familiar and well-worn. Leeds, throughout Bielsa's tenure, have been adept at creating chances. They have also been habitually guilty of wasting them. In his first year, the club's xG of 83 over 46 games compared to an actual goal tally of 76. In his second, the difference was more pronounced again: 89 goals expected versus 77 scored. Ultimately, the disparity came at no cost. Leeds secured promotion and when it came to it, they won the Championship by a 10-point margin. But Bielsa was prone to a little smile whenever anyone asked about his side's finishing, or their 'efficiency' as he described it. Yes, he would say, we are not efficient but not because of a shortage of practice or a fundamental lack of care. In 2018, he detailed a fourteen-point routine used by him in training sessions to try and improve Leeds' conversion rate. For a period of ten to fifteen minutes, his coaches would create multiple shooting opportunities from different ranges and different angles. In each scenario, the players were allowed only one chance to shoot. Bielsa's rationale was that the same opportunity would never come up twice in a game so if you missed it, it was gone. The theory was sound but Bielsa was unconvinced that practising finishing was a good use of time. 'I wouldn't say it improves the finishing of a team,' he said. 'Being efficient in training does not mean you have the guarantee to be efficient in the matches. As head coaches we work on chances. You can work on the chances to score. But what you can't work on is how well you finish.'[8]

There are echoes of that comment again when Leeds travel to Everton a week after their draw with Arsenal. But in between, news arrives from Argentina. Diego Maradona has passed away at the age of sixty. The country's greatest sporting icon is dead. Three days of mourning are declared by the Argentinian government and at Napoli, where Maradona inspired two Scudetti, they announce that their stadium will be renamed after him. Bielsa never coached Maradona and there were extreme differences in the way they looked at football and lived life. Maradona's incomparable talent allowed him to carry teams and his country on his shoulders. Everything revolved around him (though perhaps on the insistence of others, rather than his). Jorge Valdano, who won the World Cup with him in 1986, wrote in *El País* in the days after Maradona's death of the playmaker 'applying for the post of God of football'.[9] Bielsa's teams, by contrast, were always units and collectives, line-ups in which the combination of parts mattered more than the individual parts themselves. There was also a very stark comparison between Maradona's excesses and Bielsa's humble existence. But Bielsa's respect for Argentina's number 10 was absolute. If one superstar could have found a place in Bielsa's strict machine, even just for a while, Maradona might have been it. As Bielsa digests the loss, he sits and reads a range of obituaries, reliving the legend. 'He was an artist,' Bielsa says. 'In terms of what he signifies to us [the Argentine people], Diego made us feel a fantasy.' I ask Bielsa how it must have been for Maradona, living and playing for Argentina and Napoli with immeasurable expectation placed on him; expectation which was social and cultural as much as sporting. 'Players with such individual brilliance, they don't know what it is to play with pressure,' Bielsa says. 'The creativity of a player like Diego would not have been able to develop if he felt pressure. In football, pressure means that it affects your performance in some way. But the best players in the world, they don't feel this.' Carlo Ancelotti, Everton's manager, played against Maradona for AC Milan during the spell in Italy which best defined Maradona's club career. As Leeds and Everton hold a minute's silence before their meeting at Goodison Park on 28 November, Ancelotti is almost moved to tears. Then he and Bielsa draw swords.

Everton's strength is their front three of James Rodríguez, Richarlison and Dominic Calvert-Lewin. Bielsa does not base his game plans on containment of the opposition but it is apparent that if Leeds are to win, his defence and Phillips will have to hold off Everton's attacking line. Phillips heeds the warning and steals the show. His defending is consummate but his distribution is exceptional, over short and long ranges as he picks Everton apart pass by pass. In his own half his completion rate hits 95 per cent. Even in Everton's, it stays above 90. Everton have two goals disallowed for offside but Jack Harrison heads against a post before half-time and as the game passes the hour, Leeds look fitter and fresher.

Nonetheless, it looks a little like the goalless draw against Arsenal. Bielsa's side have been creative again, with more than 20 efforts on goal, but have nothing to show for it. Another stalemate looms but with 10 minutes left, Raphinha hits a speculative shot from 25 yards and arcs it skilfully inside Jordan Pickford's left-hand post. Leeds are within touching distance of victory but they cannot refrain from attacking in numbers, even in injury-time when Helder Costa draws a point-blank save from Pickford. At 1-0 up, other coaches would be trying to kill time. With 30 seconds to play, Ian Poveda declines an invitation to count the clock down by taking the ball towards a corner flag and nutmegs a defender instead, setting up Costa's chance. Costa is one of six Leeds players in or around Everton's box as Pickford blocks it. 'They had chances, we had chances,' Ancelotti says. 'Whoever took the first chance won the game. Leeds are a really, really good team.' And utterly relentless.

In between the clashes with Arsenal and Everton, *The Athletic* journalist Michael Cox publishes an article discussing what he calls 'The Bielsa Paradox'. There is, Cox says, a widely held view that Bielsa's coaching is seminal and instructive, the influence behind other top-level managers in Europe and South America. Yet increasingly, it is hard to find any team with a style like Bielsa's Leeds – teams who man-mark, teams with their formation or teams who attack to the final whistle irrespective of the scoreline. 'He's fascinating tactically not because he's influential, but for the opposite reason,' Cox writes. 'In the age of the influencer, Bielsa is something very different – he's a complete outsider.'[10]

Towards the end of 2020, I was put in touch with Fabian Costello, a former striker living in Ireland who had played in the first youth team Bielsa ever managed at Newell's Old Boys. It was 1982 when they first crossed paths and Costello was sixteen. Bielsa

Above Bielsa stops for a selfie with a fan prior to the game against Huddersfield on March 7, 2020. The last game before the Covid-19 lockdown.

Left Bielsa perches on his bucket during the home game against Birmingham, 2018.

Below left Bielsa's famous touchline crouch, away at Nottingham Forest.

Left Relief and a rare show of emotion at full-time beating Rotherham after a week of 'spygate' drama. Hugging his assistant Pablo Quiroga.

Below Scarves at Elland Road.

Far below Banner flown over Elland Road on Good Friday 2019.

Top Cameras all around
Bielsa at Brentford.

Above Ordering Leeds and
Pontus Jansson to let Villa
score on a controversial
day at Elland Road.

Right Bielsa and Lampard
in the 2019 Championship
play-offs. Spygate rivals.

Left A dejected Stuart Dallas as Derby celebrate victory in the play-off semi-final.

Below Tension on the faces of Andrea Radrizzani, Angus Kinnear and Victor Orta as the semi-final second leg kicks off.

Far below Smiles all round and a scramble for photos as Bielsa gets off the coach at Elland Road.

Above Supporters massed around Bielsa outside the Elland Road West Stand. Spot Bielsa.

Right A rare yellow card for Bielsa against West Bromwich Albion.

Below Luke Ayling euphoric after an injury time win at Aston Villa.

Above The scoreboard from Forest away 2020. A pivotal moment in the promotion season.

Left A signal box painted in Bielsa's honour in Leeds.

Below Bielsa and staff celebrate the winning goal at Middlesbrough in February 2020.

Above Luke Ayling on the volley against Huddersfield.

Right Bielsa takes the knee before a 3-0 win against Fulham. The first home game back after the Covid-19 shutdown.

Below Crowdies used to fill empty seats at Elland Road.

Left Swansea away, 2020. A crucial day which just about seals promotion.

Below Pablo Hernández sprints away after scoring the winner at Swansea. Substitue, Jamie Shackleton, runs to celebrate with him.

was still to turn thirty but he was pursuing his interest in coaching having retired after a short professional career as a centre-back. Costello told stories of their days together in Rosario and of the way in which Bielsa made the boys in his squad abandon their ideas about how football should be played and how players should train. It was an education in tactical intelligence. When it came to Bielsa's attacking streak (and his refusal to back off even when a game appeared to be won), one memory of Costello's stood out. Bielsa asked his players to tell him how many times a team could realistically expect to score over the course of 90 minutes. The boys spoke among themselves and decided to go with six. 'It takes 1.35 minutes on average to score a goal,' Bielsa said. 'So the correct answer is 66.' He was, as Cox said, a one-off in the way he thought about and dissected the game, the innovative figurehead Leeds had been yearning for through two long decades of in-fighting and collapse.

6.

THE DEMISE

The roots of Leeds United's decline went back as far as 1999, two years before they played in the semi-finals of the Champions League and two years before they burned £18m on Robbie Fowler and Seth Johnson. Those transfers represented the worst of Leeds' extravagances, the signings that melted the credit card, but it was many months earlier that the club's board of directors and chairman Peter Ridsdale began sowing the seeds for sixteen seasons in the EFL.

Leeds were growing in strength towards the end of the twentieth century and looking for ways to improve more rapidly. They had money to spend but in an ideal world they would have access to more. As wealthy as English football was becoming, external credit could be hard to come by. But in 1999 the club found a source of fresh finance: a banking loan scheme arranged by Ray Ranson which would give them more freedom in the transfer market. Ranson, a former Manchester City defender, had moved into the insurance sector after his retirement and was offering a route to hard cash. He facilitated payments from established lenders which Leeds were able to spend on players.[1] Repayment of the loans would be made at staggered intervals over the course of a new signing's contract and in good times, no one at Elland Road saw much inherent risk. The game was getting richer and Leeds as a team were showing immense promise, a renewed European force. More money meant more scope to improve but as transfer followed transfer – £18m on Rio Ferdinand, £6m on Mark Viduka, fees thrown in all directions as Leeds rode the wave of Champions League qualification – their debts spiralled beyond their means. Fowler and Johnson are considered to be the straws that broke the camel's back but the damage was done before they joined in late 2001 and Leeds by then were a gambler chasing significant losses. The club's results were on the wane, the value of their squad was decreasing and desperate measures, like the sale of popular centre-back Jonathan Woodgate to Newcastle United in January 2003, merely slowed the inevitable implosion. Ridsdale's reputation was shot and in his autobiography, *United We Fall*, he wrote about the moment when he and Newcastle chairman Freddy Shepherd agreed on Woodgate's £9m fee: 'I shook Freddy's hand and said "you know this deal is going to cost me my job!" Freddy winced and sympathised.'[2]

Sympathy for Ridsdale in Leeds was non-existent and he had left Elland Road by the time I joined the *Yorkshire Evening Post* as a football writer in March 2004. He had resigned a year earlier, leaving behind debts of close to £100m, but the rot continued to spread. In the *Evening Post*'s newsroom they knew the club had passed the point of no return in the Premier League. It was the tail end of the 2003–04 season and Leeds were fighting to avoid relegation under caretaker manager Eddie Gray but confidence in his team had burned out. In mid-February, on the day of a critical game against Wolverhampton Wanderers, the newspaper reprised the *Sun*'s famous front page published before the 1992 general election with a back-page splash reading: 'If United fail to beat Wolves tonight will the last person out of Elland Road please turn off the lights?' Gray was so caught up in his job that he did not register the headline at the time. 'But it was basically right,' he said. 'That's how everyone was feeling.'[3] Leeds won 4-1 with one of their best performances of the season but the squad were still doomed. There was no way back from a flurry of nine defeats in the first thirteen matches of the season, most of them played under former boss Peter Reid. 'Even after the Wolves game I still felt we were struggling,' said Gray, who accepted the caretaker role out of a feeling of obligation to chief executive Trevor Birch. Leeds were Gray's club and he respected Birch's attempts to keep them afloat but the dressing room was uneasy at best and badly split on the issue of possible wage deferrals. 'With hindsight, I shouldn't have gone back,' Gray said. 'So many things were wrong.' One of the players involved in that season said a section of the dressing room was 'like poison'.

There was no way, without endless time and devotion, for Marcelo Bielsa to fully digest the insanity of the years preceding his own appointment at Leeds, or to understand the causes of it. He could see Leeds' stature and potential and he liked the fervent support in the city but when it came to the complexity of their recent history, how to grasp it properly or grasp it at all? This was a tale of decay and under-achievement with no precise beginning, and a tale which looked like having no end until Bielsa arrived and tamed the beast. The cynicism in Argentina about what the Championship title he won represented, or how credible a trophy it was, could be easily countered by the stories of crisis at Elland Road and the cast of thousands involved in them. Richard Naylor was Leeds' captain in 2010, the year the club won promotion from League One at the third attempt. Before 2007 they had never played in England's third tier before. They had never fallen so low in the pyramid. 'What people don't always realise is that the players at Leeds aren't just dealing with the games in front of them,' Naylor once told me. 'As well as that, you've got to deal with the frustration of all the things that built up over a period of time, some of the stuff you had nothing to do with. You feel it in the stands every time it goes wrong, the feeling of "here we go again."' Almost like playing against ghosts.

Not long before the end of the 2003–04 season, Leeds were bought out by a consortium called Adulant Force, made up of five local businessmen. The face of the group, Gerald Krasner, was an insolvency specialist and a familiar face in the city's business community but his knowledge of football and his expertise in running a professional club was minimal. The same went for most of the consortium but in terms of purchasing Leeds, no one else was interested. The debts were sky-high and it would take administration to resolve them. In the background as the takeover went through was Geoffrey Richmond, a man blamed by many for crippling Bradford City through overspending on transfers and wages. Richmond's son David, the owner of a taxi firm, joined Leeds as managing director. Another member of the group was Simon Morris, a property developer who would later go to prison over allegations of blackmail unrelated to his involvement at Elland Road.[4] Morris, a loud and brash individual, liked to use the club's training ground at Thorp Arch for personal five-a-side games. Staff there remember him wearing a T-shirt with 'The Boss' written on it. Champagne flowed in the boardroom on match days and there was a sense of Adulant Force enjoying the sensation of club ownership for as long as it lasted. One person who was close to Leeds at the time told *The Athletic*: 'The personalities involved meant the consortium was virtually unworkable. The one thing you can say about them is they got the debts down and kept Leeds going at a time when the club might otherwise have died, because no one else would have touched the books. But if we're talking about running a football club long-term, they weren't up to it. Everyone knew it. It was never going to last.'[5]

Krasner put himself up for questioning by the media on 19 March 2004, the day when Adulant Force's buy-out went through. Leeds were bottom of the Premier League and a matter of weeks away from relegation but Krasner, in front of an audience in the conference centre at Elland Road, put on a brave and optimistic face. The debts were manageable if Leeds stayed up, he said. And if they went down, there was a separate plan which would kick in place and maintain some stability. 'The club is off life-support and can move forward,' Krasner insisted, and the *Yorkshire Evening Post* marked the takeover with the headline 'Brave New World' but it was a turbulent stop-gap. David Richmond resigned as managing director in July after returning home one day to find the gates to his driveway padlocked. There was a sign attached to the gates telling him to quit the club (it was assumed that his father's chequered association with Bradford was behind the intimidation). The younger Richmond had spent much of the summer after Leeds' relegation selling players who wanted to leave or were simply too expensive to keep. Alan Smith's contentious £6m move to Manchester United – a Leeds boy and crowd favourite joining the club's most bitter rivals – was fractious and poisonous, creating resentment which still exists today. The board at Elland Road believed Liverpool were willing to offer £10m for Smith but a firm bid from Anfield did not arrive. Smith wanted Champions League football and saw Manchester United as the best option for him, the only top-four club who were knocking on his door. Richmond warned him about the potential fall-out if he left for Old Trafford but in heated discussions, the striker refused to be dictated to. As speculation mounted and anger in Leeds intensified, Smith took himself out of the firing line by escaping to Glasgow and hiding away for a few days in an apartment owned by his team-mate Dominic Matteo. The transfer to Manchester United was so delicate that Smith and his agent, Alex Black, asked his new club to include a clause in his contract agreeing not to introduce him at an immediate press conference. The unveiling would wait until a little of the bad blood in Leeds seeped away.

James Milner to Newcastle was a simpler process, if no less depressing. Eighteen-year-old Milner was far too good for the Championship and too valuable not to cash in on. Newcastle picked him up for £5m. Matteo and others left too, the Champions League team of 2001 virtually wiped out. Leeds succeeded in removing Mark Viduka's hefty salary from their wage bill by selling him to Middlesbrough but only by taking Michael Ricketts off Middlesbrough's hands in return. Ricketts had been an England international once but was rapidly losing his way. Leeds signed him despite being told by a senior official at The Riverside that an out-of-shape Ricketts was likely to contribute nothing. 'He'll make you look like Twiggy,' the official told them. Still, it was a better alternative than trying to pay Viduka in the Championship. One of the legacies of the Ridsdale regime was that Leeds found themselves picking up a percentage of the wages earned by players like Fowler and Danny Mills long after they left for other clubs. When Leeds went into administration in 2007, Mills was still owed more than £200,000. His last competitive appearance for them had come in 2003.[6] In the face of overwhelming debts, Leeds had no bargaining power.

Kevin Blackwell, a retired goalkeeper who first joined Leeds as assistant to Peter Reid in 2003, was named as manager for the 2004–05 season but mundane football and very flat Championship results were a sideshow for events in the Elland Road boardroom. Very quickly, Adulant Force ran out of ideas and lives. In

November 2004, the group sold Leeds' stadium and Thorp Arch training ground to Jacob Adler, a landlord from Manchester, in a sale-and-leaseback deal. Adler paid a combined £12m for both properties and negotiated for Leeds to continue using them for an annual rent. The leases were set to run for 25 years and included the right for Leeds to repurchase Elland Road and Thorp Arch within a set timeframe. Andrea Radrizzani subsequently repurchased the stadium for £20m after his takeover in 2017. The buy-back clause on the training ground elapsed in 2009, denying Leeds the opportunity to own it again. Adler's acquisitions were pitched to the press as a sensible way of raising funds for a destitute club. What very few people realised was that Adulant Force intended to use some of the money to pay off personal loans used by the group to finance their original buy-out of Leeds. The loans had been provided by Jack Petchey, a shareholder at Aston Villa, and the *Independent* quoted Leeds director Melvyn Levi as saying that the consortium would have been personally liable 'for millions of pounds' had they missed a repayment deadline and triggered a penalty clause.[7] Under the terms of the property leases agreed with Adler, the rent at Elland Road and Thorp Arch rose by 3 per cent every October. By the time Radrizzani reclaimed ownership of Elland Road, Leeds were paying £1.7m a year to use it.

The rush to do business with Adler came after a proposed £25m takeover by Sebastien Sainsbury, the great-grandson of the founder of the Sainsbury's supermarket chain, fell through after many weeks of wrangling and arguing. Sainsbury claimed to have provided Leeds with satisfactory proof of funds, held by an American fund called Nova Financial Partners. Adulant Force said there was insufficient evidence that Sainsbury had enough cash to push the purchase through. But even as Sainsbury walked away, Leeds' incumbent owners were scrambling to find an exit strategy. After several months in the boardroom, the challenge of restructuring the club was overwhelming them. They craved a buyer and in January 2005, they found Ken Bates.

Bates was the polar opposite of Adulant Force. In his eighties and as forthright and cantankerous as ever, he had been in football for much of his life, most notably as owner of Chelsea. His manner was uncompromising and his attitude was ruthless. Krasner's group were constantly in need of guidance, a long way out of their depth. Bates took advice from no one and made it clear from the start that he would run Leeds as he saw fit. In the week after he signed a cheque for £10m and gained control at Elland Road (as the representative of an opaque offshore company called the Forward Sports Fund), I sat through a fans' forum staged by Bates and his wife Suzannah. Supporters were invited to attend and ask questions but Bates snapped at those who were slow in delivering them or tried to address him at length. Fatigue and frustration oozed from the crowd, some of whom harboured a suspicion that Bates and Leeds would mix like water and oil. Bates brushed the negativity off. He promised, in the words of Cilla Black, to have 'a lorra, lorra laughs' but within months he was driving season-ticket prices through the roof. Concessionary deals in parts of Elland Road disappeared. For a child in the West Stand, seats were being sold at an exorbitant £726. The reaction to the rises was savage. Bates, though, stood his ground. If you want Premier League football again, he said, you have to pay Premier League prices. That comment would follow him around for years as Leeds meandered in the EFL. 'What amuses me is that people pay increased council tax, petrol and every other tax you can think of and they don't complain,' Bates said. 'But put up the cost of their season tickets and they go apeshit.'[8]

The battle lines drawn during the season-ticket furore remained until Bates vacated the chairman's seat eight years later. Initially there was meaningful investment in the squad and deals for high-calibre Championship players like Rob Hulse, Robbie Blake and Richard Cresswell. But Leeds' defeat in the 2006 play-off final was another tipping point. That game, a 3-0 loss to Watford at Cardiff's Millennium Stadium on a torrential Sunday afternoon, caught Blackwell and his team at their worst. They were timid and startled, captured on camera jumping out of their skins a few minutes before kick-off as fireworks went off behind them. Promotion and the return of Premier League income would have helped the accounts at Elland Road. Instead, Leeds were beset by liabilities and unable to settle them. There was no prospect of the club maintaining a top-six place in the 2006–07 season and within two months of it starting, Blackwell was sacked. Bates dismissed him on the grounds of gross misconduct after Blackwell revealed in a press conference that Leeds had been hit with a large and unexpected tax bill, reducing their ability to invest in the transfer market, but results were backing him into a corner too. He has said he felt his sacking was unlawful. At his final league game, away to Coventry City, Blackwell was faced with banners calling for him to resign. For his part, Blackwell had warned Bates at a pre-season lunch that the modest level of expenditure in his squad meant Leeds could be at risk of relegation. Bates's wife was so incensed by the suggestion that she got up from the table and left the room.

The job of managing Leeds had been thankless for a while and the prospect of accepting it created mixed emotions. Any coach who carried the club out of the EFL would earn the city's eternal gratitude, as Bielsa discovered. The people who feted Bielsa outside his house after promotion in 2020 were not calling him God for no reason. They were the Israelites emerging from the desert after forty years. But the jeopardy involved in trying to tame Leeds was huge. John Carver, Blackwell's assistant, was initially earmarked to replace him by Bates but Carver's audition as caretaker went down in flames and he was gone within weeks after a horrible 5-1 defeat to Luton Town. His side were humiliated on the pitch at Kenilworth Road and ridiculed off it after a Pizza Hut delivery arrived at the team bus as they prepared for the journey home. Carver dismissed the jokes, saying pizza was a means of his squad refuelling with carbohydrates quickly post-match, but he was re-signed to his fate. After avoiding the post-match press conference, he called around a group of local journalists in Leeds later that night. 'I'll take the blame because I deserve it,' he said, 'but don't let these players off lightly either.' Carver's exit was telling. Like the Champions League side before them, the Blackwell era and his play-off final team were finished.

Bates's mind was made up about what to do next before the de-bacle at Luton. In spite of the reaction it would cause in Leeds, he decided to recruit Dennis Wise, the fiery midfielder he had taken from Wimbledon to Chelsea in the 1990s. Wise was as bold and brash as Bates. The story went that when he signed for Chelsea, he walked into Bates's office as the deal was about to be completed. Bates looked at Wise, five-foot-five of him, and asked if that was all he was getting for his money. 'Yeah,' Wise said, grinning and banging on his heart with his fist, 'but you'll get a big one of these as well.' In the only one-on-one interview I ever did with Wise, in October 2007, his thick skin shone through in every comment. There were people in Leeds who despised him and Wise knew it. No love was lost between Leeds and Chelsea and Bates and Wise were Chelsea men. The vitriol amused Wise and the objections to him were cause for motivation. I wrote in the *Yorkshire Evening Post* that his tone reminded me of a well-known Russian proverb: 'If you're afraid of wolves, stay out of the forest.'[9]

When Bates contacted him about coming to Leeds, Wise was in charge of Swindon Town. He accepted Bates's offer almost instantly and asked to bring Gus Poyet, his number two and another ex-Chelsea player, with him. As Carver licked his wounds, waiting to be dismissed the day after the loss to Luton, Wise and Poyet were flying out to Bates's home in Monaco for conversations about strategy and personal terms. Wise was one of the few people who knew how to handle his elder. Staff at Elland Road were in the habit of addressing Bates as 'chairman'. In impudent style, Wise liked to call him 'Batesy'.

Allied to Gwyn Williams, the one-time Chelsea scout who had turned up as technical director at Leeds (Bates's eyes and ears, as some called him), the smell of Stamford Bridge was everywhere. As Wise arrived for his first press conference, photographers captured him walking past a black-and-white picture of Billy Bremner, the juxtaposition between a local hero and a pantomime villain. Bates, drawing on Greek mythology, said Wise would be charged with cleaning out 'the Augean Stable', a reference to Hercules mucking out the livestock owned by King Augeus in ancient Greece. It suggested the atmosphere among the players at Leeds was rotten. Very quickly, Wise informed captain Paul Butler and defender Sean Gregan – two senior professionals with a tight grip on the dressing room – that they would be leaving. Other players felt ostracised too. 'I don't think he liked me,' said defender Matt Kilgallon, who left for Sheffield United in Wise's first transfer window. 'I don't know why but I just wasn't his cup of tea.'[10] Gregan talked of Wise dispatching him in a conversation which lasted a matter of seconds.

Wise was never far away from a fight. In February 2007, he accused one of his players of leaking his line-up to Crystal Palace before the teams met in a Championship game at Elland Road.

The saga became known as 'Molegate' and while Wise refused to name names, it filled column inches externally and caused friction internally. Midfielder Shaun Derry resented the fact that fingers were pointed at him on account of his past career at Palace (Derry vehemently denied any responsibility and Wise accepted as much, without ever exonerating Derry publicly).[11] The cracks were everywhere.

At the end of a torrid Championship campaign, Leeds were relegated to League One. The killer blow came at home to Ipswich Town on the season's penultimate weekend and supporters invaded the pitch after Ipswich equalised late in the game. Some protested against Bates in the directors' box. Others pelted Ipswich's fans with missiles. If relegation felt like the bottom of the curve, more depressing news was to come. Six days later Leeds announced that they were entering administration with debts of over £35m.

No part of their sixteen-year period in the EFL generated more chaos than that insolvent summer. Even as Leeds were declared insolvent, Bates was hastily arranging a so-called phoenix takeover with administrators KPMG. KPMG had accepted an offer from him to buy the club back and settle liabilities owed to non-football creditors by paying them a penny in the pound. HM Revenue & Customs, which stood to lose almost £7m, took umbrage and challenged the sale in court after it narrowly received the support of more than 75 per cent of creditors (the precise figure of 75.02 per cent was so tight that KPMG was forced to recount the votes). Bates, sensing that HMRC's legal action would drag on for a while, countered it by repurchasing Leeds without the Company Voluntary Arrangement (CVA) that the EFL insisted on as a way of ensuring that a large majority of creditors were satisfied. The governing body was unimpressed by Bates's manoeuvre and took a hard line: if no CVA was in place, it would suspend the transfer of Leeds' share in the EFL to Bates's new company. Other aspects of the deal between Bates and KPMG raised serious questions, too. Two of Leeds' biggest creditors, off-shore firms Astor Investment Holdings and Krato, were owed millions of pounds in secured loans, entitling them to major voting rights in any CVA process. Despite Bates claiming that neither company had any connection to him, Astor and Krato informed KPMG that they were only willing to support his takeover. For Bates they were willing to write off their debts. Any other buyer would be asked to repay them in full. It gave Bates a huge advantage in negotiations.

In the eye of a storm, KPMG and Bates drove his takeover bid over the line, facing down widespread public opposition. There were rival offers for the club, including one fronted by former Hull City chairman Adam Pearson and another involving Simon Morris and the enterprise firm Redbus. After presiding over relegation and insolvency, Bates was short of support in Leeds. In the absence of a CVA, the EFL intended to mete out punishment for what it saw as a breach of its rules. Demotion to League Two was considered as a sanction but in the end, the EFL's clubs voted by a large majority to impose a 15-point deduction on Leeds, leaving Wise and his players a mile adrift at the bottom of League One before a ball had been kicked in the 2007–08 season. Bates would spend the following eight months contesting the penalty, only to lose an arbitration case the day before the season finished. A transfer embargo forced Leeds to throw a squad together at the last minute, with Wise famously accusing the EFL of 'cutting my balls off', but the club overcame their points deduction spectacularly and made the play-off final. An exhausted Wise had resigned by then, sick of so much time away from his family in London and tempted to defect to a less demanding director's role at Newcastle.

With Gary McAllister in charge for the final, Leeds lost 1-0 to Doncaster Rovers at Wembley.

Play-off defeats were the club's cross to bear in the lower divisions. Bielsa continued the trend in 2018 when his squad succumbed to Derby in the Championship semi-finals and since the play-offs were inaugurated, Leeds have appeared five times without winning promotion once. Simon Grayson, who replaced McAllister a few days before Christmas in 2008, finally navigated a way out of League One via automatic promotion in 2010 but that achievement did little to cure entrenched divisions between the board at Elland Road and Leeds' support. Bates was criticised for allowing the buy-back option on Thorp Arch to expire in 2009, even though the club had sold academy midfielder Fabian Delph to Aston Villa for £6m (the exact amount needed to repurchase the training ground). To Bates's annoyance, Leeds City Council refused a request from him to provide a loan on the basis that the official owner of the club, the Forward Sports Fund (FSF), was shielded by anonymity. Council officials wanted to know who they would ultimately be loaning the money to before they released it. Bates was under pressure to reveal the beneficiaries of FSF but claimed to be unaware of their identities. It was not until 2011 that he bought out FSF for an undisclosed sum, becoming owner of Leeds in his own right. In response to questions about how and why the deal was done – and more to the point, from whom he had acquired the shares – Bates merely said he was trying to end 'scaremongering' about the anonymous ownership structure.[12] The detail of the process was hidden from view.

Whenever he came under pressure, he fought back with relish and he fought to win. A remarkable spat developed between him and Leeds' former director Melvyn Levi after Bates's 2005 buy-out of Adulant Force. The pair fell out and Bates went for Levi by criticising him repeatedly in his matchday programme column, accusing Levi of undermining the club. One weekend in March 2007, Bates upped the ante by using the column to print details of Levi's address (a week later he did the same with Levi's telephone number). Levi sought a last-minute court injunction and when we arrived in the press room ahead of kick-off against Sheffield Wednesday, staff at Elland Road were busy redacting the offending line with black markers. The feud would end in a harassment case which Levi won.

As Bates dug in and time passed, Leeds became more stagnant. The club went close to the Championship play-offs in 2011 but finished seventh and fell short. Having been second in the league at Christmas, much was made of a perceived lack of investment in the January window. Officials at Leeds briefed privately that Grayson had declined to spend money available to him for fear of unsettling his dressing room. Grayson later claimed he had asked for specific signings which did not materialise.[13] When that season finished, Bates spent £7m renovating Elland Road's East Stand. Two thirds of the cash was borrowed from Ticketus, a loan secured against future season-ticket revenue. In comparison to that, spending on players looked meagre and unambitious and Bates's satisfaction in turning annual profits did not chime with a fanbase who saw a team going nowhere fast. Grayson struggled to maintain results and was sacked at the very end of the January window in 2012. On deadline day, his side were trounced 4-1 by Birmingham City, conceding four times to Birmingham's giant striker, Nikola Žigić. Grayson spoke afterwards and bemoaned the fragility of a young and inadequate defence. His only signing in the closing hours of the transfer window had been Tottenham's Adam Smith, a twenty-year-old right-back with no Championship experience. The contradiction exposed a lack of joined-up thinking at every level.

Grayson's tenure ran for 169 games but after his exit, the turnover of managers was dramatic. Neil Warnock, a promotion specialist in the EFL, succeeded Grayson but was caught up in the protracted sale of the club by Bates to Gulf Finance House, a Bahraini investment bank. GFH tabled an offer for a 100 per cent stake in Leeds after an American group including Joe Januszewski – a figure in Fenway Sports Group's purchase of Liverpool – declined to consolidate tentative interest. Bates also sidestepped an approach from a Saudi Arabian party who, led by Prince Abdullah bin Mosaad bin Abdulaziz al Saud, subsequently bought into Sheffield United. GFH was neatly branded and good at extolling its own virtues but in footballing terms it was a Middle Eastern equivalent of Adulant Force: devoid of any knowledge about the sport and guilty of a chronic lack of realism about the money that could be made from club ownership in the EFL. The bank's vision was brazen and simplistic: if it bought Leeds from Bates for around £17m and did a little window dressing, it could sell its shares at the first opportunity and exit English football with a profit. The concept was known as 'flipping' and for the seventeen months in which GFH controlled Leeds, from November 2012 to April 2014, the club was listed in its accounts as an asset 'held for sale'. The bank tried to portray one of the men behind its takeover, lawyer David Haigh, as a lifelong Leeds fan despite doubts about whether he had ever followed the club previously. Claims that Haigh had been born in Beeston, a stone's throw from Elland Road, were cast in doubt after a member of the public sourced his birth certificate. Some time later, Haigh was imprisoned in Dubai after GFH accused him of defrauding the bank of funds, allegations unconnected to Leeds. It was, in its entirety, a world of muddy waters.

Leeds and Warnock, in many ways, were as unlikely a fit as Leeds and Bates. A native of Sheffield and a coach whose repeated

successes in management failed to translate into widespread pop-
ularity, Warnock's arrival at Elland Road in February 2012 was a
marriage of convenience. He was ready to have another go at promotion, the target he prided himself on hitting. Leeds embraced
his marmite personality in the hope of escaping from the EFL. But
the 2012–13 season was another ordeal. Bates's transfer of shares
to GFH dragged on for months and football became secondary.
Warnock's transfer budget was so small that at the outset of the
season he gambled on an out-of-contract El Hadji Diouf, happy to
take on a difficult character for the sake of adding another forward
to his squad (and one who was costing only £5000 a week). The
crowd at Leeds tolerated mixed form for a while but started to lose
patience with Warnock around Christmas. At the training ground,
a problematic divide developed between the first-team ranks and
the academy, the two departments suspicious and unsupportive
of each other. Warnock said the attitude of Leeds' youth-team
coaches was like 'a cancer in the club'.[14] By Easter Monday in 2013,
after six games without a win, relegation had become a real possibility. GFH pulled the plug on Warnock in the hour after a 2-1
defeat to Derby and sent for Brian McDermott, a manager who
was out of work after leaving Reading. A year earlier McDermott
and Reading had won the Championship title but the atmosphere
he was walking into at Elland Road was summed up by Ross
McCormack – unhappy with his role as a substitute – shouting
'fuck off' in Warnock's direction after scoring in the loss to Derby.

McDermott went on to feature in some of the most extraordinary events Leeds can remember, caught up in an ownership
struggle more severe than that which hindered Warnock. In his
first January transfer window in 2014, McDermott asked Leeds
to explore the possibility of a deal for Brighton striker Ashley
Barnes. GFH came back to him and told him in all seriousness

that Barnes's statistics on the computer game *Football Manager* were lower than those of Leeds winger Luke Varney and on that basis, the signing made no sense. McDermott had the club in the play-off positions midway through the 2013–14 season but his team came off the rails badly in January. A day of reckoning arrived on 11 January when they were thrashed 6-0 by Sheffield Wednesday at Hillsborough, two goals short of Leeds' worst ever defeat. McDermott brought in two new wingers in the build-up to the Yorkshire derby, Jimmy Kebe and Cameron Stewart, but chose to go with an unfamiliar 4-3-3 formation rather than the expected 4-4-2. The performance was so poor that it was said that GFH representatives discussed sacking McDermott at half-time. Soon after, he was emailed by Hisham Alrayes, a Leeds director and a senior figure at GFH, with strict orders. From now on, his line-up for each match was to be submitted to the board for approval at least twenty-four hours before kick-off. He would be expected to explain his tactical plan in detail too. Alrayes's email read: 'We would like to express dissatisfaction with the way the team has been managed. Whilst we will continue to support you further if positive results and the performance of the team is turned around, we expect you to take the points raised in this memo seriously and report to the board with the required action plan.' McDermott's job was hanging by a thread and even more so after a 1-0 defeat to Leicester City the following weekend. Leeds competed well enough against the Championship's dominant team, losing to a late goal from David Nugent, but what mattered most on that afternoon was the quiet attendance at Elland Road of Massimo Cellino, an Italian businessman who had flown into England with designs on buying Leeds.

Cellino was a wild-card, renowned in Italy for a volatile, erratic and maddening style of ownership at Cagliari. He had tried to buy an insolvent Crystal Palace in 2010 but was ruled out of the running by the club's administrators, owing to convictions for fraud in Italy (convictions which were later overturned). GFH, though, paid no heed to his background. The bank's enthusiasm for running Leeds had waned completely and, by the end of January, GFH and Cellino were on the same page. He would take a 75 per cent shareholding in the club as part of a long and detailed Share Purchase Agreement (SPA) which made astonishing concessions to GFH. Cellino agreed to stump up £11m for his majority stake. On top of that, he would repay loans in excess of £20m which GFH said it was owed, all while leaving the bank with a quarter of the equity in Leeds. None of this reflected GFH's shambolic management but as Cellino said himself, he was not inclined to perform due diligence. If he looked too closely at the accounts of a football club, he would find too many skeletons and he would never buy one. At around 5 p.m. on 31 January, Salah Nooruddin – a GFH associate and chairman of Leeds who had caused trouble some months earlier by trying to slip the son of a business associate into the club's academy – sent a text message to Cellino congratulating him on completing his takeover, even though the deal was still to be approved by the EFL. Cellino took this as his cue for bloodletting. What ensued that evening would come to be known as Mad Friday.

Within an hour or so, McDermott was sacked. The phone call to him came from Chris Farnell, a solicitor who was advising Cellino and planned to join the board at Elland Road. Cellino wanted to appoint former Middlesbrough defender Gianluca Festa as Leeds' new manager and had tried without success to put Festa on the bench for a game against Ipswich earlier in the week (a request McDermott refused to give in to). As news of McDermott's departure leaked out, two major club sponsors, Enterprise Insurance and the local theme park Flamingo Land, threatened to withdraw their support. McCormack, who scored 29 goals that season and was Leeds' most valuable commodity by a distance, asked to leave for Cardiff City before the January deadline but could not persuade Cellino to agree. Haigh, Leeds' managing director, was in mid-air and flying to Europe for a holiday with friends. As he was one of the EFL signatories required to approve transfers, Leeds and Cellino were unable to complete any signings without him. Cellino tried to loan midfielder Andrea Tabanelli from Italy but the EFL rejected the paperwork and blocked the transfer. Tabanelli spent a week in a hotel before receiving the bad news and returning home.

By the following morning, and with a PR disaster all around him, Cellino was backtracking rapidly. Irrespective of his agreement with GFH, he had no power to sack McDermott until the EFL gave his takeover the green light. Any decision on McDermott's future still fell to GFH. A plan to hand Festa control of the first team for a game against Huddersfield Town on 1 February was abandoned at short notice. McDermott's assistant, Nigel Gibbs, received an urgent call and was asked to take charge instead. Festa sat in the East Stand, shouting audibly as Leeds struggled in the first half against Huddersfield but then falling into silence as they sealed a rousing 5-1 win in the second. Supporters around Festa taunted and abused him mercilessly. With around twenty minutes of the match left, and almost twenty-four hours after Cellino's attempt to eject McDermott, GFH published a statement on the Leeds website confirming that he was still their manager. 'He has not been dismissed from his post as has been suggested,' the statement read, with bizarre simplicity. Though Enterprise Insurance had offered McDermott the use of its hospitality box at Elland Road for the clash with Huddersfield, McDermott declined and stayed away.

After a weekend of intense discussions, McDermott returned to work the following Monday. He spent an hour at a press conference walking the media through the events of Mad Friday. 'I've had certain assurances about my position,' he said. 'All football matters are down to me but who's going to be the future owner, I don't know.' His final comment said everything. Cellino had vanished temporarily, keeping his head down, but he was committed to dispensing with McDermott as soon as the EFL allowed his buy-out to proceed. GFH, meanwhile, was increasingly reluctant to fund the club's wage bill with Cellino's investment pending. In March, the salaries of McDermott, his staff and his players dropped into their bank accounts late. Haigh and GFH were faced with questions about why no one had been told in advance that the wages might be delayed.

McDermott looked hunted from Mad Friday onwards, his authority in the dressing room compromised and the Championship season out of control. It was customary for coaches at Leeds to be left looking over their shoulders – Marcelo Bielsa was a rare case insofar as he was able to work at Elland Road without any tangible threat to him. When Uwe Rösler was dismissed by Cellino in 2015 after just twelve games in charge, Steve Evans was in his car near the training ground waiting to drive in once Rösler left. Evans and Cellino had been in close contact for the previous twenty-four hours and a contract was already agreed. On the day in 2014 when Darko Milanič succumbed after thirty-two days in the job, Neil Redfearn, Leeds' academy coach, sat with Cellino in the directors' box throughout a 2-1 defeat to Wolves, preparing to step into the breach.

Cellino's lack of patience with head coaches was part of his psyche. He would make outlandish appointments and then regret them almost instantly. David Hockaday, his first pick after McDermott, went to a meeting with Cellino at a hotel in London thinking he was about to be offered a youth-team position.[15] His previous role had been at non-league Forest Green Rovers and he was no one's idea of a Leeds United manager but Cellino, after speaking to him for several hours, handed him the main job. Within weeks, the Italian was calling me late at night after a 2-0 defeat to Brighton to express doubts about the suitability of Hockaday (a man who would only shake your hand if you looked him in the eye first). Hockaday survived for six games; very nearly sacked after a 4-1 loss at Watford and then actually sacked after a League Cup defeat to Bradford City the following week. Cellino attempted to court Steve Clarke, who politely said no, and then called Carlo Ancelotti to ask about the availability of his assistant at Real Madrid, Paul Clement. Ancelotti told Cellino that Clement's salary was well into seven figures. That revelation ended the conversation instantly.

Attention turned next to Milanič, a Slovenian who, like Hockaday, appeared on Cellino's radar without any explanation as to who had recommended him. Milanič received a two-year contract worth £400,000 a year, quitting Sturm Graz in Austria for England. His thirty-two-day reign was the shortest in Leeds' history, so short that at the match where his time in charge ended, his family were at Elland Road for the first time. Milanič spent the rest of 2014 and all of 2015 on gardening leave, pulling in a wage at Leeds' expense.

The controversies around Cellino were endless. His takeover of Leeds ran into immediate trouble when the EFL tried to block it because of a tax conviction imposed on him by a judge in Italy. Cellino had been found guilty of avoiding duty owed on a private yacht called *Nelie* and the case was classed as a breach of the EFL's owners' and directors' test. He battled to salvage his buy-out and successfully overturned the EFL's decision against him by virtue of a technicality but the governing body bided its time after the takeover proceeded and imposed a four-month ownership ban on him in January 2015 when the same Italian court rejected an appeal by Cellino against his tax offence. Internally, he was at the centre of an employment tribunal case which resulted in the club's former education and welfare officer, Lucy Ward, winning compensation for unfair dismissal and sex discrimination. When Hockaday's appointment left Nigel Gibbs without a specific role (the two men did not see eye to eye), Cellino told Gibbs to fill his time by 'doing some cleaning at the training ground'. Gibbs walked out and was awarded more than £300,000 for constructive dismissal.[16]

Cellino also faced awkward questions after six of Leeds' foreign players declared themselves injured shortly before a 2-1 defeat at Charlton Athletic in April 2015, a spate of withdrawals which was seen as a direct challenge to Neil Redfearn's authority. The whispers around Elland Road said Cellino was tiring of Redfearn as manager and thinking about replacing him. That group of players became known as the 'Sicknote Six' and saw their reputations trashed. Steve Morison, who started and scored in the loss to Charlton, told *The Athletic*: 'It was odd – everyone training and then at the end of training, these guys were all injured. I'd never seen anything like it. The club, for the time I was there . . . Jesus Christ. It was insane.'[17]

And so it went on. Cellino threatened to shut Sky Sports out of a game at home to Derby in 2015 in protest at the number of times Leeds' fixture list had been disrupted for live broadcasts. The EFL threatened punitive sanctions and Cellino, who was directing the pantomime from his home in Miami, caused the rigging staff to scramble by relenting at the last minute. Steve Evans revealed that the Italian always intended to back down after making his point and making some headlines.[18] He removed the number 17 from the squad list at Elland Road, saying it was unlucky. He had a dislike of the colour purple too and his appearance at a game prior to his takeover had GFH panicking when it transpired that passes for the directors' box were printed on purple cards (new passes were produced in haste to keep him happy).

The superstitious quirks were of little consequence but some of Cellino's decisions were debilitating. Leeds' training ground was mothballed in his first summer as owner, a means of cutting costs. When the club shut the swimming pool down, the tiles dropped off the walls. Players were told to bring packed lunches with them because the canteen was no longer functioning and some were forced to drive to nearby Boston Spa to provide food for the general staff. 'It got to the stage where we went to make a cup of tea one day but the milk was off and nobody had bothered to buy any fresh,' said Leeds' former striker, Matt Smith. 'Noel Hunt was with me and completely lost it. It was a case of being goaded once too often. The wheels of the entire club had fallen off.' On another occasion, Cellino decided to cook the pre-match meal – tomato pasta – before a meeting with Bournemouth at Elland Road. When the food was served to the squad, one player did a double take and asked: 'Where's my fucking chicken?'[19] Benito Carbone, the flamboyant ex-Sheffield Wednesday forward, appeared from nowhere in 2014 to become Leeds' new academy boss. 'I'd never met Massimo until a month or so ago,' Carbone told the *Yorkshire Evening Post*, 'and I was worried I'd be sacked after two days. But I like him.'[20] Carbone agreed to work for free so long as Cellino picked up the bill for his accommodation and travel. Not long after, Cellino cut the financial support and told Carbone to pay his own way. Carbone promptly left.

Only in 2016, twelve years after their relegation, did Leeds regain some lasting equilibrium. During the summer before the 2016–17

Championship season, there was a tangible change in mindset. Cellino made a solid appointment by recruiting Garry Monk as manager. Monk had done well as Swansea City's head coach in the Premier League and boasted a good reputation. Leeds leaned more towards domestic signings and away from the obscure deals Cellino had been fond of doing abroad. Among the biggest failures was Granddi N'Goyi, a midfielder Leeds loaned from Palermo without putting him through a medical. N'Goyi had a thigh strain and played only once. Cellino's mind was focused further by Andrea Radrizzani contacting him to discuss an investment at boardroom level. It suited Cellino to talk. After two-and-a-half years of constant fighting and battles on all fronts, he was tired. The deal the two men struck saw 50 per cent of shares transferred to Radrizzani in January 2017, with the remaining stake to be sold by Cellino at the end of the 2016–17 season. Cellino would walk away with almost £50m – and for all of his shortcomings, it was widely accepted that Leeds were a more saleable asset than they had been when he first replaced GFH, with a lower cost base, a smaller wage bill and fewer liabilities. 'Because the talks with Radrizzani were going on in the background, Cellino kept himself in check more,' said a source who was close to the negotiations between the Italians. 'He wasn't going to do anything stupid while Radrizzani was close to buying him out. And by then, he'd had enough anyway.' There was, however, one more twist to come. A few months after Cellino relinquished control at Elland Road, he was suspended by the Football Association for eighteen months over an illegal payment made to an agent working on behalf of Ross McCormack when McCormack was sold to Fulham for £10.75m in 2014. Cellino had left England by then and was already installed as the new owner of Brescia. Despite the time spent seeking a guilty verdict, the FA chose not to ask FIFA to enforce his ban worldwide. Leeds, as a club, were hit with a fine of £250,000, the final act of the Cellino drama.

For Radrizzani, life without Cellino was not entirely plain sailing. Monk resigned unexpectedly before the start of the 2017–18 season, frustrated that Radrizzani had not offered him a long-term contract. Leeds suspected Monk had better offers elsewhere and he duly turned up as Middlesbrough's new boss. Radrizzani's first two managerial appointments – Thomas Christiansen and Paul Heckingbottom – failed to get to grips with the job. Christiansen sold himself with a presentation to Radrizzani and Leeds' director of football Victor Orta in Barcelona but lost his job midway through the 2017–18 term, dragged down by mediocre results and indiscipline in his squad. Heckingbottom, having cost £500,000 in compensation when he arrived from Barnsley, made no impact at all and looked like a lame duck after Leeds allowed media reports claiming they had lost faith in him to pass without comment or clarification. He won four of his sixteen matches in charge.

The club risked the wrath of their fanbase by trying to change their badge from the established shield design drawn up by former manager Howard Wilkinson in 1996. The reaction to the new crest – based on the well-known 'Leeds salute' but more akin to an image from the Pro Evolution Soccer games console series – was so scathing and ferocious that the club's chief executive, Angus Kinnear, quickly kiboshed it during a live radio interview. At the end of the 2017–18 season, Radrizzani insisted on Leeds travelling to Myanmar for two friendlies, ignoring criticism from the media and several sitting MPs who called the trip 'highly inappropriate' in the face of accusations of genocide levelled at Myanmar's government. A defiant Radrizzani said he was 'not interested in playing politics. I'm honest with myself that we are not doing anything bad.'[21] It did not take long for his Eleven Sports broadcast network to sign a nine-year TV rights deal with the Myanmar National League.

In repurchasing Elland Road, though, Radrizzani made symbolic progress. Rent payments on the ground ceased immediately and he dealt with another unhelpful legacy in 2020 when the club paid off the last of the debt owed to GFH, ridding themselves of the bank's fingerprints. Like promotion, repayment of GFH's money was part of a long and gruelling cleansing process. Few things epitomised the length of the journey more than James Milner's playing career. He was a couple of years out of secondary school when Leeds sold him in the firesale of 2004. On the first weekend of the 2020–21 Premier League season, when Leeds and Liverpool met at Anfield and Milner was an unused substitute for the reigning champions, he was a few months short of his 35th birthday.

As he decided whether to accept Leeds' offer of employment in 2018, Bielsa spent days studying the club's squad and infrastructure, working late into the night to satisfy himself. He was not familiar with the ins and outs of their decline and he had more pressing things to concentrate on. The timeline of carnage at Elland Road meant nothing to him. His remit in England was to attack the here and now. All those years after Bates asked Wise to get his hands dirty, the Augean Stable was still waiting for someone to clean it. And Bielsa did.

7.

DECEMBER

A month before Christmas, English football secures a minor win against Covid-19. Pressure has been building on the government to facilitate the return of reduced crowds and in the last week of November, Whitehall relents. The concessions are small. In the parts of England with the lowest coronavirus infection rates, maximum attendances of 4000 are permitted. In the middle tiers, the limit is set at 2000. In cities like Leeds – still under strict tier-three mixing guidelines – supporters are forbidden from attending games. The rules create an imbalance, preventing Leeds United from selling tickets but allowing Chelsea to issue 2000 for their game against Marcelo Bielsa's side in London on 5 December. It is the first time in eight-and-a-half months that either club will have played in front of fans. Many of Chelsea's tickets are priced at £75, prompting the Chelsea Supporters Trust to criticise what it says is a 'clear exploitation of supporter loyalty', but they sell in a flash.[1] Premier League clubs, Leeds included, had hoped that a phased return of crowds would allow them to fill their stadiums to a quarter of capacity. The sale of 2000 tickets at Stamford Bridge leaves 39,000 seats vacant. But it is better than nothing.

At a Premier League meeting ahead of the game, Leeds vote in favour of the new rules, irrespective of the fact that Elland Road will remain empty for the time being. As a member of their senior management team admits, the direction of travel is what they want and nobody thinks that 2000 fans inside Stamford Bridge will give Chelsea a meaningful advantage. Nonetheless, Bielsa highlights the disparity in allowing certain grounds to open while others sit vacant. 'Perhaps there could be a rule that states that if fans are not allowed in all stadiums they should not be allowed in at all, until everybody is allowed to have them in,' Bielsa says. 'It shouldn't be about the category [of the government's Covid restrictions] or the consequences of being in a category. It should be about trying to keep the competition as equal as possible. I'm looking at it with common sense – but perhaps that doesn't work.' Leeds, though, have been pushing for grounds to reopen since the earliest stages of the coronavirus lockdown. As a club they are reluctant to obstruct the first sign of progress. Their chief executive, Angus Kinnear, uses his matchday programme notes to accuse the government of taking too long to relax the rules and of 'discriminating in their treatment of football in favour of other comparable industries'.[2] Three days before the game at Chelsea, Leeds announce that all of their season tickets for 2020–21 will be rolled into the 2021–22 term and subject to a price freeze. Refunds are offered to supporters who simply want their money back (the take-up of refunds is predictably small). It means a financial hit of around £10m but there is no alternative with the season already ten games old.

Chelsea versus Leeds means Bielsa against Frank Lampard, bringing together the two protagonists of the 'Spygate' controversy which blew up in January 2019. Many months have passed since an intern of Bielsa's was caught in the act of observing a Derby County training session (at a time when Lampard was managing Derby and Bielsa was in his first season as head coach of Leeds) but the saga is always there in the background and both managers know they will be asked about it ahead of the game. Bielsa denies that his relationship with Lampard is in any way strained. 'It's similar to the one I have with the rest of my colleagues,' he insists. Lampard also sidesteps questions which are angling for 'Spygate' headlines or a hint of bad blood. 'The story's in the past,' he says. 'It's gone now. I'd rather dwell on the respect I have for [Bielsa] as a coach.'[3]

Respect for Bielsa's performance in England is coming from other directions too. At the start of December he makes FIFA's five-man shortlist for the men's coach-of-the-year award, alongside Liverpool's Jürgen Klopp, Real Madrid's Zinedine Zidane, Bayern Munich's Hansi Flick and Sevilla's Julen Lopetegui. Bielsa says he 'appreciates the distinction' but there is amazement in some quarters that the Championship title was enough to earn him a FIFA nomination. Marseille coach André Villas-Boas is vocal about it and perplexed by the omission of Thomas Tuchel, who dominated domestically in France and took Paris Saint-Germain to the 2020 Champions League final (Tuchel, as it turns out, will be sacked by PSG a month later). 'FIFA are sleeping,' Villas-Boas says. 'Bielsa? Bielsa has to win a prestigious trophy. He's not among the best five coaches in the world in 2020. It's a scandal. He won the Championship.'[4]

At Stamford Bridge, and for the first time this season, Leeds are comprehensively outclassed. In their 4-1 defeats to Leicester City and Crystal Palace there were opportunities to pinch something from each game but although Patrick Bamford scores in the fourth minute in London, Chelsea from then on look as complete as they ever will under Lampard. Lampard's players combat Bielsa's high press and bypass it, equalising through Olivier Giroud in the first half. They attack aggressively at set-pieces and punish Leeds' frailty at the back. The Leeds defence is unsettled by the loss of Robin Koch to injury in the opening minutes, an injury which results in knee surgery seventy-two hours later. The

Germany international has been carrying the problem since the first weekend of the season and a collision with Giroud worsens the damage. He will be absent until March. Bielsa is able to replace him with Diego Llorente – fit again after his groin strain – but Leeds' weakness in defending corners and free-kicks is more about structure and philosophy than personnel. Bielsa's side, in a defensive sense, are a small team with limited aerial power. They have been like this since selling Pontus Jansson to Brentford in 2019 and their make-up is a conscious decision on Bielsa's part. His football requires ball-playing defenders and he prefers them to old-fashioned centre-halves, which was why Ben White appealed to him so much. Across the squad, Leeds rate poorly in analytical comparisons to the ability of other Premier League teams in the air and they organise themselves differently to most teams too. Bielsa has never embraced zonal marking. His team go man-to-man in open play and man-to-man when they defend set-pieces. The approach to corners in particular is rigid: one player (in this instance, Raphinha at Stamford Bridge) stands on the byline as close to the corner-taker as possible, creating a distraction and also putting themselves in a position to break quickly if Leeds recover the ball. Bamford operates as a free man close to the near post. Leeds always ensure they have a numerical advantage (six on five more often than not) and Bielsa's players have specific orders on who to track.[5] Liam Cooper, their strongest weapon in the air statistically, is always given responsibility for competing with the best header in the opposition line-up – Kurt Zouma, in the case of Chelsea – but the risk of going man-to-man is that a lapse in concentration or congestion in the box often leaves an attacker unmarked. Leeds suffered like that at Liverpool on the first day of the season when Koch became trapped in a mass of bodies and Virgil van Dijk nodded in a corner. They come undone in the same way in the second half at Chelsea as a collision between Giroud and Cooper leaves Zouma to glance an easy finish inside the far post. Lampard's side wrap up a 3-1 win in injury-time when Timo Werner breaks away down the right and sets up a tap-in for Christian Pulisic. A retreating Llorente pulls a hamstring as the goal goes in. There is no arguing with the result, save for the claim that Leeds might have had a penalty for a challenge on Ian Poveda while Chelsea were 2-1 ahead.

Bielsa knows that set-pieces are where Leeds are most likely to wobble. Over the course of two-and-a-half years in England, 44 per cent of the goals conceded by his side have come from those situations, penalties included. Almost 20 per cent have come from corners. 'We failed to neutralise Chelsea in this aspect and in the end it was an important factor,' Bielsa says. He promises that Leeds will address the problem in training but he thinks the focus on set-pieces by the media is over the top. Bielsa complains that nobody is paying attention to fouls and obstruction inside the box. Nor are they considering that in allowing Zouma and Van Dijk to score, Leeds have conceded to two of the strongest headers in the division. But six days later the shortcomings bite again as West Ham United come to Elland Road and win 2-1. Mateusz Klich draws first blood with a retaken penalty but West Ham reply when Tomáš Souček, a big presence at six foot three, gets above Stuart Dallas to convert a corner at the far post. Leeds toil from then on and concede for a second time ten minutes from the end, on this occasion from a free-kick. Angelo Ogbonna steals a yard on Cooper and is free to finish from close range. 'There's no mystery to the things we have to do,' Bielsa says. 'Set-pieces can be improved by continuously working on them in training. But then you have to reproduce that in a game.' David Moyes, West Ham's manager, denies that he targeted dead-ball situations specifically.

'We didn't do any more practice on them than we would have done normally,' Moyes says. 'In fact, we did none.'

Two aspects of the defeats to Chelsea and West Ham interest Bielsa more than set-pieces. He notices that at Stamford Bridge, Chelsea's physical output was 20 per cent higher than their average for the season. West Ham as a unit also covered two kilometres more against Leeds than in any of their previous games. Energy and movement is integral for Bielsa and his squad have earned a reputation for outrunning and outworking their opponents. The data is evidence of rival managers responding by attempting to push their own players further. Lampard's strategy was to match Leeds physically and then look for Chelsea's superior quality to make the difference. In a list of ways to beat Bielsa, it was undeniably effective.

Leeds' own output is steady and consistent, according to their in-house analysis. Bielsa has seen no drop in their running stats but the West Ham defeat provokes questions about their stamina. This form of scepticism comes at Bielsa's teams in cycles: the belief, built up over many years, that the strenuous nature of the way he asks his squads to train and play results in an inevitable dip in performances. Tim Sherwood, the former Tottenham Hotspur and Aston Villa manager, picks up on that theme before Leeds meet Newcastle United at Elland Road on 16 December. He is part of the punditry team for Amazon Prime's live broadcast of the game and in the pre-match chat, he reviews Leeds' loss to West Ham. 'These look like they've blown a gasket already,' Sherwood says. 'They looked tired against West Ham. They're supposed to be the fittest team in the league.'[6] What follows undermines his opinion. Leeds concede first to Newcastle against the run of play and ship another goal from a corner but they have Newcastle penned in for most of the match and control 68 per cent of possession. With the game poised at 2-2, Leeds turn the screw in the last 12 minutes. Dallas scores with a header, Gjanni Alioski smashes in a shot on the break and although the contest is already over in injury-time, Jack Harrison rounds off a 5-2 win by sprinting over 40 yards and finding the top corner from a mile out. Behind him, Ciaran Clark and the rest of Newcastle's trailing defence look shattered. Leeds' gasket is intact.

For the closing stages, Bielsa sends Pablo Hernández on from the bench. It is Hernández's first appearance since his show of petulance against Leicester but he and Bielsa have tried to settle their differences over and in eight minutes Hernández weighs in with two assists, showing that his touch and vision are still there. Bielsa has avoided speaking about Hernández's transgression but afterwards he strikes a sympathetic tone when someone asks about the midfielder's situation. Hernández is 35 and into the twilight of his career. Six years have passed since he last played in the Premier League with Swansea City and the chance to play at this level will not come around for him again. He can see that and so can Bielsa, even if the manager is not about to make concessions for him. Hernández was drifting when Leeds signed him in 2016, an experienced footballer on the books of Al-Arabi in Qatar. The Middle East was an adventure for him and Hernández tried to paint it as a serious transfer but in reality, the money on offer in Qatar was too good to turn down. When he went there from Swansea, his partner Mar (the sister of golfer Sergio García) and his first son Eric went back to Spain and the coast near Castellón. Qatar looked like a retirement home, despite Hernández being in his twenties, but Leeds had invigorated him. He won the club's player-of-the-year award in the season before Bielsa arrived and won it again in both of Bielsa's two seasons in the Championship. His form in the run-in when Leeds claimed the title was magical, arguably the form of his life. Kalvin Phillips would say that when the ball came to him, his first thought was always to 'look for Pablo. It's just instinctive. He's always available and he always knows what his next move's going to be. Pablo's the person I look for. Every time.'[7] Hernández thought of football like chess in which the best players screened the pitch and worked out their next pass before possession came to them. 'It's not about how fast you are,' Hernández once said. 'It's about how fast you think or how fast you realise you have a pass to a team-mate [on]. I try to manage this before I receive the ball because it means that when I do receive the ball, I need less time to do things.'

There had been points where Leeds wondered if Hernández would leave England and go back to Spain to finish his career. His parents, Alfonso and Carmen, lived in Castellón and in 2018 Hernández and his father became part-owners of the city's professional club, investing in an attempt to stop it going out of business.[8] He had a sports shop there, run by his sister, and numerous ties to the local area, but in 2019 he accepted a new two-year contract at Elland Road, committing him to Leeds until the age of 37. In Bielsa's first year, he ran the show from the right wing and amassed 12 goals and 13 assists, a player with the knack of making something out of nothing. But it went without saying that time would catch up with him eventually. 'The day when I go to a game and I feel that the rest of the players run more than me, are faster than me or I arrive late to the ball – on this day I'll say goodbye to football,' Hernández said two months after promotion. 'I don't think this is that moment. Physically I feel better than 10 years ago.'[9]

Bielsa's training sessions and tactics asked a lot of Hernández's body but the occasional hamstring strain aside, he held up to the demands well in the EFL. In the Premier League, minutes are proving harder to come by. Leeds, as they have to, are moving on from Hernández gradually. His brilliance in the last eight games of the club's promotion campaign – goals, assists, killer touches and major interventions off the bench – could not have come from anyone else in Bielsa's dressing room, but Leeds cannot rely on much more of it either. 'For any player, it's difficult for them to be a substitute,' Bielsa says. 'For the prestigious players and those who are idols, it's even more difficult. Before a season starts nobody is guaranteed how many minutes they will play but there's no doubt that it's difficult to put this into practice in a harmonious way.' Bielsa reveals that he recently watched a foreign game on television and heard the commentator talk about players reacting badly to substitutions that annoy them. 'I understand the dissatisfaction,' Bielsa says. 'Without doubt it's very difficult to manage that.'

Every member of the squad at Leeds wants to play on the last weekend before Christmas. The fixture list is sending Leeds to Manchester United, a resumption of one of the fiercest rivalries in England. Nobody can quite explain why the clubs' mutual enmity runs deep. Some see it as classic antipathy between two cities which lie fifty miles apart and fall into the counties of Yorkshire and Lancashire, historically opposed over many centuries. Some say it stems back to the 1960s and the days when Matt Busby and Don Revie ran two of the finest European teams. In Manchester they think Leeds are jealous of Manchester United's consistent success, particularly under Sir Alex Ferguson. In Leeds they see arrogance, entitlement and commercialism in a club who have long since become a global brand. What everyone agrees on is that these fixtures were never dull. They were often prone to crowd trouble and kept the local police forces busy. The teams have not played in a league match since 2004 and their last meeting came in a League Cup tie at Elland Road in 2011. On the day of that game, police vans were sent to the Crowne Plaza hotel in Leeds to guard Manchester United's squad from a crowd of Leeds fans who had gathered outside the entrance. The match itself saw twenty-four arrests and injuries to two police officers as fighting broke out behind the South Stand. 'Liverpool–Manchester United games have always been fierce,' Ferguson said afterwards. 'Sometimes supporters can play a bad part in that but it never reaches the levels of Leeds United. I don't know what it is between Leeds and Manchester United. It's not nice.'[10]

For Bielsa, the sting is taken out of the rivalry by the absence of a crowd at Old Trafford. The bus journeys over the Pennine hills, the rush for tickets, the skirmishes on the industrial estates around Manchester United's stadium; normal service has been suspended by Covid. But Leeds appreciate the importance of the fixture. Kalvin Phillips, a lifelong Leeds fan who was eight on the day of the club's most recent Premier League appearance at Old Trafford, spends the days beforehand chirping at his team-mates and making sure they grasp the depth of the history. 'We've got Raphinha and I'm not sure he knows the importance of the game,' Phillips jokes. 'I've given him a little slap on the back of the head and told him.' Bielsa thinks back to his time as manager of Newell's Old Boys and the derbies he experienced against Rosario Central. 'Ask a Newell's fan if they want to be the champion of South America or win [against Rosario Central] and they'll say the champion of South America,' Bielsa says. 'But if you ask the day before [playing Rosario Central], they would prefer to win the game. That's exactly how I feel.'

Bielsa has won at Old Trafford before. In 2012, his Athletic Bilbao team lit up the Europa League with a 3-2 victory there. A magnanimous Ferguson said that 'what we've seen tonight is a team whose work rate is higher than anyone I've seen in Europe.'

Elimination from the Europa League annoyed the Scot but Bielsa had earned his respect. It surprised Ferguson, and tickled him, to discover that on the morning of the match, Bielsa broke from convention by putting Athletic through an hour-and-a-half-long training session. Most coaches would do no more than tell their players to rest or take them for a short walk. 'I never forgot that comment from Ferguson,' Bielsa says. 'The training session we did showed the players where to run. It co-ordinated them. It allowed them to run less in the game because they were in the right positions.' Method behind the madness, in other words. Everything good about Bielsa's football was showcased in that Europa League tie: ambition, durability, technical complexity and fearlessness. To English viewers, the myth of Bielsa – mentioned only in brief dispatches from Spain – was made real in those 90 minutes. 'It's a wonderful thing to see such energy and determination,' Ferguson conceded.[11]

Eight years on, Bielsa's second experience of Old Trafford is brutal. Manchester United are 2-0 up inside four minutes as Scott McTominay scores twice. Bielsa's midfield is torn apart by Bruno Fernandes pulling Phillips around the pitch and McTominay and Fred exploiting the gaps created by Fernandes's running. By the 37th minute, Leeds find themselves 4-0 behind. Liam Cooper reduces Manchester United's lead to 4-1 before half-time but Bielsa's side have been broken structurally and are paying a heavy price for allowing Ole Gunnar Solskjær's midfield to drive through theirs. Bielsa gets his players together at half-time and instructs them to continue attacking. Fight to get back into the game, he tells them, and attack to the last minute, no matter the scoreline or how bad it gets. Leeds lose 6-2 but the contest is a peculiar one. Manchester United create 26 efforts on goal, Leeds 17. There is a pivotal moment at 4-1 when David de Gea, Manchester United's goalkeeper, claws a volley from Raphinha away from under his crossbar, a save of immense difficulty. On a different day the afternoon could have yielded twice as many finishes. Solskjær is asked by a journalist, quite seriously, if he is disappointed that his side failed to hit double figures. 'It could have been 12-4,' Solskjær says. 'It was that type of game.'

Ferguson is there to watch and is overheard saying that Leeds are one of the best attacking sides he has seen so far this season but the media coverage that ensues is highly critical of Bielsa. He is questioned again about his refusal to implement a 'plan B'. If his tactics result in Leeds trailing 4-0 at Old Trafford, why does he not think about changing or redrawing them? Bielsa made two substitutions at half-time but there was no significant alteration to his system. Is it acceptable that when Leeds lose they concede goals in spades? And if Bielsa is as intelligent a manager as his reputation suggests, why does he appear so unwilling to adapt? Reporters want to know if the defeat in Manchester explains why sections of the population in Argentina consider him to be overrated, or a 'smoke-seller', as Bielsa puts it. Bielsa expects this scrutiny and tries to pre-empt them before they gather pace. 'Of course, when we lose there are questions about our style of play,' he says. 'But when we win we are praised for it. All around are people with the intention that the team plays in a more pretty way, with less pragmatism.' More negatively, to use a word which Bielsa will not. Bamford is asked in a pitchside interview if he or any of the other players at Leeds would consider asking Bielsa to adjust his tactics, to prevent similar thrashings. 'We're fully behind the manager,' Bamford says. 'Ultimately, if we play exactly the way he wants to play then we'd win every match. But we're human and sometimes we aren't quite at it.'[12]

Bielsa picks up on the exchange with Bamford and it frustrates him. It is, he says, an attempt to 'destabilise' the dressing room by suggesting to a member of his squad that their strategy is flawed or too one-dimensional.

Bielsa's distant relationship with the media does not speak to ambivalence about the content of the reporting. In the mornings at Leeds, his secretary is tasked with translating reams of articles about Bielsa and his team, converting them from English to Spanish and allowing Bielsa to digest the narrative. There are no instructions to filter out either overly positive or overly negative pieces. He wants as much copy as he can get, to give him an insight into how he is being perceived and portrayed. Throughout his reign as manager of Leeds, he has taken to either naming his line-up publicly before a game or giving away so many hints that his line-up was easy to guess. Information seen as sacrosanct by the average coach is neither here nor there to him. He does the same before Leeds' defeat to West Ham, listing his eleven starters in full, but the attention that draws makes him wonder if other managers might start to see him as over-confident or disrespectful. 'For me, knowing the eleven of the opponent does not give you a significant advantage,' he says. 'But from now on, to avoid any backlash, I will not give answers on players who can or cannot play at the weekend. Imagine that the manager of West Ham says I name the team due to vanity. It's something I shouldn't do.' Bielsa claims not to worry about the impact of coverage on him or his players. In the main, it is easy enough to shut criticism out of a training ground. But it concerns him that critical writing will influence the public or the public's way of thinking. For all that Leeds' fanbase are enamoured with Bielsa, he is anxious that attention on his perceived lack of flexibility might take hold. 'The press has no influence over the team I manage,' he insists. 'But the press is there to influence people and what worries me is the effect that it has on the public.'

On Christmas Eve, he sits down on Zoom for his pre-match media briefing before Leeds' game against Burnley on 27 December. After a couple of routine answers, he embarks on a forty-five-minute defence of himself and the performance at Old Trafford. Comments in so much detail invariably come when Bielsa feels under attack or under pressure to explain himself. It was the same during 'Spygate' and the same at the midway point of the 2019–20 season when Arsenal cut short Eddie Nketiah's loan at Elland Road due to a lack of games. Nketiah's exit led to accusations that Bielsa had failed to manage the England Under-21 international as he should have done by playing him more. Bielsa resented that view and railed against it for several weeks, returning to the subject of Nketiah time and again. He admits that he has been thinking at length about how to respond to the criticism of the defeat to Manchester United. 'It takes me a whole day to reach these conclusions and ensure I'm not saying the wrong thing,' Bielsa says. He tries to make the point that Leeds had chances on the day. He holds his hands up and accepts that he made a mistake by failing to realise how aggressively McTominay and Fred would attack his midfield. He says once more that in the midst of the debate about Leeds' defending of set-pieces, few people are willing to highlight fouls against them. A reporter on the call misquotes Sean Dyche, the Burnley manager, by asking what Bielsa thinks of Dyche's comment that Bielsa valuing style over results is 'peculiar'. (Dyche in fact said that he was 'pretty sure Bielsa is not just thinking about style'.) 'I've never said this,' Bielsa replies. 'It clearly indicates that [people] hear what they want to hear. Nobody can say I put style over results. I've never said that I do. It's just another way to ridicule me.' The press conference goes on for so long that the club's head of communications steps in and ends it after an hour. Bielsa's players are arriving for training and are due to start in a couple of minutes' time.

At Elland Road there is a sense that Bielsa is being held to unreasonable standards. Leeds are a newly promoted team sitting in mid-table but every loss leads to discussions about naivety or shortcomings on the part of him or his players. The club are very happy with him and the mood at Christmas is one of contentment. Bielsa runs his annual raffle and, as usual, gives his squad the choice of whether to train in the morning or the afternoon on Christmas Day.[13] The reality of the Manchester United fixture is that in the context of remaining in the Premier League for a second season, it was always less significant than Burnley at home or West Bromwich Albion away two days later. Burnley lose 1-0 at Elland Road but find a way to make Leeds sweat. They push Bielsa's side back after half-time, restricting Leeds to just 12 completed passes in the final third. Leeds are rarely so devoid of possession or territory but an early penalty from Bamford, his tenth goal of the season, is enough to register a victory which takes Leeds onto 20 points. Forty points is seen as the standard benchmark for survival, although it is a decade since Wolverhampton Wanderers needed that tally to stay up and send Birmingham City and Blackpool down. Realistically, Leeds are more than halfway there.

West Brom away on the 29th is a completely different battle. Leeds play in West Brom's half throughout, keeping the ball up the pitch. Bielsa sees a high attacking line as the most effective way of defending, forcing the opposition to build and counter from around the edge of their own box. Romaine Sawyers sells West Brom down the river with an early own goal but Leeds have the measure of Albion and canter to a 5-0 win. West Brom are so far removed from Illan Meslier's net that they come up with only one shot on target and fail to complete a single pass into the Leeds box. It is Sam Allardyce's second game as West Brom manager and the result deflates him. He is supposedly here to rescue them but in this form, they look doomed. Leeds' performance and goal-scoring ooze quality. It is telling to think that six months earlier, the two clubs were vying with each other for the Championship title. But Allardyce sees another factor too. Over 90 minutes, the distance covered by Bielsa's team reaches almost 120km. They have gone further than before and destroyed West Brom physically. 'Leeds didn't just outplay us tonight,' Allardyce laments. 'They outran us too.'

8.

MURDERBALL

Wednesday at Leeds United is murderball day. The players brace themselves for it and love it and dread it in equal measure. The spectacle is mayhem, like nothing any other coach has made them do before, but in comparison to it, a competitive match can feel like a breeze. 'I hate it at the time but then you get to the next game and it feels easier,' one Leeds player told me. 'The games are never as intense as murderball. Not even close.'

Murderball is Marcelo Bielsa's *pièce de résistance*, the part of the training week which defines him and resonates most. His ideas have inspired or enlightened the careers of other elite managers but none of them replicates or wants to replicate the session Bielsa stages when Leeds have no midweek fixture. Andoni Iraola was a right-back who played for Bielsa at Athletic Bilbao and went into management with Spanish clubs Mirandés and Rayo Vallecano after retiring. When I speak to him about murderball, he knows exactly what it is and I tell him that I cannot imagine other managers trying to mimic it – or other managers being brave enough to push their squads through a routine so physically brutal. 'No,' Iraola says. 'Neither can I.'[1]

Bielsa's coaching philosophy has its roots in murderball – the belief that extreme fitness levels and the ability to focus in an exhausted state are fundamental factors in dominating matches. The difficulty in facing Bielsa's Leeds, as Sam Allardyce said, is that they never stop running. Jürgen Klopp discovered as much on the first day of the Premier League season, when Liverpool edged a 4-3 win over Leeds at Anfield. 'They performed outstandingly,' Klopp said. 'It was very difficult for us. And for 95 minutes, by the way.' Opposition teams would soak up pressure in the hope that Leeds' batteries were likely to go flat. Murderball and Bielsa's training regime as a whole gave his players the stamina to go all night.

The concept of murderball is as old as Bielsa's own career and it goes back to his days as manager of Newell's Old Boys in Rosario. Back then his team called the 11 versus 11 session 'opposition' (the players at Athletic Bilbao would nickname it 'Champions'; it was only at Leeds that 'murderball' entered the Bielsa lexicon) but the structure was the same: no corners, no throw-ins, no goal-kicks and no referee. It was a contest without rules and the purpose of it was simply to keep the ball in play and run as hard as you could. Murderball has a keen influence on the line-ups Bielsa chooses. After every session he reviews the data, analyses the distance covered by his squad and grades them accordingly. At Leeds they say that if you cannot cope with murderball, you have no prospect of playing at the weekend. It is the examination Bielsa expects the players to pass consistently. The strain of it is greater on a player like Pablo Hernández, well into his thirties and a little prone to muscular injuries, but Bielsa makes very few allowances and the physical output goes off the scale. 'If the ball never goes out of play then you can't stop running,' says club analyst Tom Robinson. 'So the numbers go up. Compared to a normal game, it's not comparing apples with apples.'

The murderball skirmishes are so gruelling that Iraola recalls how he used to remind himself to eat 'a big bowl of rice the night before'. Most sessions are shorter than a 90-minute match and is split into multiple segments. When those segments end, Bielsa calls his players in briefly to make tweaks to the line-ups or his formation before starting the game up again. Balls are scattered around the edge of the pitch to make sure it continues without a pause. His staff are on hand too, there – as another player puts it – 'to shout orders and get into the lads'. Wild and unstructured though the football is, the technical standard is high and nobody wants to lose. Nobody wants Bielsa to look at them and question their effort either. One team often consists of his strongest XI and the other will be padded out with youngsters, some of them rotating to make sure the weaker side stays fresher. 'You have all the coaches by the pitch, screaming all the time,' said Mateusz Klich in Bielsa's first season. 'Basically you can't stop running.' Will Huffer, the club's former academy goalkeeper, enjoyed the chaos and had seen nothing like it. 'I'd have someone standing next to my goal and any time the ball went out, another one would get thrown to me and I'd get verbals straight away,' Huffer said. 'All you'd hear was, "Play the ball! Play the ball!" You had to find a pass even if it wasn't on. Just play it and keep it going. The games were madness but at the same time, really good fun.' It is very different to the 'shadow play' of Arrigo Sacchi, the two-time AC Milan manager who put his side through sessions with an imaginary ball to improve their positioning and their reading of the game, but it is no less singular. 'He doesn't let a player waste time on the pitch,' said Claudio Vivas, Bielsa's assistant at Bilbao. 'The day-to-day is so intense. You start at a certain hour and you don't know when you'll finish. You train like you play and you play like you train. People often say that's one of [Pep] Guardiola's mantras but it's been one of Bielsa's for a long time.'

There are two essential strands to Bielsa's football: exceptional conditioning and a rigid tactical model. It sounds like the blueprint for any successful coach but Bielsa pushes the boundaries on both fronts. Jonjo Shelvey, the Newcastle United midfielder, was bewildered by Leeds' vigour after coming up against Rodrigo. 'He was meant to be playing centre midfield and he was just all over the place,' Shelvey said. 'I said to him, "Geez, can you just stand still for one minute? Because you're running around like a nutcase." Some of it was like pointless running but he goes, "I must do, I must do. The manager tells me I must do."'[2]

Bielsa's attention to fitness stems from the 1980s and his earliest seasons as a coach, when he taught his youth teams at Newell's about the effect of lactic acid. Bielsa confused the boys by making them run hard in the twenty minutes before a game. It seemed counterintuitive and felt like a waste of energy but the boys soon discovered that lactic acid flowing in and out of their muscles made them feel physically stronger when the match kicked off.[3]

When Bielsa took over at Leeds in 2018, almost every player was told to lose weight and reduce their body fat percentage. Right-back Luke Ayling, who had stuck to the target weight set for him by a different coaching team at the end of the previous season, shed half a stone on Bielsa's orders – 'There ain't no cereal in my house any more,' Ayling said. Unavoidable weight checks deterred the players from deviating from a strict diet plan. One who was sold by the club after Bielsa arrived stopped for a final chat with the security staff as he drove out of Leeds' training ground. 'At least I can eat whatever I like now,' he said. The canteen at Thorp Arch was filled with fruit, yogurt and smoothie makers, removing all traces of free sugars. At the DoubleTree Hilton hotel, where Bielsa's squad stay overnight before home matches, he asked that bowls of sweets laid out for guests be removed from the floor Leeds were on, to cut out the temptation. There was no leeway at all. Bielsa signed Jamal Blackman from Chelsea in the summer of 2018 but refused to play him initially because Blackman's weight was not up to scratch. The keeper's loan ended early after he broke a leg in an Under-23s game but by that stage, four months later, he had lost 12 kilograms. The impact was seen immediately in Bielsa's football: fast, fluid and impossible for many Championship teams to live with. Stoke were destroyed in Bielsa's first game. For two seasons Leeds barely dropped below the division's top three and their win rate held at above 50 per cent. The remarkable aspect was that Bielsa was achieving this with a majority of the footballers he inherited.

For disciples of his, though, Bielsa's tactical thinking is where the enchantment lies. To the uninitiated, there is a madness about the way his teams play. It is possible to sit through a game without being able to determine the precise formation he is using or how Leeds avoid becoming tangled in their movement and rotation but, in Bielsa's eyes, everything is coordinated and synchronised. There is an element of artificial intelligence in the way he develops footballers as reliable as robots but with the scope to think for themselves. His training programme, in big groups and small, involves constant repetition, drilling and drilling the principles of passing, moving and positioning.

In the second season of Amazon's *Take Us Home: Leeds United* documentary series, the cameras spotted Leeds' schedule for pre-season before the 2019–20 term. Bielsa likes to put his squad through as many as three daily sessions in pre-season and that particular document spelt out a typical day: breakfast, training, lunch, siesta, training.[4] It started at 9 a.m. but as Vivas would say, the day tends to finish whenever Bielsa chooses to ring the bell, a grind on repeat. There is little or no room in his thinking for *enganches* or playmakers, the Juan Román Riquelmes of the football world who thrive on instinct and play off the cuff. Everything is focused on the machine as a whole. There are very few gentler days either. After Ian Poveda signed for Leeds from Manchester City in January 2020 he started doing bits of extra work after training, trying to push himself on. He was taken aside by members of the backroom staff and told that if he had the energy to do extra work once Bielsa was done with him, he was not pushing himself hard enough.

There are basic starting points in Bielsa's manner of preparing Leeds for individual matches. The first is that his team should always have a spare centre-back against any frontline they meet. So if the opposition use a lone striker in attack, Bielsa employs a flat back four with two centre-backs. If, as Chris Wilder's Sheffield United did in the first month of the Premier League season, the opposition field two strikers, Bielsa switches to a back three with wing-backs either side of them. His formation of choice is 4-1-4-1 with Kalvin Phillips in the holding midfield role but the 3-3-1-3 system he devised at Newell's Old Boys in the 1990s – the novel set-up which helped to earn Bielsa his 'El Loco' nickname – has been reprised in England too. At Bramall Lane, Bielsa's system was too flexible to strictly define. Stuart Dallas, nominally Bielsa's left-back, roamed the pitch throughout, leaving Jack Harrison to patrol the left side of it alone. It should, in theory, have created an imbalance down that flank but Harrison's discipline and stamina allowed him to keep a tight rein on Sheffield United. It was his cross which set up the winning goal for Patrick Bamford two minutes from time.

The most striking difference between Bielsa and most Premier League coaches – in truth, most coaches in the modern era – is his devotion to man-marking. It creates scenarios where individual contests count and individual contests have to be won. Man-marking requires a high level of concentration, to avoid the gaps which a zonal strategy can compensate for. Bielsa's centre-backs will stray out towards the halfway line or beyond to track opposition forwards who drop deep. Klopp's Liverpool used that tactic with Roberto Firmino trying to stretch Leeds by drawing Robin Koch or Pascal Struijk out, but they found that the attempts by Mo Salah and Sadio Mané to take advantage were thwarted by Bielsa's full-backs tracking them tightly. Kalvin Phillips's first reaction when Leeds lose possession is to look for the player he is supposed to be marking, rather than the ball. 'If my man gets the ball and I'm not with him, it's a problem,' Phillips says. 'We've always played man-to-man so keep track of your own player and you'll be in a good way. I keep that thought in my head.'[5] For 20 minutes against Guardiola's Manchester City, Leeds found pressure hard to exert. Phillips and Mateusz Klich were given the slip by Phil Foden and Kevin De Bruyne and struggled to control the middle of the pitch. But as Bielsa's pair grew into the game, Foden and De Bruyne began to fade. Over 90 minutes De Bruyne alone lost the ball 18 times. It was one of several matches in which Leeds could feel themselves acclimatising quickly.

Bielsa's style is predicated on the retention of possession. He and Guardiola are very similar in that respect. In the case of a manager like Klopp, keeping the ball is less of a concern for him. Klopp wants Liverpool to be dominant and aggressive but is more focused on using an organised press to spring traps and create transitional situations in dangerous areas. In Bielsa's first season at Elland Road, Leeds controlled an average of 64 per cent of possession per game, according to stats compiled by Opta (other teams like Birmingham City coped with less than 40 per cent). His second season was identical. Even in the Premier League, teams are finding it hard to deny Leeds the ball. Against City and Liverpool, Bielsa's side saw more of it. They attempted more passes too. Possession allows his defence to hold a high line and gives his full-backs the freedom to push on, overlap or, as Ayling likes to, drive through the middle of the pitch. Phillips provides the cover by creating a back three and monitoring the space out wide if Leeds lose the ball and are hit on the counter. In season one under Bielsa only three Championship players made more tackles than Phillips. It is risk versus reward in which very little is left to chance.

*

The extent to which Bielsa prefers to worry himself about things he can control was summed up by the draw for the 2002 World Cup which took place in South Korea. Bielsa, Argentina's coach, declined to travel to the ceremony in Busan. He was absent as the balls placed his team in the same group as Sven-Göran Eriksson's England. There was no point in me being there, Bielsa told the Argentine media, when the outcome was essentially random. 'I didn't go because my presence would have contributed nothing,' he said. 'You can't suggest, give instructions, participate or evaluate. You can only accept the luck of the draw.'[6] The thought of flying to South Korea on the basis that coaches traditionally attending these events did not cross his mind. Leeds soon encountered his reluctance to go with convention. He won the Championship's manager-of-the-month award at the first time of asking in 2018 (the first Leeds manager to receive it in more than seven years) but refused to be photographed with it. The trophy sits on the top of a filing cabinet in the office of the club's head of communications at Elland Road. He relented when he received the prize for a second time, allowing pictures to be taken, but gave the award away to his captain, Liam Cooper. 'To recognise the manager is one way to recognise everybody,' Bielsa said. 'But of course what's more important is the input of the players.'

Penalties are an isolated area where Bielsa takes a more

laissez-faire approach. Leeds tend to have a designated penalty-taker – Kemar Roofe in their first season, Mateusz Klich in their second after Roofe left for Anderlecht, and in the Premier League, Bamford – but the pecking order is not strictly enforced. Bielsa's staff take notes during training to decide who is most accurate and assured but, contrary to so much of his management, Bielsa is happy for his team to sort out spot-kicks in the heat of the moment. 'Usually the player who picks up the ball has an advantage,' he said. 'This shows he is confident.'

That relaxed thinking aside, the football Leeds play is neatly programmed. In possession they start at the back with short passes from their keeper to either the back four in front of him or Phillips beyond them. They use patience, width, overlapping full-backs and switches of play to find exit routes out of their own half and cut through defensive shapes. Bielsa, despite the basis of his philosophy, is happy for his team to use purposeful long balls and, every now and again, they rely on diagonals to hit space out wide or beat the press. But Leeds are more suited to working their way out of tight corners with a combination of one-touch passing and rotation. Bielsa likes his midfield to trade positions in possession and during two years in the Championship, his squad came to understand each other implicitly. When Phillips drifted to receive the ball, Klich would quickly occupy the open ground left by him.

Persistent passing and moving would give Leeds chances to push the button and break forward at pace. It was in this way that Leeds got on top of Guardiola's Manchester City at Elland Road. Whenever Ayling advanced and cut inside from right-back, his team-mates ahead of him gravitated towards his flank, anticipating that the opposition's left-back would be sucked out of position. Leeds attacked in the EFL like many teams were attacking in the

Premier League, committing in numbers and creating a forward line of five or six. Television pundits were surprised to see them play so aggressively at Anfield on the Premier League's opening weekend but it was how Bielsa's team were tuned and their transition between divisions is made easier by an inherently top-flight mentality. Liverpool's midfielders found it difficult to resolve the dilemma of where to place themselves when Leeds had possession. If they advanced on a deep-lying Phillips, they ran the risk of Klich and Hernández ghosting in behind them. If they stood off Phillips, they risked him picking passes in the surgical manner which set up the first goal for Jack Harrison. Leeds' big advantage as a newly promoted club is their confidence in Bielsa's tactics; their confidence in knowing how to make them work. Bamford, as a number 9, takes responsibility for leading a high, man-to-man press and helping Leeds do damage in transition. A very high turnover rate allows for regular counter-attacks and the squad showed in Bielsa's first two seasons that they were technically sound enough to cope with the complexities of his plan.

Their winning goal at Swansea City on the penultimate weekend of the 2019–20 Championship term provided a perfect snapshot of Bielsa's instructions. To many, it was the straw that broke the camel's back and ensured the title would come to Elland Road, despite the efforts of West Bromwich Albion and Brentford. The reaction of Bielsa's players and staff, all of them euphoric as Hernández scored, told its own story but the celebrations disguised the clarity of thought in the attack leading up to the midfielder's finish. Leeds were 60 seconds from injury-time at the end of a tight and gruelling match. The decisive burst began a few yards from their own goal-line, with the ball at the feet of Ayling. Rather than going long, Ayling carried possession out and took Leeds to Swansea's byline in the space of 12 seconds by exchanging passes with

Klich and Helder Costa. At the point where he squared the ball to Hernández, a pass Hernández buried with the help of a deflection off the far post, Leeds had six players inside Swansea's box and Ayling out of play beyond the net, gambling almost everything. 'It's nothing new for us or for people who watch Leeds normally,' Hernández said afterwards. 'We fight for 90 minutes and we don't stop running for 90 minutes. It's the only way we can play.'[7] Yet for all that Bielsa fixated on ball retention, in the Championship he built a side capable of scoring some exceptional goals on the break. The best of them were like flicking a switch: the opposition giving up possession in or around Leeds' box and Bielsa's players reacting instantly. They would sprint into space, make quick one-touch passes and swarm towards the other end of the pitch as defenders fought to recover. It worked six times during the 2019–20 season and made the point that Leeds could hurt a team with the ball and hurt them without it.

*

The question Bielsa keeps hearing, and the question he has faced for longer than he can remember, is whether his football is sustainable. Are this Leeds squad made to last or will his team hit the wall as a result of Bielsa cracking the whip? The narrative of burn-out has stalked him for thirty years. Bielsa's tenure at Newell's Old Boys was a golden era for *Los Leprosos*, bringing two domestic titles and an appearance in the final of South America's Copa Libertadores, but Bielsa was drained by the time he resigned in 1992. His players were jaded too. Ricardo Lunari, a regular presence in the Newell's midfield, remembered the parting of ways with sadness. 'We had a lot of respect for everything he taught us and how he improved us,' Lunari said, 'but in the end we weren't willing to blindly follow all the instructions. We won Argentine titles and reached the Libertadores final but we started to relax a little bit after that. I think some of us [players] developed attitudes Marcelo was not willing to accept.' The same was said of Athletic Bilbao, where Bielsa's first season ended with defeats in the finals of the Copa del Rey and the Europa League. It was, as a whole, a phenomenal campaign but Bilbao came up short and were never the same again. Bielsa left his job at the end of the following season. 'Our legs said "stop",' Ander Herrera, the former Bilbao midfielder, admitted during an interview with *The Big Interview* podcast in 2018. 'To be honest, we were physically fucked.'[8]

In the second half of Bielsa's first season at Leeds, the burn-out theory reared its head. Leeds were away at Queens Park Rangers in the last week of February, a game in hand and a chance to climb back to the top of the Championship table. They played poorly and lost 1-0, and a rare appearance from Izzy Brown off the bench added to the sense that Bielsa was grasping for solutions on the night. Leeds' form showed five defeats from ten matches and Bielsa was pictured by a *Yorkshire Evening Post* photographer after full-time, crouched down in a corridor near the dressing rooms and staring intently at the floor. It was an image of dejection and people seized on it (Bielsa would say privately that he regretted exposing his emotion in that way). Asked afterwards if his team were running on empty, he bit. 'Your question doesn't have any basis,' an angry Bielsa replied. 'It's clear that you don't know what you're talking about because if there's something this team doesn't lack, it's energy.'

As if to prove his point, Leeds annihilated West Brom at Elland Road three days later. Hernández found the top corner from 20 yards after 16 seconds and West Brom were beaten 4-0. Crisis averted, or so it seemed. But when the season reached its most delicate stage, Leeds needed a maximum of 10 points from four remaining matches to beat Sheffield United to automatic promotion.

Norwich City were already heading for the title. Suddenly the composure of Bielsa's players evaporated. They lost 2-1 to Wigan Athletic on Good Friday despite Wigan conceding a goal and losing Cedric Kipre to a red card early in the first half. They travelled to Brentford on Easter Monday and offered little in a 2-0 defeat. In a flash, second place was gone and Leeds were consigned to the play-offs.

What happened? Did Bielsa's squad burnout? Were tired bodies and minds to blame? To the naked eye, it seemed less about exhaustion than it did about tension. Leeds appeared to be riddled with nerves and nothing was more demonstrative of that than their loss to Derby in the play-off semi-finals. With 44 minutes of the second leg gone, Bielsa's side led 2-0 on aggregate. Then Cooper and Kiko Casilla contrived to gift Derby a goal before half-time and the tie descended into the most nervous mess Elland Road has ever seen. Mason Mount scored immediately after the restart, waltzing through the Leeds midfield to bring Derby level at 2-2. Cooper gave away a cheap penalty, pulling unnecessarily on Mason Bennett's shirt, and Gaetano Berardi was sent off for a rash lunge on Bradley Johnson. Derby substitute Jack Marriott dinked in an 84th-minute chip to send Derby through to the final at Wembley with a 4-3 aggregate win. From 44 minutes onwards, everything about Leeds was wrong: their judgement, their decision-making, their professionalism. Later that night the club's senior management team had the ignominy of handing over 40,000 play-off final tickets to Derby's directors who packed them into the boot of a car and drove home. For the next forty-eight hours, and with the season over, Leeds sat and wondered if they were about to lose Bielsa too.

Hernández was not convinced that the painful ending to that season, an ending which left him in floods of tears, was indicative of burn-out. To him, the downturn in results was the consequence of rising anxiety. 'I think one of the differences is that in the last part of [Bielsa's] first season, we felt the pressure,' he said a few weeks after Leeds were promoted. 'In the last six or seven games we only won one of them. But this year we changed that. In the crucial moments we took forward steps and we won important games. We didn't give any chance to Brentford or West Brom to close the gap.'

The 2018–19 season was proof of something Bielsa often says about himself: that he is fallible. Imaginative and often touched by magic but fallible all the same. He has his weaknesses and so do Leeds. They can be vulnerable at set-pieces and fairly ineffective with the set-pieces that are awarded to them. Bielsa's system becomes more fragile when teams accurately block off the passing lanes from his keeper and his defence. He rarely hides from tactical issues and early substitutions became a trademark of his reign. Phillips's 100th club appearance ended unceremoniously after 28 minutes away at Swansea in 2018 as Bielsa sought to rebalance a midfield which was being overrun. 'I just saw it as me needing to learn,' said Phillips diplomatically. Even Rodrigo, Leeds' record £27m signing, was not immune from changes like that. On his full league debut against Fulham, the Spaniard was replaced after 45 minutes without having much chance to shine. It was not personal – with Bielsa, it rarely is. The same rationale was behind his refusal to indulge Riquelme's genius while Bielsa was in charge of Argentina and picking a squad for the 2002 World Cup. As former Argentina striker Jorge Valdano said, it was almost impossible to pick Riquelme 'without giving him all of the responsibility'.[9] Players fit into Bielsa's system. His system does not fit around individual players.

The philosophy worked for him in the Championship and it

is working for him again in the Premier League. By the turn of the year, Leeds have 23 points from 16 games and are thriving in the division. The best of their performances are eye-catching. The worst of their defeats are heavy but Bielsa's penchant for attacking leaves no middle ground (demonstrated by his refusal to try and limit the damage when Leeds found themselves trailing 4-0 to Manchester United). When it clicks, his counterparts in the dug-out learn the lesson given to many of the managers in the league below: that studying Bielsa's methods is only half the battle of smothering Leeds on the pitch. Burn-out? There is no sign of it yet.

9.

JANUARY

Leeds are in such good shape by the end of December that they decide to leave the January transfer window alone. Victor Orta speaks with Marcelo Bielsa, who agrees that more recruitment is unnecessary. The club will allow some fringe players to go, either on loan or permanently, but they are a good distance clear of the Premier League's relegation places and there are no signs in the data of results exceeding the quality of their performances. Orta devotes his time to working on potential deals for the end of the season. One of the players who interests him is Romain Perraud, a left-back and a rising star at Stade Brestois in France. Perraud has just signed a new contract but the extension is seen as a way of maximising his market value. A left-back will be one of Leeds' priorities when the summer arrives.

Orta is sceptical about the merit of the January window in general. Mid-season signings tend to be expensive and, in his view, finding value is increasingly difficult. There is also the issue of uncovering players who are physically ready to adapt quickly to Bielsa's coaching. Many of the players under Bielsa have gone through two-and-a-half years of adjustment and learned to cope with the strain of his training sessions. The resounding failure of Jean-Kévin Augustin's move from RB Leipzig at the start of 2020 was an example of how challenging it could be to slot into Bielsa's team – and it was only because of unforeseen circumstances that

Augustin arrived at all. Bielsa had signed Eddie Nketiah in the first week of the 2019–20 season, taking the England Under-21 international on a year-long loan from Arsenal. Leeds fought hard for Nketiah, beating Bristol City and Fortuna Düsseldorf to his signature after Orta was invited to make a detailed presentation to the striker, his agent and some of Nketiah's academy coaches at Arsenal's London Colney training ground. Orta's slides revealed how he and his staff had watched Nketiah live a dozen times in ten months. The presentation talked of Leeds having a manager 'with an international reputation and a track record of developing young players'. It used video clips to show why Bielsa had 'identified him as a player who takes our team to the next level' and included a page detailing how Nketiah was 'the perfect fit'. Arsenal were convinced and in Bielsa's mind, he had his back-up for Patrick Bamford. Nketiah would not feature too regularly, stuck behind Bamford in a formation which needed only one centre-forward, but he was up to speed, he trained well and he chipped in with important goals. It was Arsenal's decision to recall him in January, bemoaning his lack of game time, which prompted Leeds to approach Augustin. Augustin was blessed with talent but had drifted out of favour at Leipzig and completed an unremarkable loan at Monaco. His body was not up to changing gear suddenly and the failure of his move was a potentially expensive lesson for Leeds. By far the best time to recruit players for Bielsa was in pre-season. That was when the most concerted work on fitness and tactics took place.

Financially it suits Leeds to have a quiet January too. Their outlay on new players in preparation for the Premier League season was vast by their standards and comprehensive analysis in FIFA's annual global transfer report shows that only five clubs across Europe – Chelsea, Manchester City, Manchester United,

Barcelona and Juventus – spent more.[1] Leeds chairman Andrea Radrizzani rules out any further investment, saying they are 'financially exposed' by the signings completed in the summer window. He and the club's board hoped that crowds would begin returning to Elland Road before the midway stage of the season but the UK is subjected to another substantial lockdown in the second week of January as schools close and restrictions tighten once more. By then, Premier League clubs are resigned to a season without significant attendances – and some, like Leeds, will see none at home until the final day.

More attention is being paid to ensuring that the 2021–22 season brings supporters back through the gates. Leeds are managing gaps in their accounts but January brings the announcement of a major deal in the form of fresh investment from the club's minority shareholder, 49ers Enterprises. The subsidiary of the San Francisco 49ers raises its stake in Leeds from 15 per cent to 37 per cent, substantially increasing its influence. An agreement was reached shortly before Christmas but Covid delays completion of the formalities until the end of January. Radrizzani tells the *Financial Times* Business of Football summit that the latest deal values the club at around £300m, a big spike on the £45m he spent buying Leeds in 2017. His comments indicate that 49ers Enterprises has paid around £60m for its new batch of shares.[2] Some of that money goes to Radrizzani, paying off loans used to cover Leeds' costs in the Championship. Documents at Companies House show that £23m has been channelled into the club's accounts, in return for an issue of new equity. It is valuable working capital at a time when Leeds have no matchday or corporate income. 'Part of the money will keep the club going,' Radrizzani says. 'The investment in the summer and last year was very heavy and this gives a bit of stability.'

Paraag Marathe, the president of 49ers Enterprises, is named as Leeds' vice-chairman and Radrizzani wants the NFL franchise to actively invole themselves in infrastructure projects like the proposed redevelopment of Elland Road into a 55,000-capacity venue. Though 49ers Enterprises is the face of the new investment deal, there are other entrepreneurs behind the money including the Australian Lowy family, YouTube co-founder Chad Hurley and Nick Swinburn, the man behind the creation of the online US clothing retailer Zappos. Both Hurley and Swinburn are investors in San Francisco's basketball team, the Golden State Warriors. Swinburn, who was born in the UK and moved to the USA when he was seven, also featured in an American takeover of Swansea City in 2016. A source close to him says investing in Leeds was 'an opportunity he had to see if he could be part of'.

*

Bielsa keeps his distance from the boardroom reshuffle and the implications of it. 'These are aspects to do with the commercial side of the club, which I don't deal with,' he says, and the fixture list in January gives him other things to think about. Leeds start 2021 away at Tottenham, where they lose 3-0. They compete well for half-an-hour but hand Spurs the initiative when a misplaced pass from Illan Meslier draws Gjanni Alioski into conceding a penalty by fouling Steven Bergwijn. Harry Kane converts it and with a 1-0 lead, Tottenham are able to employ José Mourinho's tactics without any difficulty. They contain Bielsa's side and Son Heung-Min scores a second goal before half-time with a cute finish from Kane's cross. Toby Alderweireld kills the game early in the second half when his header from a corner slides off Meslier and into the net. The goalkeeper takes some of the blame for the defeat but Bielsa is protective of him afterwards. 'The question you are asking is about an undeniable error,' Bielsa says, referring to the first goal. 'But we have to look at how the goalkeeper performs in all games, not just in one fixture.' At twenty years of age, Meslier (a baby-faced giant with a stick-thin frame and a surprisingly deep voice) is a project of Bielsa's and exceptionally raw by both the standards of the Premier League and European football. Across the continent's five big leagues, he is the youngest keeper to have made 10 or more starts this season. He is on course to break the Premier League's record for starts made in a single campaign by a keeper under the age of 21. Leeds paid Lorient £5m to sign him but they think he has the potential to be worth considerably more, a France international in the making. Bielsa sticks with him as first choice and tells Meslier to continue taking risks with his passing and his distribution. This is what keepers in Bielsa's team are there to do. The Argentinian is willing to accept the consequences.

Defeat at Spurs was not unlikely but what happens the following weekend is more difficult to excuse. Leeds are drawn away to Crawley Town in the FA Cup's third round and despite indicating beforehand that he was minded to field a strong line-up, Bielsa makes numerous changes. His squad are going well in the Premier League and in a season where many clubs are feeling the pressure of a truncated schedule, there is a chance for them to make meaningful impact in the cup. From Leeds' perspective, progress in the FA Cup is long overdue. They have not reached the semi-finals since 1987 or appeared in the final since 1973 (the club won the trophy for the first and only time in the year of the competition's centenary, 1972). They also have a recent history of humiliating exits: Histon in 2008, Sutton United in 2016 and Newport County in 2018, a result which exhausted most of Radrizzani's remaining faith in former head coach Thomas Christiansen, who was sacked a few weeks later. Crawley are a League Two side but are in form with a nine-game unbeaten run. Nonetheless, Bielsa creates a rigid plan for the tie, mapped out in full. He rests Patrick Bamford, Stuart Dallas, Mateusz Klich and Luke Ayling, four of the players he has used most in the Premier League. He names only seven substitutes on the bench because he already knows who he wants to replace and when. Liam Cooper is returning from an abdominal injury and completes the first half. The tie is goalless at the interval and Leeds' performance has been laboured but Bielsa presses ahead with three changes regardless, removing Cooper, Rodrigo and Pascal Struijk. Academy defender Olly Casey drops in at centre-back and Jack Jenkins is given a debut in defensive midfield. Jack Harrison, Bielsa's left-winger, steps off the flank and takes up the role of centre-forward. As Leeds lose their shape and their cohesion, Crawley seize the moment and score in the 50th and 53rd minutes. The tie feels lost long before Crawley seal a 3-0 win when Jordan Tunnicliffe stabs in from close range. There are mistakes from Kiko Casilla in goal and an overwhelming sense that Bielsa has got it wrong. He has no way of explaining himself at full-time because Crawley have no facilities for an online press conference and Leeds, despite the insistence of the Football Association that every coach should be available to the media, refuse to expose him to a pitchside huddle of journalists. Covid is too much of a concern.

With a few exceptions, Bielsa and his squad have been able to avoid the coronavirus. A bout of it prevents Tyler Roberts from featuring at Spurs or Crawley and two of Leeds' development squad forwards, Sam Greenwood and Joe Gelhardt, come down with Covid in early January. But shortly after the FA Cup defeat, Meslier tests positive and is ruled out of the next league game against Brighton. With their first-choice keeper in isolation, Leeds are more than happy to co-operate when officials from the Premier League approach them to discuss the postponement of a home meeting with Southampton, scheduled for 20 January. Southampton and Shrewsbury Town are trying to fulfil a Covid-affected FA Cup fixture and a rearrangement works for Leeds on a number of levels. It will allow Meslier to recover and limit his absence to one game. It will also allow the club to address a pitch at Elland Road which is damaged beyond repair.

Leeds' ground staff hoped the pitch would limp through to the end of the season, surviving until the entire surface could undergo full reconstruction, but a combination of historic problems and persistently wet weather has worsened it. There is no way of salvaging it or making it playable to Bielsa's standards. Issues with the drainage at Elland Road have been apparent since the pitch was first laid a quarter of a century earlier, caused by a layer of natural film developing over some of the gravel beneath the turf.[3] It was another area of infrastructure which the club neglected in the years when they were stuck in the EFL, devoid of the money needed to bring it up to scratch. When it rains heavily, water is liable to pool on the grass, particularly in front of the tunnel. Bielsa's instructions to the ground staff are simple – keep the surface 'short, fast and wet' – but beyond keeping it saturated, they are fighting a losing battle.

A turgid, messy 1-0 defeat to Brighton on 16 January brings matters to a head. The state of the pitch is not the only factor in the result and Leeds suffer from the absence of Kalvin Phillips through suspension but their expected goals calculation drops to 0.3 over 90 minutes, the lowest figure they have ever recorded in over 100 games under Bielsa. Brighton's manager, Graham Potter, is generous about the surface and Bielsa refuses to condemn it publicly but in private, the quality of it is a frustration. His coaching team can tell from his demeanour that any days off planned for the week ahead will be cancelled. Radrizzani and the board accept that they cannot ask Bielsa to continue working with a pitch which compromises his style of play.

In a matter of days, Angus Kinnear finds a solution. Tottenham have asked a firm in Leicestershire, Hewitt Sportsturf, to grow a spare top layer of grass for them and Spurs agree that Leeds can buy the pitch for a little over £300,000. Tottenham were holding it in reserve in case the hybrid football pitch at their new stadium was affected or damaged by a separate synthetic pitch used for NFL fixtures and concerts but Covid has cancelled all events aside from Premier League fixtures and Leeds are welcome to have it. Hewitt Sportsturf has already secured the contract to carry out a full refit of the Elland Road pitch at the end of the 2020–21 season, replacing the drainage and undersoil heating and resolving the shortcomings which had bothered Leeds for almost 25 years. The postponement of the Southampton game provides a two-and-a-half-week window between home games, enough time for a new layer of turf to be laid. Leeds know the solution is only a temporary measure. The £300,000 they are spending now will not avoid more major work or an outlay of over £1.5m in the summer. A complete overhaul is the only means of bringing the club in line with technological advances.

In the interlude after Brighton, Bielsa doubles up on murder-ball sessions as Leeds prepare to play at Newcastle United on 26 January.[4] One of the players who stands out in the sessions is Diego Llorente, fit again after the hamstring strain he suffered at Chelsea in early December. His running stats are impressive and mentions in dispatches from Thorp Arch speak of him impressing the other players with his aggression and his competitive streak. It is almost as if Llorente suspects a door might be opening for him again. His intuition is correct. For the previous fortnight Bielsa has been considering turning to the Spaniard. He held off on using him against Brighton but in the week before that match he withdrew Llorente from an Under-23s game at Burnley and sharpened him up by putting him through a full range of drill sessions instead. In an attempt to end a run of three consecutive defeats, Bielsa names him in his side at Newcastle. With eight minutes gone, Llorente pulls up with another hamstring injury.

A shortage of centre-backs has been a topic of discussion at defending champions Liverpool throughout the season. The loss of Virgil van Dijk to an ACL was the start of a string of injuries which have decimated Jürgen Klopp's defensive resources. But Bielsa and Leeds have it almost as bad. Llorente, an £18m Spain international, is yet to start and finish a full game and has only played twice since signing from Real Sociedad. Robin Koch's knee is still on the mend after surgery. Cooper has been sidelined three times and Bielsa's preferred partnership of Cooper and Koch has been used just six times. Struijk steps off the bench to replace Llorente at St James' Park and Leeds, despite a disjointed second half, hold on for a 2-1 win. Raphinha and Jack Harrison score in either half, negating Miguel Almirón's goal, and with half of their fixtures gone, Bielsa's side are 14 points above the Premier League's bottom three. In a couple of weeks' time they will move past 30 and towards the brink of safety. Bielsa, still, is in no doubt that after a downturn in form, a victory at Newcastle was required. 'It was important for us,' he admits. 'The quicker you get out of these runs the better.'

Leeds' next opponents, Leicester City, have a keen admirer in Radrizzani. They come up in interviews carried out with him after 49ers Enterprises completes its equity increase. Radrizzani says he will try to emulate Leicester, describing them as a 'model to follow'. 'I love what they have done in the past ten years and in six seasons in the Premier League,' Radrizzani says. Leicester were famously the 5000-1 shot who won the Premier League title in 2016 but their success and sustainability came from the long-term planning of the Thai ownership group who bought into them in 2010. Leicester, like Leeds, had tired and outdated infrastructure. They had also lost substantial amounts of money by employing Sven-Göran Eriksson as manager in the Championship and backing him in the transfer market with no tangible return. Having fixated on promotion initially, Leicester's new board saw the sense in playing the long game. Upgrades were made to the King Power Stadium and a new training ground was financed and built at a cost of almost £100m, opening on Christmas Eve in 2020. They altered their recruitment strategy to look for value in less fashionable markets and showed common sense in selling their most valuable players when offers for them went through the roof. For example, in the summer of 2020, Ben Chilwell moved to Chelsea for £50m; Leicester replaced him at left-back with James Justin, a £7m signing from Luton Town. In Radrizzani's eyes, Leicester had succeeded in blending sustainability and ambition without losing sight of their size as a club. Radrizzani is not talking about the Premier League title. Aiming for that would be ludicrous. What he imagines is Leeds competing in the Europa League with a re-vamped stadium at Elland Road. 'I give myself five to seven years to build the Leeds I dream of,' he says. 'My dream is to have one of those big European nights.'

The most astute of Leicester's signings, Jamie Vardy, does not feature during Leeds' visit to the King Power. He has undergone minor hernia surgery and Leeds are asked to deal with the benign presence of Ayoze Pérez instead. In the clubs' first meeting this season, Bielsa's side paid heavily for mistakes and poor judgement which allowed Leicester to wound them in transition. The game in Leicester starts badly as Leeds lose possession on halfway and allow Harvey Barnes to sprint forward and beat Meslier. But Stuart Dallas equalises within two minutes and Leeds adopt an intelligent approach in the second half. Brendan Rodgers' switch to a back-three helps Leicester to control more possession but Leeds lie deep and limit their risks. They repel Leicester's attacks until the 70th minute when a deft pass from Raphinha and a brilliant finish from Bamford put Leeds 2-1 up. Raphinha is developing into the sort of purchase Leicester would be proud of: bought for £17m but already worth considerably more. Leicester throw everything forward but six minutes from the end, Leeds break out from a corner and Harrison completes a 3-1 win on the counter-attack, given a tap-in as Bamford chooses to square the ball instead of shooting himself. 'I've got myself in my own fantasy team,' Bamford jokes in the post-match interviews. 'But if I shoot there and I miss, it's not worth it. For the team, we needed that extra comfort.'[5] England coach Gareth Southgate is there to watch.

Bielsa wants his players to think like Bamford does, to occupy themselves with collective aims. The long analysis sessions, the clips sent to his squad before every game, the hotel video meetings on the night before a match, the fixation on data; the purpose of the schooling is to make complex football second nature and to guard against anyone coasting or plateauing. Perfection would never be reached. As Bielsa said himself, footballers were human and humans had flaws. The same went for coaches. But it did not stop him trying.

10.

ANALYSIS

Before becoming manager of Athletic Bilbao in 2011, Marcelo Bielsa gave the club the same forensic going over he would later give Leeds. Bilbao had played 42 games in the season just gone, finishing sixth in La Liga, so Bielsa sat down and watched every one of their matches. Then he watched every one of them again, to 'deepen the data' and check if there was anything he had missed. The information he compiled from the footage in front of him was exhaustive, categorising every starting line-up, the formations at kick-off, the substitutions made and the way in which tactics changed mid-match. He did this for Athletic and he did it for their opponents, storing the findings in computer files and outlining them in a video which he sent to Spain for Bilbao's hierarchy to study. Bielsa had worked in Spain and La Liga before but only very briefly with Espanyol in 1998. If he was to last for any length of time at Bilbao, his research of Spanish football thirteen years later would have to be meticulous. And even then, the offer of the job depended on a certain candidate, Josu Urrutia, winning an election to become Bilbao's president.

Patience is one of Bielsa's virtues when it comes to preparation. There is no limit to the time he is willing to spend on analysis or the time he is willing to wait for others to supply it. In the 1990s he developed an acute fascination with Louis van Gaal and Van Gaal's remarkable Ajax team, a team whose principles were wholly

European and wholly derived from Van Gaal. Argentina had a passion for flair and individualism, a nation brought up on free spirits like Maradona. When Maradona died in November 2020, Bielsa talked about him 'making us feel a fantasy', of Maradona being an 'artist' who allowed the poorest people in Argentina to drift off and dream, but Ajax were more in tune with Bielsa's ideology. Van Gaal devoted a lot of thought to structure, a studious man who saw collective endeavour as the route to special football. Over the course of Van Gaal's tenure at Ajax, Bielsa arranged for VHS cassettes and files documenting Ajax's games to be mailed to him in South America. They arrived slowly, dropping on his doorstep long after news of the results had reached him, but from Bielsa's perspective they were worth the wait. In 2016, speaking at the Aspire Academy's global summit in Amsterdam, he told the audience that he had watched more than 200 of Ajax's matches with Van Gaal as manager. All of them were a window into Van Gaal's world, the best way for Bielsa to uncover the Dutchman's philosophy. After a while Bielsa stopped looking at the match files in advance and asked his wife, Laura, to tell him when Van Gaal made substitutions in each game. Using his knowledge of previous fixtures, Bielsa would try to predict the player Van Gaal replaced, the player he sent on and the way in which it affected Ajax's formation. If he was right, he was starting to understand Van Gaal. If not, he had more to learn. 'I never believed I knew what Van Gaal knew because I didn't know what he felt,' Bielsa told the Aspire summit. 'This was the only piece of his mind I could get hold of. It was minimal but it was a way to access his knowledge.'[1]

Bielsa never tired of these discoveries, however small they were. If anything, as he got older his addiction to analysis intensified, to the point where even he admitted that the amount of data he gathered was 'stupid' and excessive.[2] He realised as much but he could not help himself. At Leeds he was a modern-day Don Revie, the godfather of the dossier who embraced scouting and analytical work like very few coaches in the 1960s and '70s. Unlike most of his peers, Revie cottoned on to the fact that studying and understanding the opposition was a means of outwitting them and beating them. His staff, like scout Maurice Lindley and coach Les Cocker, travelled all over England and Europe producing handwritten notes on the strengths, weaknesses and strategies of teams and individual players. Reports were typed up by Revie's secretary, Jean Reid, and distributed to the squad at Elland Road before each game.[3] Some in Revie's dressing room valued the files. Others thought the detail was superfluous. Peter Lorimer, Leeds' record goalscorer, would complain that Revie was capable of making a fourth-division full-back sound like the world's greatest footballer. Eddie Gray used to joke that it was hard enough to persuade Lorimer to 'read the *Sporting Life*' and Lorimer was not alone in finding the dossiers hard going. But they soothed Revie's paranoia, the fear that he might overlook something crucial if he let his analysis slide. Bielsa was the same. Some of the data Bielsa amassed was abstract and some of it was of no tangible value. In 2019, he referenced the file he compiled on Barcelona before his Bilbao team played Pep Guardiola's Barcelona in the 2012 Copa del Rey Final. Afterwards Guardiola was given a copy by Bielsa and could not believe the depth of it. 'But the report was useless,' Bielsa said, 'because they scored three goals against us.' Even so, it was better than Bielsa feeling under-prepared as the final kicked off.

Bielsa's insistence that Leeds install an enhanced camera system around the pitches at their training ground allowed his assistants and analysis team to monitor sessions more closely and produce video clips as quickly as possible. Everything was filmed and fed back into the complex's main building in real time. On any given afternoon, and in the hours after the morning training session ended, his backroom staff could be found in a room on the first floor of Thorp Arch, sat quietly and intently in front of laptops and tablets. They were renowned for arriving early each day and they were often among the last to leave at night. Even on the evening in July 2020 when West Bromwich Albion's defeat to Huddersfield Town confirmed Leeds' promotion to the Premier League, they were all at their desks planning for Derby County away two days later, a dead rubber as it turned out. Leeds' players joked with Bielsa about having the day after promotion off. His concession was to delay the start of morning training by two hours. In Bielsa's first season, the partner of one of Leeds' foreign employees flew home after complaining that they barely saw each other. The hours were long and there was very minimal downtime. Bielsa set projects for his assistants, like one task which involved studying the 2018 World Cup and establishing training drills which would have created or prevented every goal scored in the tournament. During the Covid-19 lockdown, they were asked by him to go back over matches in six of Europe's big leagues – the Premier League, La Liga, Serie A, the Bundesliga, Ligue 1 and the Championship – and gather new ideas.[4] The result of their work was an extraordinary amount of insight for Bielsa to draw on. Leeds were astonished to find that within the documents put together for the 2019–20 campaign was an eight-page breakdown of Luton Town goalkeeper Marek Štěch. Štěch was third choice at Kenilworth Road and did not play once that season. Nobody expected him to play either. But at least Bielsa was covered if he did. Friendlies were given the same treatment. Before Bielsa's very first pre-season game, away at Forest Green Rovers in July 2018, he wrote to Forest Green to request permission to film three of the League Two club's other friendlies. All of those matches were against minor non-league opponents based in the south-west of England – bounce games designed to shake off some rust – but Bielsa did not want to play Forest Green without casting a proper eye over them first. 'I was a bit bemused,' said Forest Green's manager, Mark Cooper, when I spoke to him on the night of Leeds' visit. 'We said yes quite happily because there wasn't any reason to say no. It wasn't like there was anything to hide. I just couldn't understand why anyone would be so interested. I've never had a request like that.'

The players at Leeds adjusted very quickly to an increased load of analysis. Bielsa changed their pre-match routine so that nights before home games, as well as nights before away games, were spent together in a hotel. He and his staff used those spare hours to sit with the squad individually, run through aspects of their recent performances and the plan for the following day. They reviewed the decisions each player had made, the decisions they should have taken, the effectiveness of their movement and any avoidable mistakes. Bielsa liked to arm them with a laser and ask them to track themselves on the screen, a test of their concentration.[5] 'The way he sees the game is incredible,' winger Jack Harrison told the *Telegraph*. 'You can imagine the amount of work it takes. You can see the exact situations he's drawn out.' Bielsa's post-match de-briefs are long, exacting and unpredictable in tone. Leeds can play well and win and find him dissatisfied. They can underperform, lose and find him supportive. 'There are times when he'll cane you when you're not expecting it,' one of his players told me. 'You just have to take it. But sometimes when you are expecting it, he'll go easy on you. It keeps you on your toes.'

His squad were ready for a morning of criticism and ire after a 2-0 defeat to Nottingham Forest in February 2020. The result was a watershed moment in a season which was in danger of losing its way. Leeds were on a run of two wins in 10 league games. The loss at Forest and the mood at full-time were summed up by Luke Ayling (one of Bielsa's more optimistic and charismatic players) giving a demoralised interview to Leeds' in-house television station, LUTV. 'We played nice football again,' Ayling said, 'but no cutting edge. So the same old story.'[6] They were worrying comments and by the time the team bus left for home, they had already spread across social media. It was unusual to hear anyone in Bielsa's camp talk like that.

Confidence in Bielsa was so high and the cohesion of his team so solid that in both of his seasons in the Championship, Leeds reeled off seven straight wins around Christmas. Doubt did not creep in easily but the anxiety caused by Forest's win put pressure on Bielsa to read the room. In moments where form and results dipped, he was inclined to plough on and redouble his demands no matter the strain his squad were under. Training never eased, not even in the closing weeks of a season when some coaches would taper the workload to compensate for bodies and minds tired by forty-plus games. But on this occasion Bielsa had his eyes open to the atmosphere around him and in the analysis session after the defeat to Forest he changed tack and turned the meeting into a pep-talk. Much about the performance was good, he insisted. On a white board he made a list of the things Leeds had done well. It might be one win in eleven, Bielsa told them, but you are better than these results. You are as good a team as you were before, the best in the division. The meeting finished with a spontaneous round of applause from everyone in the room. 'It was powerful stuff,' Ayling said. 'We all felt it. It was a big part of the turnaround.'[7]

That weekend asked more of Bielsa than standard man-management. On the day of the game at Forest, Liam Cooper's newborn son was taken ill and admitted to hospital in Hull. Leeds' medical team drove Cooper straight to the ward after full-time and the defender and his partner, Abbie, spent three nights crossing their fingers and waiting for news. Out of the blue, Bielsa arrived at the hospital to offer moral support. He said a prayer for Cooper's family and told Cooper to concentrate on nothing else. Leeds had a midweek game at Brentford looming but they could manage without him. It was only football. Deprived of sleep but invigorated by Bielsa's visit, Cooper started at Griffin Park and scored in a 1-1 draw. Brentford were one of the slickest sides in the Championship but having warned beforehand that an out-of-form Leeds 'couldn't pick a worse place to play on Tuesday night', their manager Thomas Frank watched Bielsa's team outplay his own completely.[8] In an instant the negativity was gone and, from there, Leeds' last 14 matches yielded 12 wins and the title. Bielsa's interventions were perfectly pitched.

*

It was no secret that in performing so much analysis, Bielsa liked to cover every base. Anyone who had read about his interest in Louis van Gaal or his fastidious way of considering job offers understood how particular he was, but his techniques were the cause of bitter controversy and national scrutiny in January 2019. An encounter between police officers and one of Bielsa's interns on a roadside in Derby was the start of a dispute in which he and his methods came under attack. The media dubbed it 'Spygate' and a month-long saga gave journalists access to the deepest reaches of Bielsa's analytical machine, an unprecedented look at the way an elite coach worked. By the time the dust settled, Spygate had cost Bielsa a fine of £200,000. What worried him more was the impact on his reputation.

Bielsa, unbeknown to almost everyone at Elland Road, was in the habit of sending analysts and interns to watch opposition teams train before Leeds played them. The staff were dispatched with instructions to look at the shape and systems used and to find anything else which might give Bielsa an edge. To him it was a legitimate method of scouting. Argentinian clubs did this all the time and in Spain, every one of Bielsa's training days at Athletic Bilbao had been carried out in public, his sessions and drills on show. Analysing them was standard practice in other countries but in England, attitudes were different. Bielsa was treading a fine line between ultra-professionalism and cheating. He had stumbled into a clash of cultures.

One Thursday morning, 10 January 2019, Derbyshire Police received a phone call from a member of the public. The caller had spotted a man dressed in dark clothing hovering in the bushes opposite her house, next to the fence surrounding Derby County's training ground. Officers arrived at the scene and spoke with the man but saw no grounds for arresting him. There was no damage to the fence and no sign of an attempt to force entry to Derby's complex. But when the police ran a database check on the man's vehicle, they discovered that it was a pool car registered to Leeds United. The officers put two and two together. Derby were due to play Leeds at Elland Road the following night and it was no coincidence that a French intern with a club car was loitering near Derby's training ground. After he left the scene, Derbyshire Police used Twitter to publish a photo of the intern inside their van, accompanied by the hashtag '#Spyingischeating'. Case closed.

Derby were aware that something was afoot. A separate call had been made to their reception, alerting them to the intern's presence. The police later denied passing on details of his identity to the Championship club but Derby knew he had been sent by Leeds. They were furious and wanted answers. Why was he there? And was he there on Bielsa's instructions?[9] Had the training ground been compromised or was the intern merely peering through the fence? There was, as it turned out, some useful information to be gleaned from Derby's Thursday morning session. Harry Wilson, their on-loan Liverpool winger, was injured and absent, indicating that he would miss the game at Elland Road. To that end, the intern's trip offered an advantage. But when Leeds began to receive word of what had happened in Derby, they were caught by surprise and unclear about Bielsa's involvement. They planned to sit tight and say as little as possible until they had spoken to him and asked him to explain. Bielsa, though, saw no reason to be coy. The decision was his and he would answer for it. He told the club to get him Frank Lampard's number and he phoned Derby's manager directly.

Bielsa, with the help of his translator, Salim Lamrani, confirmed to Lampard that the intern was there on his behalf. The responsibility lay with Bielsa, not the intern. There was, however, no apology offered during that call or when Bielsa was pressed on the dispute in a live Sky Sports interview ahead of the match between Leeds and Derby. 'I don't feel I cheated,' Bielsa said. 'My goal was not to get an illegal advantage. I can explain my behaviour but my intention is not to be understood or to justify it. I have to respect the norms of the country where I work.' Bielsa had a point. In the EFL's rulebook, there was nothing governing the security or the sanctity of a club's training ground. A new regulation was subsequently introduced at the governing body's annual general meeting, banning scouts from going near a rival team's training complex in the seventy-two hours before a game. Leeds, as part of their settlement with the EFL, voted in favour of the rule. Technically, there was nothing forbidding his staff watching a training session from a vantage point on public land. But culturally, England was less inclined to tolerate it. The day after the

Championship clash with Derby, which Bielsa's players won 2-0 at a canter, Leeds published a statement on their website apologising for his actions and saying they would 'work with our head coach and his staff to remind them of the integrity and honesty which are the foundations Leeds United is built on'. Leeds chairman Andrea Radrizzani said sorry to Derby owner Mel Morris personally. Radrizzani was under the impression that the apology would placate Morris and limit any sanctions.

Spygate, naturally, led the media agenda. There was support for Bielsa in some quarters but Leeds resented much of what was being said and written. Lampard had spoken about Bielsa's intern crawling around with 'pliers and bolt-cutters' but all the police found in his car was a pair of secateurs for cutting through bushes. Leeds' players saw the controversy as something of a joke – Mateusz Klich marked the end of the win over Derby by pretending to gesture with a pair of binoculars and others in Bielsa's squad did likewise when the *Mirror* sent a photographer to take pictures of them training from woodland near Thorp Arch[10] – but Bielsa took the criticism seriously. His integrity was being picked apart and when Leeds lost at Stoke City the following weekend, a request for no questions about Spygate in the post-match press conference was ignored. Bielsa was asked whether the defeat was a result of him no longer being able to snoop on the opposition. He shook his head in bewilderment.

The negative coverage convinced him to go on the offensive. Five days after the victory over Derby, around 3 p.m., phone calls were made to local journalists by the media department at Leeds. Bielsa had called an impromptu briefing for 5 p.m. Be there and be on time. There was no hint about what he planned to say because virtually nobody at Elland Road had been told. Was he about to resign? Or was he in any way considering his future? It would not have been the first time he had left a managerial post overnight. The fact that the club's players had trained with him as normal in the morning was a reassuring sign (Leeds, at that stage, were five points clear at the top of the Championship). And the little Bielsa said to director of football Victor Orta made Orta confident that Bielsa was not about to quit in frustration. When we got to Thorp Arch, a small group of us huddled in reception waiting to be summoned upstairs. The meeting room where Bielsa planned to speak – the usual setting for his pre-match press conferences – was small and cramped, with most of his staff bunched together at the back of it. The air was heavy and tense. Bielsa had overhead projectors ready and two big screens to the left of his seat. He looked worn down and exasperated. Once we were settled, his opening gambit was to admit quite openly that his staff had 'observed the rivals we played against and watched all the training sessions of the opponents before we played against them'. It was an unambiguous admission, albeit from a man who did not think he had crossed a line in the first place.

What ensued was an extraordinary, sixty-six-minute presentation in which Bielsa ran through the finest details of the analysis done by Leeds on other teams. There were no questions from the floor and no breaks in the flow of it, except for the odd moment when one of Bielsa's staff was asked to explain something specific. On a couple of occasions, a journalist was given the chance to pick an individual game for Bielsa to focus on. And at the end of it, he thanked us for our patience and walked out. Bielsa paid particular attention to Derby because Derby were at the centre of Spygate. Everything about them was laid out in front of us: formations, substitutions, the signals used by Lampard's players at set-pieces, the different roles given to certain players and the minutes each one of them had played. For good measure and, perhaps, the benefit of others, Bielsa displayed a comprehensive profile of Harry Wilson, put together before his intern made the journey to Derby. He showed how his analysts had gone through all fifty-one of Derby's games from the 2017–18 season, the season before Bielsa took over as head coach at Leeds. It amounted to 200 hours of research, or four hours per game, and focused purely on the players who were still on Derby's books (County had a new manager in Lampard and therefore a different tactical set-up to that of his predecessor, Gary Rowett). 'It's not very useful,' Bielsa admitted. 'But the way to respect football is to make the effort to know the players and the teams. We try not to be ignorant about the competition we play in. I can't speak English but I can speak about the twenty-four teams of the Championship.' The insight went further still, to staggering lengths. A few days after the presentation, away at Stoke, Leeds would be meeting a side with a new manager, Nathan Jones. Jones, who was previously at Luton, had been in the job for only a week but in that short period Bielsa's staff had analysed the last twenty-six matches he handled before leaving Kenilworth Road. 'To play Stoke is hard because they have a new head coach who has had just [two] games,' Bielsa said. 'So what did we do? We analysed twenty-six games he had at Luton and the tactical structures. I would like to be seen with the maximum humility.'

The avalanche of data was designed to make a deliberate point. If Bielsa had this information – all of it sourced legitimately – then how much difference could spying on an opponent's training ground really make? Was there much left to learn? 'What I'm trying to explain is that I didn't have bad intentions and I didn't try to get an unfair sports advantage,' Bielsa insisted. 'I am not trying to gain an advantage because I already have all the information.' Which begged a question. What, then, was the purpose of those scouting trips, if not to find a marginal gain? 'Because it's not forbidden,'

Bielsa said. 'I didn't know it would create such a reaction and even though going and watching an opponent is not useful, it allows me to keep my anxiety low. Why do I do it? Because I'm stupid.' In other words, unable to say enough is enough. With files on various clubs stacked on shelves behind him, you heard that comment and imagined Revie saying the same.

The impact of the press conference was twofold. To those in the room, it offered access on a level that very few managers would be happy to give. But elsewhere in the Championship, Bielsa's presentation was taken as a dig; the implication being that his analysis was superior to that of other clubs (despite his efforts to avoid giving that impression). As an employee of a rival side said: 'If it hadn't been for that, other clubs might have let the spying thing go. But it pissed a lot of people off.' Deep down, Radrizzani agreed. 'The press conference of Marcelo was unnecessary,' he said. 'It was pointless to do it in public, in my opinion. He could have explained the same content to the federation and the league. Why to the public?'[11]

The EFL and the Football Association were facing calls to punish the Leeds manager, irrespective of the gaping hole in their regulations. Bielsa claimed he had called his press conference to 'make the investigation easier' and when he took the train down to Wembley to speak to FA officials in person, he made it clear that he would tell them everything. 'I will answer any question,' Bielsa said. In the absence of rules governing training grounds, Leeds were in a position to fight Bielsa's corner but when the EFL charged them with a breach of its 'good faith' charter, the club pleaded guilty. The saga had not reached a point where it was distracting their players but Leeds reasoned that it might if it dragged on too long. And by accepting a £200,000 fine, they would kill the threat of a more damaging penalty like a points deduction.

Radrizzani was ready to pick up the tab but Bielsa insisted on paying the £200,000 himself. 'It's a sanction the club received, not me,' Bielsa said, 'but I am responsible and that's why I paid.'[12] In brief moments, and away from the cameras, he was able to treat the dispute with levity. A local cartoonist, Graeme Bandeira of the *Yorkshire Post*, sent him a couple of drawings of Bielsa standing on his bucket and using binoculars to stare over a hedge. Bielsa autographed one and sent it back. The other he kept.[13]

None of Bielsa's players were aware of his scouting methods and very few of them cared. His coaching had transformed them as a team and as individuals, yielding the technical improvement Bielsa prided himself on. In assessing a footballer, he would look first to see if they had the core set of skills he wanted. If they did, he would back himself to enhance them. None of this would be done by massaging their egos. Bielsa rarely speaks to his players on a personal level or engages with them outside of training. Ex-Chelsea defender Frank Leboeuf, a critic of Bielsa's, once said crassly that his impression of the Argentinian was of a man who was 'a bit autistic' in the way he shunned social interaction.[14] Hayden Evans, a Leeds-based agent who managed former Leeds midfielders David Batty and Gary Speed, represents a number of the younger professionals at Elland Road, including midfielder Jamie Shackleton. 'Whether it's fantastic psychology on Bielsa's part or a genuine thing from him, I don't know,' Evans said. 'But when the players get five minutes of appreciation from him, they're buzzing. They'll phone you and say, "He said this or that to me." My perception is that he gives a player far more awareness of what needs to go into a game. He gives a complete awareness of what needs to happen.'[15]

In rare flashes the facade can crack, like it did when Patrick Bamford drove in a glorious volley in training one misty morning.

The striker was on his way back from a second knee ligament injury, trying to get himself going. As the ball dropped into the net, Bielsa ran forty yards with his arms in the air to give him a hug. 'It caught me by surprise,' Bamford said. 'Honestly, you never see him like that.' It was like the outpouring of emotion prompted by Leeds' promotion to the Premier League, when Bielsa joined his squad in one of the hospitality boxes at Elland Road and finally let his hair down. 'He turned from your coach into your favourite grandfather,' Bamford said.[16] And then, just as swiftly, the carefree smiles were gone.

At different junctures in Bielsa's two years in the Championship, there was clamouring for him to drop Bamford, not least in the face of sharp finishing from Eddie Nketiah in the early months of the 2019–20 season. Bielsa resisted the pressure, convinced that Bamford's attributes were essential in allowing Leeds to function properly as a team. Even if Bamford fell below his expected goals ratio – a stick used to beat him with regularly – Bielsa was not going to have his arm twisted by public opinion or make a big deal of supporting Bamford privately either. Bielsa's faith was implied by Bamford's inclusion in the starting line-up, rather than explicitly stated to him, but the selection policy spoke volumes. In Bielsa, Bamford found a manager who genuinely believed in him. Bamford had played in the Premier League before but with no real success. At Crystal Palace they knew so little about him that some of Alan Pardew's coaches were surprised when it transpired that Bamford was left-footed. At Burnley he banged heads with Sean Dyche who, in Bamford's view, classed him as arrogant and overly privileged; the schoolboy who was privately educated, played the violin and spoke several languages. It seemed that in Dyche's head, Bamford was too comfortable or aloof to make it as a Premier League footballer. Bielsa, in contrast, had no interest in

his background. If Bamford was a good fit tactically, his upbring-
ing was irrelevant. And by early 2021, with 11 Premier League
goals behind him, there were increasingly credible shouts for the
striker to be handed a first international call-up by England coach
Gareth Southgate.

It was better, Bielsa thought, to work with existing players than
fixate on the transfer market, unless expenditure was unavoidable.
Bamford was the marquee signing in Bielsa's first transfer window
and in order to fund a £7m deal with Middlesbrough, Leeds sold
midfielder Ronaldo Vieira to Sampdoria for the same fee. Vieira
was young and precocious, with a wonderful name given to him
by parents who loved Brazilian football (his brother, who also
played in the Leeds academy for a while, is called Romario) and
while Bielsa sanctioned the bid for Bamford, he wanted to keep
Vieira too. Radrizzani explained to him that they could only meet
Middlesbrough's asking price if they took Sampdoria's money.
Bielsa relented but told Radrizzani that Vieira would be worth
much more before long. 'To give me advice, Marcelo said "to take
£7m this year, you would take double next year for the way [Vieira]
will go,"' Radrizzani revealed.[17] In other words, leave Vieira with
Bielsa for twelve months and Leeds would have a bigger asset on
their hands. It was a promise rather than bravado, soon backed up
by the evolution of Bielsa's squad.

In the case of Kalvin Phillips, no player evolved more. The midfielder was a respected academy product, someone of good stock,
but prior to Bielsa's appointment he had struggled to find his niche.
He thought of himself as an all-action midfielder with attacking
capabilities but spent two or three years changing roles. Thomas
Christiansen tried to employ him as more of an attacking outlet,
with a licence to get beyond the last man. Other coaches saw him
as a generic number 6 (and Steve Evans hardly used him at all, to

the extent that Phillips had begun to think about leaving on loan). When Bielsa arrived and introduced himself to his squad, Phillips was surprised to be told that Bielsa saw him as a number 4, the defensive pivot in front of the centre-backs. Phillips was not familiar with that position or defensively trained to Bielsa's standards but Bielsa's perception of his strengths was astute. Phillips made the EFL's team of the year at the end of the 2018–19 season and was targeted by Aston Villa after Leeds failed to win promotion. At one stage in the summer of 2019, a transfer to Villa Park looked close. Leeds, who were being offered more than £20m, did not want to sell but were resigned to the fact that if Phillips wanted Premier League football there and then, they would have to give in to him. Bielsa made it clear that if Phillips were to stay, he had to commit unconditionally or not at all. It was pointless keeping the midfielder if he was in two minds. Orta took an alternative view. If Phillips were set on joining Villa, he could go. But if there were any doubts in his head, Orta would not sanction the sale. 'I was basically on the verge of leaving,' Phillips said. 'Us losing in the play-offs killed me a bit. It was hard to take. Victor said, "Listen, if you want to leave then just let me know. If you want to leave, tell me right now and I'll sell you." I said, "I don't know." So Victor said, "If you don't know then I'm not selling you."' The significance of that decision sunk in fully when promotion materialised twelve months later; deliverance for Phillips with the club he grew up supporting and signed for in his mid-teens. It was one in the eye for the headteacher who warned Phillips' mother that he would be making a mistake by leaving school and chasing a career in football.[18]

There were other major success stories, too. Klich, from the outside, appeared to be on the way out of Elland Road prior to Bielsa's appointment. He had signed for Leeds just a year earlier, a £1.5m purchase from FC Twente in Holland, but finished the 2017–18 season on loan with another Dutch club, FC Utrecht. Klich was ostracised by Christiansen who gave up on the Pole in a matter of months. Klich's perception was that Christiansen had taken against him after he lost his footing during a game at Cardiff City and gave away the first goal in a 3-1 defeat. In wet conditions, the midfielder had worn blades instead of studs – 'the wrong choice of boots', as Klich put it[19] – and from there on he and Christiansen barely spoke. Klich knew what it was like to be stuck on the fringes of a squad. At VfL Wolfsburg he had battled unsuccessfully for appearances under the eccentric Felix Magath. The biggest kick in the teeth came when Magath took him to a Bundesliga match at Borussia Dortmund, tempting Klich to think that he was about to break into the matchday squad. Magath left him out and told him later that a seat in the stands was Klich's reward for an improved performance in training. He was damning Klich with faint praise.[20]

Bielsa's appreciation of Klich's talent was a slow burn. In Bielsa's first pre-season, he split his players into three groups: the main group of professionals Bielsa rated, a second group who he was undecided about and a third group – 'The Bomb Squad', as they were nicknamed – who were surplus to requirements and finished. Klich found himself in group two, someone Bielsa initially considered training as a centre-back, but he climbed the ladder with the help of circumstances and his own persistence. When he left for Utrecht, Klich told Orta that he would come back to Leeds and compete again once his loan in Holland was over. He would find a way to make the transfer work. And then, a fortnight before the 2018–19 season started, Adam Forshaw broke a bone in his foot. A midfield position, the number 8 role, was vacant and with Vieira poised to sign for Sampdoria, Klich took it. It was apparent early on that Klich suited Bielsa's style. His recoveries and his interplay beyond halfway – short, sharp passes rather than long dribbles with the ball at his feet – helped to bring up goals and assists and win after win. He played in every league game in Bielsa's first season and all but one in Bielsa's second, a streak of 92 starts back-to-back; never injured, never reliant on rest and very rarely out of form. Bielsa went as far as saying in November 2020 that Klich was a player who could 'play in all the best teams in the world'. He was also the embodiment of a slogan painted on a wall in the gym Klich part-owned in his hometown of Tarnów in south-east Poland: 'People come in asking "where are all the machines?" I tell them: "We are the machines."'

In Cooper, Bielsa fashioned a ball-playing centre-back who broke preconceptions about him. Cooper, for a while, had been taunted with the nickname 'League One Liam', implying that he fell short of what was needed in the Championship, let alone the Premier League. Bielsa invested in him by keeping Cooper as captain and trying to improve his passing. Leeds' attacking verve and dominance of possession made a difference. 'When you've got people freeing themselves constantly, putting themselves in space and asking for the ball, it plays into my hands,' Cooper said. 'I think that's one reason why I struggled to find my form [before Bielsa arrived]. We were defending way too much.'[21] Even Pablo Hernández said Bielsa had found something new in him. The art of creating and scoring goals was inherent in Hernández but with Bielsa he had gained a better understanding of shape, discipline and how to press; of how to influence a game without having the ball. Many of the players at Elland Road could relate to the comments made by goalkeeper Steve Mandanda after Bielsa resigned as Marseille manager in 2015. 'He developed almost the entire squad,' Mandanda said.[22]

Robin Koch, Leeds' £13m signing from SC Freiburg, was a prime example of how far Bielsa's fixation with video analysis stretched. Leeds were first given permission by Freiburg to formally engage with Koch in May 2020, well in advance of promotion. Koch had one year left on his contract and Freiburg realised that the time had come to cash in. Bielsa asked his analysts to package up footage for the German to watch, showing him how Leeds played and explaining what a right-sided centre-back would be expected to do. Orta, for his part, knew Koch inside out. He had been monitoring him since reading positive mentions of Koch in dispatches from a game between Kaiserslautern and Hannover three-and-a-half years earlier but Bielsa insisted on the files being sent to Koch regardless. Koch admitted he had 'never really seen anything like it.'[23] The information was so detailed that it was as if Leeds and Bielsa were treating him as their own player, despite two caveats. The Championship season was still in lockdown and Leeds were not yet promoted. The club also had Ben White on loan from Brighton in their squad. Orta was frank with Koch: if Leeds failed to reach the Premier League, they would not be able to afford him (and Koch, a Germany international, might not want to leave the Bundesliga). And if Orta managed to talk Brighton into a permanent deal for White, Leeds were unlikely to have the budget to sign Koch as well. Koch dived into the clips and watched them anyway. He was being analysed in a way he had not experienced before and the presentation captivated him. It might be that the transfer disappeared into the ether. But when it came to Bielsa, he was transfixed.

11.

FEBRUARY

Leeds United's new pitch, all £300,000 of it, gets its first proper test against Everton on 3 February, a shivering Wednesday night. The grass at Elland Road looks relatively plush – Garden of Eden-like compared to the turf the ground staff have removed – but the coldest snap of the winter is the worst time to be replacing it. The surface is smoother and Marcelo Bielsa can see that the ball is moving more cleanly but for the players it is slippery and treacherous. Throughout Everton's 2-1 win, both teams struggle to stay on their feet and move around gingerly, conscious of how icy the pitch feels. As the difficulties persist over several weeks, the squad at Leeds switch from moulded blades to the longest studs they can find for their boots, trying to overcome a problem which is baffling the club and the company who supplied the surface. Much as renewing it mid-season is a necessary evil, it was not supposed to play like this.

Everton seize control of the game quickly, scoring after seven minutes as Bielsa's defence fail to track a run by Gylfi Sigurdsson and leave him to tap in from six yards. Dominic Calvert-Lewin scores a second before half-time when he arrives at the back post to finish off a corner. Luke Ayling takes the blame for allowing Calvert-Lewin to head in unmarked. 'For the second goal, it's my man and I got caught napping,' he says.[1] But there is quality in Leeds' performance and when Raphinha replies early in the second half, finding the bottom corner after a cross ricochets to him, Everton lose their composure. Raphinha flourishes again, swapping wings and running himself to a standstill. Robin Olsen, Everton's goalkeeper, keeps Carlo Ancelotti's side in front with repeated saves and Leeds are unable to force a draw, even after throwing on Pablo Hernández from the bench. Bielsa thinks the performance of his side was more threatening than Everton's but he admits that with both concessions, 'we could maybe have been more intuitive' and prevented them. As for the pitch, any concern about it is kept to himself. 'We were very happy to be able to count on a pitch which is much better than the last few games,' he says. 'It's impossible for me to make any reference for why the players were slipping.' The ground staff and Leeds' well-respected head groundsman, Kiel Barrett, feel just as perplexed.

Hernández is still part of Bielsa's squad despite doubts about his future bubbling up in the last few days of the January transfer window. There is interest in him from Castellón, the Spanish second division club he part-owns, and encouraged by Hernández's lack of minutes at Leeds, Castellón's board start making enquiries. They could do with a shot in the arm and the injection of Hernández's imagination would be good for them. After two promotions in three years, they are deep in a battle against relegation. Leeds do not want to lose Hernández and they avoid discussions before the deadline but Castellón are under the impression that the midfielder is keen to join them. It is an un-usual situation in which Hernández, as one of Castellón's group of shareholders, would almost be negotiating with himself. His wage at Leeds is far beyond what Castellón can afford to pay him, and he has eighteen months left on his contract. But he does have ways of making a transfer happen and a move would take him back to the area he knows best, out in the hills near the village of Borriol

The city of Leeds marks promotion by naming a street after Bielsa.

Bielsa with his players as Leeds lift the Championship title.

A packed Elland Road on the night that Leeds are crowned champions.

Fans gather to celebrate in the centre of Leeds.

Opposite page top A mural of Bielsa which springs up in Wortley after Leeds seal promotion. 'Marching on Together', 2020. Nicolas Dixon.

Opposite page right A second mural of Bielsa on a building in Hyde Park, Leeds. Tankpetrol.

Bielsa on socially distanced media duties.

Back in the big time. Bielsa and Klopp at Anfield on the
opening weekend of the Premier League season.

Casting a keen eye over Leeds under-23s

At home to Fulham with Scott Parker far right. Empty stadiums due to Covid-19.

Patrick Bamford completes a hat-trick at Aston Villa. The first Leeds player to score a Premier League hat-trick since Mark Viduka in 2003.

Bielsa arriving at Crystal Palace. Leeds will suffer a heavy 4-1 defeat.

Above Raphinha finds the top corner in Leeds' biggest win of the season, 5-0 at West Bromwich Albion.

Right A beaming Bielsa after Leeds' incredible win at Manchester City, April 2021.

Leeds spell out their opposition to the European Super League warming
up in 'Earn It' T-Shirts before their game against Liverpool.

An affectionate hug between Bielsa and Hernández as the Spaniard leaves
the field before the end of the 3-1 win over West Brom – his final game
for the club. Farewell Pablo.

and close to the Club de Campo del Mediterráneo golf course run by his wife, Mar, and her family. Mar and their two sons, Eric and Luca, have returned to Spain due to the Covid-19 pandemic and Hernández is alone in England but Leeds think he is worth keeping for the time being, irrespective of the fact that all signs point to a parting of ways in the summer. His elder boy, Eric, was taken on by Leeds' academy but there has long been an expectation that Hernández would go back to Spain eventually. To compound an unproductive season, he suffers another minor muscle injury after the defeat to Everton.

Leeds recover from that result quickly with a 2-0 win over Crystal Palace, a contest which looks over from the moment Jack Harrison scores in the third minute. Harrison is into a third year on loan from Manchester City and is lined up to join Leeds permanently for £11m when the Premier League season ends. The transfer would have happened in the summer of 2020 had Covid-19 not seen Leeds' original option to buy him expire. As a consequence of the delay and Harrison's form, they will pay more than the £8m first agreed. He has been steadily improving on Bielsa's watch and become one of the players on whom the Leeds head coach is most inclined to depend, already beyond 100 appearances. A fit and persistent runner, Harrison's career path was unusual in that he bailed out of Manchester United's academy as a schoolboy, choosing to head to the USA and study at college there instead. By way of the Major League Soccer draft and a transfer to New York City – one of numerous clubs in the City Football Group (CFG) controlled by Manchester City's owners – he found his way to Eastlands and then on to Elland Road, one of Bielsa's first signings. Patrick Vieira coached him in New York and was always convinced that Harrison would play in the Premier League. David Villa, the former Spain international, played alongside him there and thought the winger was 'certain' to reach the top level. Having got there with Leeds, he is acclimatising so well that by the end of this month England coach Gareth Southgate will be thinking about calling him up. When Harrison chose to quit Manchester United as a boy, a coach there warned him that he was doing what youngsters never do – in other words, that he was making a mistake – but his mother Debbie would look at pictures of kids she had never heard of on the walls at Manchester United's Carrington training ground and wonder what happened to them. 'She began thinking about a more secure pathway for me,' Harrison said in 2019. 'There are so many who go through the system but ultimately [at Manchester United] it was going to be one or two who made it out of each age group, if that.'[2]

He scores against Palace with a deflection which flicks off Gary Cahill and over goalkeeper Vicente Guaita. It is that sort of night for Palace coach Roy Hodgson. Cahill is tormented by Leeds and embarrassed late in the first half when a turn and flick from Raphinha leaves him for dead on the edge of his own box. When a frustrated Jordan Ayew is substituted in the 76th minute, someone near the touchline hears him telling Kalvin Phillips that he can 'stop kicking me now'. Palace are 2-0 down with no way back after Patrick Bamford claims his 100th career goal. They are bullied by Leeds who out-pass them by 714 to 332 and dominate possession from the start. With 32 points on the board, it feels as if Bielsa's squad are all but safe from relegation with more than three months of fixtures to go. If they maintain their average of 1.45 points per game, they will clear 50 by the end of the season, something only ten other newly-promoted clubs have done since the Premier League became a twenty-team division in 1995, but Bielsa refuses to be presumptuous. 'It's better to only make comments on things like this when it's impossible to go down,' he says.

Bielsa is prone to excessive caution at the best of times. Even when Leeds stood on the very brink of promotion, victorious against Barnsley in July 2020 and in a position where only goal difference could deny them, he could not be persuaded to jump the gun, saying simply that it was 'not convenient' to get ahead of himself. It made no difference that some of his players were almost in tears on the pitch.

Phillips plays on until the 88th minute against Palace but is carrying a calf injury and Bielsa is about to lose him for a month. The tear to the muscle is not serious but it will worsen if Bielsa pushes him and Leeds' position in the table – 10th as it stands – means there is no sense in risking Phillips. But it brings Bielsa back to a well-worn topic of conversation: if not Phillips in defensive midfield then who? Internally, Leeds are starting to debate this themselves. Bielsa has been juggling the Phillips conundrum for almost three years, aware that none of the players at Leeds is a perfect match for the 25-year-old but insistent that enough of them can fill in effectively. It seems more and more that specialist cover would be preferable and Victor Orta has been concocting a list of potential targets for the summer window, a list of midfielders who do what Phillips does. If Leeds stay up, the club are thinking of making as many as five new signings. There are also decisions to be made about existing squad members like Hernández, Tyler Roberts, Helder Costa and Gaetano Berardi.

February sees the return of Berardi from the ruptured anterior cruciate ligament (ACL) he suffered against Derby County in the 2019–20 season. The former Sampdoria defender sustained the injury twenty-four hours after Leeds were confirmed as champions and no more than a week before his contract at Elland Road was due to expire. He had agreed to extend that deal after Covid-19 delayed the fixture list, taking a gamble by playing on without the promise of a contract at Elland Road or anywhere else. Some out-of-contract players at other clubs refused to do the same, considering the potential cost of injury to be too high, and Berardi's reward was to finish the campaign on crutches. As Bielsa's side departed on holiday with Championship medals in their pockets, Leeds were sending Berardi to Barcelona for knee surgery. Three months later they handed him a new twelve-month deal to tide him over and look after him financially while he followed his rehabilitation programme. Berardi was reluctant to take the contract at first. It worried him that people might think he was drawing a wage in return for nothing; accepting a salary despite the fact that he had no chance of playing until the start of spring at the earliest. His recovery has gone to plan, however, and as January ends, Leeds start easing him back into training and Under-23s matches. As a personality, Berardi is a contradiction: incredibly quiet off the pitch but a hand grenade on it, with more red cards on his record than any other player in Leeds' hundred-year history. He became something of a cult hero and earned the lasting respect of the club's support by refusing to be part of the 'Sicknote Six' debacle at Charlton Athletic in 2015. Bielsa rates Berardi, as a centre-back and a character. He regards the Swiss as a tidy passer of the ball and very easy to coach – compliant and professional. But in four months' time, Berardi's deal will be up again and he will be almost 33. His partner Erika has recently given birth to their first child, Gabriel. Prior to his injury, Berardi had told friends of his that he expected to leave Leeds for Italy that summer. His departure might come around this summer instead.

For Leeds' next game away at Arsenal, Bielsa goes with his usual ploy of replacing Phillips with Pascal Struijk in midfield. Struijk is having a very good season and is the subject of a fight for his services internationally between The Netherlands and Belgium.

He was born in Dearne on the outskirts of Antwerp but his family moved to The Hague when he was young. Appearances for The Netherlands' Under-17s seemed to confirm stronger Dutch allegiances but contact from the Belgium camp has encouraged him to apply for a Belgian passport (in the next few weeks, he will turn down a call-up to the Dutch Under-21 squad in an effort to keep his options open). He scores at Arsenal, a towering header in the 58th minute, but the game at the Emirates is chaotic from Leeds' perspective. Pierre-Emerick Aubameyang completes a hat-trick for Arsenal in 47 minutes, including a penalty scored after Illan Meslier loses control of the ball and slides through the back of Bukayo Saka. Héctor Bellerín's finish helps Arsenal establish a 4-0 lead. Bielsa makes two substitutions at half-time and Leeds peg Arsenal back to 4-2, aided by Struijk's goal, but recovering from such a big deficit is not something Bielsa can expect his team to do. Mateusz Klich completes 45 minutes but is carrying a hip injury and has been off-colour for a few weeks, his form drying up after so much football over two-and-a-half years. 'It was an act of generosity on his part,' Bielsa says. 'I value a lot the fact that he sacrificed himself for this game.'

If the loss at Arsenal is unflattering, a 1-0 defeat at Wolverhampton Wanderers six days later is unlucky by comparison. Leeds miss several big chances, the best of them falling to Liam Cooper, and Patrick Bamford sees a finish narrowly ruled out for offside. Wolves score the only goal when Adama Traore strikes the crossbar and the ball hits Meslier in the back, rebounding off him and into the net. 'There were very few periods where we weren't dominant,' Bielsa says but he gives Nuno Espírito Santo, the Wolves manager, a warm handshake at full-time. Nuno, after a few excellent seasons at Molineux, is not enjoying this Premier League term. He is in a different country to most of his family and unable to travel abroad to see them. The absence of crowds is grating on him and at Molineux they say he and his team have lost their spark.[3]

Bielsa sympathises. He is thousands of miles away from his wife Laura and his two daughters, Inés and Mercedes. The family are accustomed to Bielsa disappearing to Europe when clubs come calling but they are extremely close nonetheless. Laura was a friend of Bielsa's sister, María Eugenia. They studied architecture together and she and Bielsa met through that friendship. Bielsa joked when he took over at Lille in 2017 that Laura had told him, before his first press conference, to smile and look into the eyes of whoever was asking him a question.[4] It was not his usual pose and she wanted him to engage. Inés became a psychologist and a talented hockey player. Newspaper articles in Argentina talk of Mercedes studying to become a playwright and film director. There is plenty waiting for Bielsa in his home country but the irony of the coronavirus impact is that he has rarely seemed happier in his own skin, at Leeds or anywhere else in his recent coaching career; so much so that Leeds would like him to stay on for another season. If they could get a contract in front of Bielsa, they would ask him to sign up for a fourth year and avoid more back-and-forth negotiations during the close season. Understandably, they want to negate the possibility of Bielsa creating a sudden void by choosing to leave. Bielsa, though, is unwilling to engage here and now. He wants to wait until the season is finished and in his view, Leeds should delay too.

Over the weekend that follows the trip to Wolves, Andrea Radrizzani gives an interview to CBS Sports in America. He is asked about Bielsa's future and confirms that Leeds intend to retain him again. 'Marcelo knows we are happy with him,' Radrizzani says. 'The players still follow him unconditionally and that's the most important element for me. It's up to him. We wait on his decision. But in any case, myself and Victor [Orta] have already analysed the options and what to do, in case Marcelo does not want to be with us.'[5] Bielsa picks up on Radrizzani's remarks in the translation of articles done for him by his staff and his secretary, Sara. He is ready for the questions when they come up at his next press conference. Is he willing to stay on? Would he be happy to sign up now? Does he understand why Leeds might be worried about another uncertain summer? 'I need to give you a complete response,' he replies and so he does, speaking for several minutes. 'There is nothing better than what Leeds represents as a job. I didn't take Leeds to the Premier League. I manage in the Premier League thanks to Leeds. I would not consider any alternatives until my job at Leeds is done and I would like to make it clear that Leeds as a project surpasses me as a coach. But there are still a dozen games to play and those games will offer conclusions which help to make decisions.' He says he respects Leeds' right to look at alternatives and discuss contingencies. He says he will give Leeds a quick answer if they insist on one. 'It could be interpreted as the club having more of a desire for me to stay than I do, and that's not the case,' he says. 'If the club need an answer before the end of the season I will respond before the end of the season. But I will take the time to tell them that they should consider what happens in the last part of the season.'

A home game against Southampton the next day underlines Bielsa's value to the hierarchy at Elland Road. Southampton have the better of the first half but fall apart once Leeds get on top of them in the second. Raphinha is impossible to deal with, hammering down the left and ripping Southampton to shreds. Southampton's manager, Ralph Hasenhüttl, complains about the pitch afterwards – 'I know they [Leeds] train on it three times a week and you could see they are more used to it' – but goals from Bamford, Stuart Dallas and Raphinha make sure of a comprehensive 3-0 win. Bielsa's players have not been using the pitch three times a week. They have staged a couple of sessions there but as one member of staff at Elland Road says, the grass is enough of a problem without training cutting it up regularly.

February has been more like the Championship than the Premier League, with six games in twenty-four days. The last of them is at home to Aston Villa, who have learned a lesson from their 3-0 defeat to Leeds at Villa Park in October. On that evening Villa attempted to fight fire with fire, opening themselves up and attacking aggressively. This time Dean Smith organises his team to hold up play and contain, with a deep line and a tight defence. He says afterwards that the pitch encouraged him to be more cautious and his tactics are aided by Villa striking in the fifth minute. Ollie Watkins slips as he shoots from the edge of the box and Anwar El-Ghazi reacts first to the striker's misplaced shot, tucking the loose ball under Meslier. Leeds have a lot of the match and plenty of the ball but no sharp edge to cut Villa with. They lose 1-0. 'We lacked imagination and precision with the final pass,' Bielsa says. Bamford is peripheral throughout, rarely on the ball and on the end of very few chances. There is no opportunity for him to impress Southgate, who is in the stands to watch him again.

Bielsa endures these days relatively infrequently; days when the football is nothing to write home about. They are few and far between and in the boardroom, he has given them what they wanted in September: a virtual guarantee of a second Premier League season, before the winter is out. They would be happy to see him go further by signing a new deal too but Bielsa will move at his own pace on the contractual front, with no hint to anyone of what he intends to do: not Radrizzani, not Orta and not the players. Even the staff around him, the men most loyal to him and the men who have been with him for years, cannot be sure if season three will lead to season four.

12.

RIGHT-HAND MEN

The interns and would-be assistants who court Marcelo Bielsa have come to be known as the *chiquillos*, or 'the kids'. They are young and they approach him from far and wide, trying to engage him and open a door into his world. Bielsa is constantly in receipt of job applications which take the form of research papers, analytical projects and coaching ideas. He studies them and responds to some of them, picking out the best and the most intuitive. Most managers have an established backroom team – a trusted group of staff which changes infrequently – and to a point Bielsa is the same but the *chiquillos* try their luck because of his history of indulging the unknown, the unproven and the uninitiated. Much is made of his influence on some of football's elite coaches but more can be said of his willingness to nurture men with meagre profiles and smaller ambitions.

In 2019 I made contact with Felipe Cañete, a Chilean born in the city of Curicó. Cañete's name was unfamiliar in England and even in the story of Bielsa's reign as Chile's national coach, it appears only sporadically, but his brush with Bielsa told a story about the way in which Leeds United's head coach recruited the people around him. When Cañete was 16, Bielsa paid a visit to Curicó. Chile had fallen in love with Bielsa's football and he was treated like royalty as he travelled around the country. Cañete was entranced by him and wanted to work for him. As unrealistic as that was for a 16-year-old boy, he wrote to Bielsa and spelt out his interest in Bielsa's coaching. Before long, a reply came through the post. 'I'll set you a project,' Bielsa said. 'Watch 150 games from start to finish and write back to me with all of your observations.' That way Bielsa could see if Cañete had an eye for tactics and an analyst's brain. Perception was more relevant than the boy's age.[1]

Infrastructure in Chile was in a state of disrepair. The earthquake of 2010 had done substantial damage to the country and Cañete's only tools were a pen, paper and a television. He had no analytical software and no laptop to work with but a few months later he completed the task and mailed a pile of documents to Bielsa. Bielsa read them carefully. The insight was intelligent and Cañete's work ethic was evident. Bielsa invited him to join Chile's staff and the proactive effort to get a foot in the door paid off. Cañete had just turned 17 and was already employed in international football. 'It's what I had to do,' he said, as if the task drawn up for him by Bielsa was standard practice. 'I had to do it to get to work with him.'

Others have taken the same approach. Towards the end of Bielsa's second year in charge of Leeds, a British coach – out of work after leaving his post at a Scottish club – compiled a file running to almost one thousand pages which looked in detail at Leeds' defensive structure. It did not lead to an offer of employment but it made the point that anyone trying to communicate with Bielsa on a professional level had to tap into the intricacy of his thinking. Bielsa disliked the trend of people, and journalists not least, reaching conclusions on the basis of results. His spiky reaction to Leeds' heavy defeat to Manchester United was an objection to what he saw as simplistic criticism and a lack of nuance. 'Some media platforms and journalists can only analyse results,' he said after that game. 'The capacity to analyse beyond results offers some way of interpreting what happened on the pitch.' It was the same when Leeds hit a run of five defeats from seven games in the second half of the Premier League season. Was Bielsa worried? 'It's a question without any content,' he replied. 'You have to analyse the five defeats. If you ask me a question based on those performances, I can answer. But if you just say that from seven games we lost five, the response is of course I am worried. And then "next question".'

Most of the relationships between Bielsa and his staff go back a long way. None of his assistants have been with him for longer than Pablo Quiroga, one of the coaches who dropped everything and flew in from Argentina when Bielsa took the job at Elland Road in 2018 (he had also been present at the very first meeting involving Bielsa, Andrea Radrizzani and Victor Orta). Quiroga is an Argentinian who was born in 1981 and grew up in Colón to the north of Buenos Aires. He played football for a local team, Atlético El Fortín and, after qualifying as a PE teacher, coached at El Fortín in his spare time. There was no money involved and no prestige. El Fortín are an amateur side and people there recount how Quiroga would get in touch with them and offer to help out whenever he and Bielsa were between jobs (Quiroga's son, Augusto, also turned out for El Fortín, extending the family connection). He was bright and had talent as a tactician but until Bielsa became aware of him, few around Quiroga expected him to carve out a career as a high-level coach. It was only as a result of a chance conversation that Quiroga became the most recognisable face in Bielsa's inner circle, following him from Chile to Athletic Bilbao, Marseille, Lille and Leeds. Bielsa tends to dominate his dug-out during matches, crouched on his haunches or yelling orders in basic English as he paces back and forward, but Quiroga is the most vocal of his assistants, often positioned on one corner of the technical area with his hands clasped behind his back.

The EFL introduced yellow and red cards for coaching staff ahead of Bielsa's first season in England and Leeds were as susceptible to them as any other club in the Championship: some issued for dissent, some issued after they exceeded the permitted number of staff allowed in a technical area at any one time. The frenetic activity around Bielsa divided opinion among his peers. Neil Harris was angered by it after Leeds scored a late equaliser in a 1-1 draw against Harris's Millwall in September 2018. 'Their reaction to the goal is completely over the top and a disgrace in English football,' Harris said.[2] Bielsa refused to take the bait, saying: 'I get involved in disputes only when I think exchanging arguments will increase the understanding of the public.' But other managers liked Bielsa's intensity and aura, and they enjoyed competing with him. Paul Warne, Rotherham United's manager, would laugh to himself at the sight of Bielsa sitting on a stool at the start of a match. The bucket-shaped seat was unusual and a source of intrigue early on. It gave him a vantage point similar to that taken by André Villas-Boas in the days when Villas-Boas coached Chelsea and liked to watch games from a crouching position. But Bielsa was baffled by questions about it. 'You want me to tell you more than what it is?' he would ask. 'I have nothing to add. It's just a bucket, a comfortable bucket. I wish I could attract attention another way.' Warne, though, thought Bielsa on his stool transmitted confidence and control. 'He's the calmest person in the stadium,' Warne said. 'By Saturday his work's done. It's like going on *The X-Factor* and being backstage next to Elvis Presley with his collar turned up. You're wearing jeans and a white T-shirt and psychologically you fear the worst. That sounds awful but it's also the reality.'[3]

Quiroga was first mentioned to Bielsa in 2007 by Horacio Garcia, a long-time friend who had worked with Bielsa at Vélez Sarsfield during the 1997–98 Argentine season (a year in which

Vélez won the Clausura title). Garcia knew Quiroga and had good things to say about his coaching at El Fortín. Bielsa arranged to meet Quiroga and warmed to his personality and outlook on football. He challenged him to go back through the 2006 World Cup and analyse the attacking and defensive strategies of the teams involved in the tournament. The information was relevant to Bielsa because he had recently been appointed as Chile's head coach and was about to embark on a complete overhaul of the national side's system and tactics. Quiroga was as diligent as Cañete. There was no knowing if Bielsa's offer of work was genuine or if the analysis would be sharp enough to merit a job. The research could amount to many wasted hours and a letter of rejection. But Quiroga pored over replays, picked them apart and earned Bielsa's confidence. Little by little the pair became closer. Quiroga was promoted up the ladder at Chile after Bielsa's assistant, the former Boca Juniors player Alfredo Berti, resigned. He was named as Chile's number two when Eduardo Berizzo – a defender for Newell's Old Boys while Bielsa was manager there – moved on to pursue his own career as a manager in 2010. For more than a decade Quiroga has been at Bielsa's side or at the end of a phone, waiting for Bielsa's next appointment to materialise. Those close to him say he turned down jobs which were independent of Bielsa and has long been unconditionally committed, despite the fact that some of their adventures in Europe were short. Bielsa's two-day reign at Lazio was so bizarre and so brief – breaking down after an argument over proposed transfers – that neither he nor his staff actually made it as far as Italy before he resigned. Appointed at the start of June 2016, Bielsa was scheduled to officially begin work on 9 July but complained that Lazio had made no progress with the players he wanted them to sign and quit forty-eight hours later. Quiroga was ready to travel because Quiroga was always ready to travel but it would be twelve months before Bielsa secured another post with Lille in France.

There is no evidence that Quiroga has ever attempted to branch out into full management himself, or any indication that he is tempted to. Very few of the elite managers who credit Bielsa with inspiring them actually coached under him themselves. Most, like Diego Simeone, Mauricio Pochettino and Gerardo Martino, played for Bielsa at stages of their career before pursuing their own paths. In the case of Pep Guardiola, he and Bielsa had never even met before 2006 when Guardiola travelled to meet Bielsa in Rosario and ask for advice about starting out as a manager. Berizzo was a rare example of someone who had cut his teeth as a coach alongside Bielsa. Claudio Vivas – just 22 when he served as assistant at Newell's Old Boys – was another who became a manager in his own right after repeated stints as Bielsa's number two (in 2019, Vivas took over at Bolívar in Bolivia's Primera División). But in general, those who were closest to him seemed reluctant to step out of his shadow. Quiroga would be at Elland Road for the duration of Bielsa's tenure but not a day more. Diego Reyes, one of Leeds' other assistants, was equally devoted and had been on the scene since Bielsa's time in Chile. A third member of the staff, Diego Flores, left Leeds at the end of Bielsa's second season, within weeks of the club winning promotion, but merely for a rest and to go travelling with his partner. Life with Bielsa was all-consuming. There was rarely any time off and the disruption caused by Covid-19 meant the 2019–20 and 2020–21 seasons were separated by less than two months. In the close-season in 2019, Flores travelled through South America with Bielsa, assisting him as Bielsa attended seminars and carried out tactical research. Bielsa did not want to lose him but in the aftermath of promotion, Flores's mind was made up.

Flores's path explained again how interns came to Bielsa by way of obscure routes. A pleasant and likeable character, Flores is Argentinian like Quiroga and played professionally as a centre-back at a lower level, including a stint for Sportivo Belgrano. People who played with him described him as 'a coach on the pitch' on account of his ability to read a game.[4] He wanted to advance his technical knowledge so having earned a degree in PE in Cordoba, he gained a qualification with Argentina's coaching school, the *Asociación de Técnicos del Fútbol Argentino*. Then, in his twenties, he decided to move from South America to Ireland to improve his English and give himself the chance of earning a UEFA Pro licence. In Dublin he linked up with a local team, Kingswood Castle, in what was a random encounter. One of Kingswood's coaches, Brian Coleman, was running a training session with a junior squad when he noticed Flores doing fitness exercises on the grass nearby. When he was finished with his routine, Flores sat down to watch the kids train. He and Coleman got talking and Coleman discovered that by coincidence, Flores was renting a room in a house owned by the mother of one of his friends. He invited Flores to play for Kingswood's senior team and Flores suggested that he might help coach the juniors too. Coleman's impression of Flores was that he 'had it all upstairs'. Flores was full of ideas and would travel to England at weekends for conferences and other football events. In 2013, he left Dublin permanently to seek full-time employment in football and carried out a small amount of work for Southampton, where Pochettino was manager (there is a picture on Flores's Twitter account of him and Pochettino standing side-by-side at St Mary's Stadium in early 2014). It was not long after that Flores became one of the *chiquillos*. Sources close to Bielsa say Flores was recommended to him by Reyes, who had become acquainted with him and was already with Bielsa at Marseille. Like others before him, Flores's aptitude was tested but he passed the examination and joined Marseille's staff. It was always the same routine with Bielsa; a case of asking prospective employees to sink or swim. As an associate of his put it: 'If the *chiquillo* can stay submerged in oil for an hour without breathing, he has the possibility to remain on Marcelo's staff.'[5]

Flores was predominantly an analyst and a more reserved member of the camp at Leeds. He kept a low profile and while Bielsa and Quiroga would patrol the touchline during matches, Flores was more often seen sitting behind them with a laptop. But he came to prominence in 2019 when Bielsa enlisted him as his translator at his press conferences. Throughout the previous twelve months, Bielsa's comments to the media had been translated to English by Salim Lamrani, a French academic and a Marseille supporter who had taken an interest in Bielsa during the latter's reign at Marseille. They subsequently met in person and Lamrani, who spoke English, French and Spanish, offered Bielsa his services. Lamrani went with him to Lille, where media briefings quickly became tense and heated as Lille struggled to find any form. At Leeds, Lamrani was officially employed as the club's discipline coach, joining in the summer when Bielsa was appointed, but translation was a major part of his brief. Not everyone at the club liked him. Certain players found Lamrani abrasive and thought his proximity to the squad was unhelpful. At the end of the 2018–19 season, Leeds and Bielsa agreed that Lamrani would move on. Sources at Elland Road said the decision was instigated by Bielsa, though one close to Lamrani insisted the club's head coach had sent him off 'with great memories and a hug'. Bielsa was subsequently displeased by Lamrani publishing a book about him after their parting of ways.

Translation duties then passed to Flores until his own departure a year later. Flores did not crave the responsibility – nobody did, because conveying the nuance in Bielsa's comments could be difficult – but Bielsa refused to employ a specialist translator and declined offers from Leeds to find him one.

*

One of Bielsa's expectations was that his staff would be as obsessive as him. Jan Van Winckel, who was with him at Marseille, told *L'Équipe* how in sixteen months together 'we took four or five days off'.[6] Bielsa is not prone to relaxing and drinks very little alcohol (he was once seen at Leeds' team hotel splitting a pint of lager into two glasses, his way of avoiding drinking the whole thing).

If two years at Leeds took their toll on Flores, Diego Reyes was impervious to fatigue. The Chilean had a reputation for slogging without a break. Players at Marseille would joke that they had never seen him without a laptop or a tablet and he was renowned for spending hours at the training ground, an 'ultra-student' as one local journalist said. Reyes, in keeping with the wider narrative, had chanced his arm by making an approach out of the blue while Bielsa was coaching the Chilean national side. Reyes was similar to both Quiroga and Flores: a PE teacher and a footballing fanatic who had picked up a coaching badge in Santiago. The story went that he turned up one day at Chile's training centre, the Juan Pinto Durán complex, and asked to get involved. Like Quiroga and Flores, he was rapidly able to persuade Bielsa that he thought like a coach and had an appetite for data. Cañete quickly made friends with Reyes and saw him as 'a genius in all of his dedicated areas, 100 per cent committed to Marcelo'. Bielsa trusted Reyes to the extent that before he took over at Marseille, it was Reyes who flew to France to compile an assessment of the club and their squad. On match days at Leeds, Reyes tends to hover behind Quiroga but is in and out of the technical area all the same. Little is known about Bielsa's assistants because none of them ever speaks publicly or grants requests for interviews. NDAs in their contracts maintain a strict silence and there is no record of extensive comments from any of them.

Only two members of Bielsa's initial backroom team at Elland Road were inherited by him: Under-23s coach Carlos Corberán and goalkeeping coach Marcos Abad. Both had joined Leeds a year earlier as part of a clearing-of-the-decks initiated after Radrizzani's takeover of the club. Abad was UEFA Pro qualified and despite never playing as a professional keeper, he had been set on a career as a coach from the moment he enrolled for a masters degree in PE at the University of Alicante in 2005. He found a way into football with Alcoyano in Spain's second division and spent time at Elche while Victor Orta was head of the recruitment team there. Abad followed Orta to Middlesbrough and then to Leeds, replacing Darryl Flahavan who quit the goalkeeping coach's role at Elland Road after Garry Monk's resignation as manager in 2017. Bielsa had strict instructions for which coaches should join him in England but he was happy to leave Abad in place. While Quiroga, Reyes and Flores were accustomed to Bielsa's manner, Abad's eyes were quickly opened by it. 'There are no limits for him in the pursuit of excellence,' Abad said in an article in the Spanish press. 'You realise you have someone brilliant in front of you. There are these geniuses who, although sometimes called crazy, dedicate all the time in their lives to becoming better and better at what they do. Not everyone is up for that.'[7]

Corberán was up for it too but when Bielsa descended on Leeds, the challenge for him was to make his face fit. Ideally, Leeds wanted to provide Bielsa with another senior coach to blend with Quiroga, Reyes and Flores. In the initial round of negotiations over his contract there were discussions about whether it might help Bielsa, at least for a while, to involve someone with a certain amount of knowledge of the English game. There had been contact between Leeds and the representatives of Alan Smith, the club's former striker who was player-coach at Notts County until his retirement in 2018. Leeds admired another of their ex-players, Lee Bowyer, who was cutting his teeth in management as caretaker at Charlton Athletic. But when Radrizzani and Orta arranged to travel to Argentina for their first conversation with Bielsa (who was accompanied to the meeting by Quiroga, Reyes and Flores), they decided to invite Corberán too. Orta's idea was that Corberán would step up from the Under-23s and assist the first team. Bielsa knew nothing of him but was happy to go with the suggestion. The Spaniard, in some respects, was built in the Bielsa mould: an ex-goalkeeper with the talent to make Valencia's academy as a youngster but not enough to build a long playing career. In his early twenties, Corberán got his head around the fact that he 'wasn't going to make it at any of those places you dream about when you are a kid'.[8] 'I was 23 when I began to feel that my future would be in coaching,' he told me in 2019 and his subsequent dive into it took him across the world, from Villarreal where he spent three years as assistant manager, to Saudia Arabia and Cyprus.[9] Some of his jobs were off the radar – played out in the backwaters of world football – but his spell at Villarreal coincided with Guardiola's appointment at Barcelona and the new era of tactics ushered in by Guardiola's genius. Corberán was as much of an admirer of Guardiola's ideals as anyone else. He talked of the Barcelona coach 'starting a revolution' as teams in Spain tried to digest and mimic Barça's tactics.

Leeds first offered him the Under-23s job after he parted company with Ermis Aradippou, the side he was managing in Cyprus.

A friend of Corberán's who knew him from Villarreal had linked up with the Aspire Academy, the vastly expensive development centre in Qatar which was run by Leeds board member Ivan Bravo. Corberán and Bravo met at a conference in England and prompted by Bravo, Corberán was brought into the Leeds academy after a successful interview. Even before Bielsa's arrival, Leeds' Under-23s had switched to a more technical, possession-based style on the instructions of Corberán and his fellow development-squad coach, Danny Schofield. To begin with, the results were poor. Corberán's ideas represented a wild shift in tactics and the squad took time to adapt. But around the midway point of the 2017–18 season, the style clicked and results took off with six wins from the last seven games. Romario Vieira was a winger in that youth team and witnessed Corberán's impact. 'That man, football is his brain,' Vieira said. 'If he's not the next Bielsa or Guardiola I'll be surprised. The way he wanted us to play, we all thought he was crazy. The results were bad at the start but when we started getting it right, when we clicked, you were thinking, "This guy's a genius."' Corberán could come across as cocky or arrogant. An employee at the academy once quipped that 'If Carlos was chocolate, he'd eat himself.' Vieira saw him differently. 'When you get to know him, he's nothing like that,' he said. 'When you get to know him, he's a lovely guy and really talented.'[10]

By the end of Bielsa's first pre-season, Corberán had acquired a dual role at Leeds. He would continue to look after the Under-23s but he would involve himself with the senior squad too, joining Bielsa in the dug-out for first-team matches. The presence of a conduit made sense. Bielsa intended to lean on the best of the club's academy prospects when injuries or suspensions left him needing cover. Corberán's involvement at both levels would allow Leeds to establish consistent tactics and give Bielsa the best idea of who was ready. Corberán jumped at the offer but there was no doubt that it was asking a lot of him.

When I went to interview him for the *Yorkshire Evening Post* in March 2019, he had been at Colchester United with the Under-23s the night before. The squad arrived home in the early hours of the morning and Corberán was back in work at Thorp Arch before 9 a.m. By that stage of the season he had already been involved in 75 matches, the equivalent of ten a month. But spreading him thinly was not compromising results. Leeds' senior squad were four points off the top of the Championship. Their Under-23s – helped by regular first-team cameos – would take their league title by a nine-point margin and win the end-of-season play-offs too. Corberán's stock rose steadily. He differed from Bielsa's other assistants in that it was plausible, if not highly likely, that he would want to manage in his own right again. If it was possible for Leeds to create a succession plan with a view to replacing Bielsa further down the line, some wondered if Corberán might be capable of stepping up. Corberán would never be drawn on the suggestion. 'My focus is to go year by year,' he said. 'That's enough ambition right now, not to think about other things that might be.'

His reputation and his potential pricked ears elsewhere and in 2020, a few weeks before Leeds' promotion was confirmed, Huddersfield Town began making enquiries about him. Huddersfield's team was in the hands of the Cowley brothers, Danny and Nicky, but avoiding relegation from the Championship had been a battle and the partnership with the Cowleys was about to run its course. Two days after Huddersfield ensured their survival, the pair were sacked. Conversations with Leeds about Corberán were already advanced and the Spaniard indicated to his boss that he wanted to go. Two years under Bielsa had been an education but Huddersfield were offering a second-tier job and it was a chance for Corberán to make himself front and centre. He was not inclined to tie himself to Bielsa indefinitely or to sacrifice his personal ambition. The two clubs agreed that Corberán would stay on at Elland Road for a short while longer, until the season finished and Leeds lifted the Championship title. On day one of the summer break, his appointment at Huddersfield was confirmed.

Corberán took much of what he had learned from Bielsa with him. Though murderball was seen as a Bielsa concept – a session which few other coaches thought they could implement with success – Corberán began using it as part of his weekly programme at Huddersfield. Left-back Harry Toffolo described it as 'carnage' and soon discovered what the fuss was about. 'The intensity of murderball sessions are outrageous,' he said. 'The stats we get are sky-high.'[11] In a mixed first season for Corberán there were flashes of Bielsa's football alongside poorer form which exposed a squad too weak to compete for promotion. By the closing weeks of the year, Huddersfield were fighting to keep themselves clear of relegation.

*

Coaching for Bielsa is as much a lifestyle as a profession. There are brief moments when he leans on his assistants emotionally – a firm embrace between him and Quiroga after a 2-1 win at Rotherham United in January 2019 felt like a burst of relief after a week in which Bielsa had been beset by the 'Spygate' controversy – but he can be distant too and the men who work for him give themselves over to him by becoming his eyes, his ears and his analytical tools. They are closer to the squad than him but not by much, limiting frivolity and avoiding a good cop, bad cop routine. 'It's business,' one of the players once said. 'Always business. They're good with us but they know who they're working for and what he expects.

They don't mess about.' In the final month of Bielsa's first season at Elland Road, Leeds were due to play Wigan Athletic on Good Friday (a match which ended in defeat and played a pivotal part in ruining their initial bid for promotion). Wigan had hosted Norwich City the previous weekend and beforehand they received an email from Elland Road asking them to set aside tickets for Bielsa's scouts. He was not just sending one. In total, he wanted six to attend the game and spread themselves around the stadium, analysing Wigan from different angles. No rest for the wicked but as Juanjo Spagnuolo, a friend of Quiroga's says, these disciples and devotees are 'forged by Bielsa', built by him and willing to fixate like him. Much like the squad at Leeds itself.

13.

MARCH

The seventh of March marks a full year since Elland Road last hosted a crowd. There was electricity in the stadium that day and a touch of apprehension too. Covid-19 infection rates were worsening across the country and though very few people felt inclined to miss the game (a 2-0 win over Huddersfield Town, in front of 36,000), there was a growing acceptance of what might be coming. People touched elbows rather than shaking hands, in a meagre attempt to stay distanced. Supporters washed their hands so frequently that the soap dispensers in the toilets were empty and required refills by half-time, the first time staff at the ground could remember that happening. Nevertheless, Leeds were careering towards promotion with four straight wins and four clean sheets behind them. Luke Ayling lit the touchpaper with a flying volley in the third minute (a goal he would watch so often on repeat that his partner Poppy banned him from showing it on their living room TV).[1] Patrick Bamford made the game safe early in the second half. Marcelo Bielsa had come up short in his first season as head coach, denied promotion in the campaign's final throes. But this occasion, season two, felt different.

Six days later, English football shut down and the fixture list was suspended, leaving Leeds hanging. As they negotiated wage deferrals and rapidly implemented Covid-19 protocols (their head of medicine, Rob Price, had been planning for almost two months after deducing that the virus was bound to reach England), the club began lobbying for the continuation of a season which was only nine games from finishing. Certain sides in the Premier League, particularly those near the bottom of it, were talking about declaring the campaign null and void if it could not be played to a conclusion. Some teams in the EFL preferred the idea of the final tables – and therefore promotion and relegation – being decided by a points-per-game (PPG) metric. Leeds stood to be promoted automatically if PPG were enforced. They were a point clear of West Bromwich Albion at the top of the Championship and every team in the division had played 37 times but PPG did not sit right with them. In general, it was an unpopular concept across the Championship as a whole. For one thing, Bielsa would not even discuss the possibility with the board at Elland Road. It was clear to Leeds' directors that in his mind, completing the season properly was the only option they should entertain. Other alternatives were off the table unless they were given no choice. And deep down, nobody at Leeds wanted to be seen to be winning promotion to the Premier League by default. After sixteen years in the EFL, they would do it over 46 games and do it properly. Otherwise there would always be an asterisk next to their name.

Did the shutdown help Leeds and Bielsa by allowing them to draw breath for the run-in? The question was raised midway through the 2020–21 Premier League term when Karen Carney, the former England international and TV pundit, discussed Leeds' Championship title win during Amazon Prime's coverage of their 5-0 win at West Brom on 29 December. 'They outrun everyone and credit to them,' Carney said. 'My only concern would be will they blow up at the end of the season? We saw that in the last couple of seasons. I actually think they got promoted because of Covid, in terms of it gave them a bit of respite. I don't know if they would have got up if they didn't have that break.'[2] This reprising of the Bielsa burn-out theory was, to people at Leeds, a poor representation of a team who were moving like a train in the Championship when Covid-19 intervened. Leeds' official Twitter account posted a pointed response to Carney at the end of the win over West Brom, prompting online attacks on her, many of them misogynistic, and resulting in her deleting her own account. The club issued a statement condemning the abuse but declined to delete the original tweet. Indeed, Andrea Radrizzani used his own account to call her comments 'completely unnecessary and disrespectful'.

In an effort to quell the controversy, Carney was invited by Leeds to visit their training ground but declined the offer. Publicly the club stood their ground and refused to apologise for fighting their corner. They had been seven points clear of third place when the Championship term was suspended. Prior to the shutdown, they had reeled off five successive victories without conceding a goal. They won the title by 10 points and were, by a distance, the strongest team in the division. Bielsa was not angling for a rest and when questions about the merits of PPG were put to him, he was unequivocal in opposing it. 'To think of us getting something without playing is very disappointing,' he said.

In the Premier League, the strain of the schedule has been nothing like it was in the Championship; fewer midweek matches, fewer logjams in the fixture list and a natural reduction in travelling time. Bielsa's squad have coped with absences from the very start but they have not flagged in the top flight or stumbled into anything resembling a chronic loss of form. At no stage by the start of March have they lost more than two league games back-to-back or gone three league games without a win.

Bielsa takes his players to West Ham United for a Monday

night meeting on 8 March with clear water between them and the relegation places, a healthy gap of nine points. He has been able to recall Diego Llorente again and despite Leeds' defeat to Aston Villa a week earlier, the Spaniard's distribution and poise were encouraging. Significantly, his fitness held up too. But at West Ham, Leeds shoot themselves in the foot with simple concessions in the first half. They are the stronger side initially and have the ball in the net twice (both finishes disallowed for offside) but when Ayling sticks a leg out and trips Jesse Lingard in the box, Lingard tucks the rebound away after Illan Meslier parries his penalty back into his path. Seven minutes later, Craig Dawson charges onto a corner from Aaron Cresswell and heads past Meslier from close range, confusing Llorente with a powerful run and a late change of direction. With Leeds 2-0 down at half-time, Bielsa gives his fitness coach, Benoit Delaval, strict instructions before heading for the dressing room. Gjanni Alioski and Jack Harrison are sent on as substitutes at the start of the second half. Bamford should score twice but puts one opportunity wide and another over the crossbar. Rodrigo comes off the bench and fails to take a chance from a few yards out, scuffing it against Dawson on the goalline.

The defeat was avoidable but Bielsa will not accept that Leeds are giving goals away cheaply, in spite of them conceding at a rate of 1.75 a game. 'I don't think we're facilitating the goals of the opponent,' he says. 'If you pay attention and if you look at the performances this season, in general the goalkeeper, the defenders and the defensive midfielder have been the most consistent. This opens up another type of analysis because having had defenders who've played so well, you then start to think about why we have conceded so many goals. In this respect, there is a responsibility on me. Because if you have good footballers who recover the ball well, the coach is involved.'

*

Alioski continues to feature in Bielsa's plans but for several weeks there have been signs of frustration in his body language. The offer of a contract extension at Leeds is on the table but it has been there for some time and Alioski has not accepted it. Leeds are more and more convinced that the 29-year-old will leave on a free transfer when his deal runs out at the end of June. Rumours emerge about the possibility of a move to Galatasaray, a Turkish club with whom Leeds have bitter history.

In April 2000, two Leeds supporters – Kevin Speight, a pub landlord, and Christopher Loftus, a telephone engineer – were stabbed to death in Istanbul on the night before a UEFA Cup tie between Galatasaray and Leeds. The events of that evening were harrowing and the aftermath was poisonous, fuelled by the sense that Galatasaray's management were dismissive of, or indifferent to, the killings. 'I don't think, even to this day, that Galatasaray would see the amount of press coverage or criticism as being fairly labelled against them,' former Leeds chairman Peter Ridsdale told me on the twentieth anniversary of the deaths. 'I'll be careful here but I didn't feel that their response was what our response would have been. I make no secret of that.'[3] One of the men who played for Leeds in Istanbul, Harry Kewell, was heavily criticised for taking an offer to join Galatasaray later in his career. Kewell grew up in Leeds' academy and experienced the impact of the tragedy at close quarters. There are photos online of him emerging onto the pitch at Galatasaray's Ali Sami Yen Stadium with the rest of the Leeds line-up, surrounded by Turkish police with riot shields. It seemed like reason enough for him to turn down that transfer. Alioski's background is different to Kewell's, with no tangible connection to the stabbings in Turkey, but the link between him and Galatasaray causes a divide within Leeds' fanbase. Some think

Alioski is entitled to look after himself at a stage of his career where a lucrative contract might be his last on that scale. Others think Galatasaray should be off limits for anyone associated with Leeds. Privately, the squad at Elland Road voice concerns about some of the criticism he is receiving online. The club, however, are in the dark about what Alioski intends to do or who he intends to sign for.

More positive from their perspective are the noises coming from the England camp. Kalvin Phillips is certain to be included in Gareth Southgate's next international squad but Leeds' performances have pushed other players onto the radar. Southgate has been monitoring Bamford for months and in the days around the defeat at West Ham, Luke Ayling and Jack Harrison are made aware that they are also under consideration. The chances of a call-up for either of them are slimmer than Bamford's but they are part of the conversation all the same. Southgate appears at Elland Road again for Leeds' game against Chelsea on 13 March, a match which finishes goalless. Bamford limps out of it in the first half after banging hips with Antonio Rüdiger but the damage is minor and he will be fit for England duty if Southgate selects him. Chelsea have a relatively new manager, Thomas Tuchel, and Leeds do well to shut them out. It is rare for Bielsa's side to be dominated at Elland Road but Chelsea control 62 per cent of possession and outpass Leeds by 588 to 330. Meslier keeps out the best of Chelsea's chances and despite the balance of the contest, Leeds produce several of their own. The scoreline is unusual. In 119 league games, it is Leeds' fourth goalless draw with Bielsa as head coach. It is only their 20th draw in all. The perception of them as a team who win or lose (sometimes spectacularly) with very little in between is backed up by the results of a coach who sees fewer than 15 per cent of the matches he takes charge of finish level. 'We had to make an enormous effort,' Bielsa says. 'Evidently we played against a team who are superior to ours but the chances both teams had were similar.'

Leeds are without Liam Cooper due to a bout of Covid-19 but defensively they are regimented and tight. Much attention is being paid to Meslier who shines in goal again and looks increasingly suited to the Premier League. There were similarities between him and Raphinha in the way their previous clubs allowed them to leave without a fight. Meslier had the opportunity to go to Chelsea before quitting Lorient to join Leeds but turned them down for fear of getting lost in the crowd of top-level players at Stamford Bridge. His arrival at Elland Road came about after Lorient upset him by signing another keeper, Paul Nardi, from Monaco on the back of their promotion from France's second division in 2019. Meslier had contributed heavily to that promotion and expected to remain as first choice. When the bid was made for Nardi, he took umbrage and asked to leave. Victor Orta had been monitoring him and was made aware of his availability, persuading Lorient to release him on a season-long loan with a permanent option worth £5m. Lorient seemed happy to lose a player who, within twelve months, would go on to be a regular in the Premier League.

The following week, the international call-ups begin. Southgate has a routine for choosing his England squad: phone calls in the morning to those who are included and personal conversations with a select few of those who are absent, followed by an announcement later in the day. Bamford was twitchy before the selection of the last England squad in November, admitting to having a sleepless night before the group was named. 'I was tossing and turning in bed and went into training the next morning absolutely knackered,' he said.[4] He could not resist badgering Phillips for details of when and how Southgate passed on good news. There was no call-up to that squad but this time there is measured confidence that Bamford, at 27, will feature for the first time. When the morning of the announcement comes, though, his phone is silent.

Leeds go through drill work first thing and then board a train for their game against Fulham the following night. They are en route to London when the squad list drops and Bamford's name is missing from it – Aston Villa's Ollie Watkins is included instead. Southgate has chosen twenty-six players but there is no space for Bamford. He keeps himself to himself until the train arrives at Kings Cross station, subdued and disappointed. The extent to which it matters to him is shown by the glaring contrast to his response when the Republic of Ireland made efforts to convince him to play for them. Bamford qualified for Eire through one of his grandparents but Mick McCarthy, the Republic coach who spent the most time trying to talk him round, gave up in exasperation after Bamford steadfastly refused to commit. The Irish connection did not stir much passion in Leeds' centre-forward but England was a dream. 'If I got one England cap in the whole of my career, I'd be over the moon,' he told the *Mail on Sunday*. 'It would be something I'd cherish.'[5]

Bamford has recovered from the knock to his hip and starts away at Fulham. The match at Craven Cottage is a chance for Bielsa's side to effectively settle their season, with nine fixtures left. Win in London (where Leeds, bizarrely, have not won a game for more than three years) and Fulham, who occupy 18th place in the table, will be 13 points behind; too far to even think of catching the Yorkshire club. An early header from Ayling is ruled out for offside before Bamford ensures that he will dominate the post-match headlines. Jack Harrison bursts onto a throw-in down the left and drills in a low cross. Bamford finds space at the near post and thumps a shot into the net, his 14th goal of the season. He leads the press effectively and Fulham take more than half an hour to get a foot into the match. As soon as they do, Leeds lose their shape at a corner and Joachim Andersen equalises with a volley. But there is more quality in Bielsa's line-up than Fulham's and in the 58th minute, Phillips leaves Fulham short of numbers with a sliding tackle near the halfway line. Bamford carries possession forward and slips a pass into Raphinha whose slick footwork allows him to shoot under Alphonse Areola. It is a seventh goal for Raphinha and, for Bamford, a sixth assist. Fulham are unable to respond for a second time. Bamford tries hard to be magnanimous about Southgate's decision afterwards. Bielsa, who appreciates the difficulties of managing an international squad, tries not to get involved. 'He plays to be picked but I don't think he played with the spirit of trying to prove [Southgate] wrong,' Bielsa says. 'The fact that he was considered has value.'

Leeds' 2-1 win is soon overshadowed by events closer to home. The next morning they announce the death of Peter Lorimer, their record goalscorer and youngest ever player. Lorimer, who was 74 and famed for having the most powerful shot in English football, is the fourth former Leeds player to have died since the Covid-19 pandemic began. Norman Hunter, their World Cup winner and tough-as-teak centre-back, died a few weeks after the suspension of the season in 2020. The seat he liked to occupy in the gantry at Elland Road lies empty. Jack Charlton passed away three months later, not long after the sudden death of Leeds' former captain, Trevor Cherry. Leeds have tried to pay tribute to them and stands at Elland Road have been named after Hunter and Charlton but in the absence of crowds, there is no way of properly sending them off. The last glimpse any of us had of Hunter was of him sweeping out of the press box at the end of Leeds' 2-0 win over Huddersfield, smiling his broad smile and supremely confident that promotion was in the bag. Then he was gone.

Bielsa delivered on promotion and at this juncture, he has gone past his thousandth day in charge of Leeds. It is a landmark for a coach who has a reputation for failing to stick at the clubs who employ him. 'I always think I'm going to stay for ever in all the jobs I take,' Bielsa says. 'I go day-to-day thinking I'm going to be here for the rest of my life. But at the same time, it's far more common for a manager to be fired than to stay in the same place for a very long time. And I don't think I've triumphed in this job. Triumph is something that evades me. I don't think there are many managers in football who have the legitimacy to be able to stay in a job for as long as they like. I can aspire to that but sincerely, with me it is not the case.'

He talks about Pep Guardiola shaping modern football, a phenomenon of the game. Guardiola is influential, Bielsa says, because his tactics have themselves generated a second style of play: a style designed to negate what Guardiola's teams do. 'Opponents think the best way to avoid defeat or to lose by a small number of goals is to recover the ball 10 metres from their own box,' Bielsa says. 'The style people adopt against him has only one objective – to lose by a small number of goals. That is real praise.'

Bielsa is not convinced that many managers are inclined to copy him or combat his football in the same way. And he is not convinced that many managers should. Was promotion not a vindication of his own methods? 'It was very difficult not to achieve promotion,' Bielsa says, 'because the level of our team deserved it.' It was the players' triumph rather than his, he insists. But the roots of Leeds' success went much deeper than their squad and deeper than Bielsa too; all the way down to the framework put in place after Radrizzani walked through the door at Elland Road and promised to deliver promotion within five years or fall on his sword. It was as Orta liked to tell everyone: squads and managers take you so far. But they will never take you far enough without a competent front office.

14.

THE HIERARCHY

One of the things Victor Orta prides himself on is his collection of football magazines. He has all the issues ever printed of *El Gráfico* and *Placar*, two of South America's most popular periodicals. He has numerous copies of *Shoot* (almost three-quarters of its entire back catalogue) and he hoards publications from around the world, including coverage of Japan's J-League which is almost indecipherable. His home in Madrid was too small for all of them so he stored most of the copies at his mother's house, put there for safekeeping.[1] The archive has been growing ever since he was young.

In Orta's office at Elland Road, the magazines are the first thing you see when you walk in, piles of them stacked on a table which was nominally put there for coffee mugs. There is a hole in one of the walls caused by him throwing his mobile phone across the room in anger after being told that Harvey Barnes had rejected a transfer from Leicester City to Leeds. Orta later wrote Barnes's name on a Post-it note and stuck it next to the hole. His appearance – the thick black beard, the dark, deep-set eyes – and the working environment around him create an atmosphere of organised chaos. It looks like mayhem but in practice the dots join up and staff around him say the limitless supply of magazines are indicative of someone who cannot leave football alone. My first article for *The Athletic* was an interview with Orta in August 2019, the first time we had spoken at length about his role as director of football at Leeds. He was a complex and guarded character with a mixed reputation; warm to chat to but happier behind the scenes. He had worked on the recruitment side of major European clubs for almost ten years. But in Leeds, twelve months in the job had yielded two managerial sackings and a hit-and-miss record in the transfer market. From a distance it did not justify the hype about him but up close he came across as an obsessive and a workaholic, cut from the same cloth as Marcelo Bielsa. Orta sat and ran me through his scouting database, filled with almost 7,000 extensive reports. Alongside it, the club had created a separate database for players under the age of 19. That list ran to more than 2,000 names. He and his recruitment staff liked to maintain what Orta called a 'Best XI', a line-up consisting of the prospective signing in each position who would rank as first choice if Leeds went into the transfer market tomorrow. They updated it regularly, adding names who came onto the radar and removing those who either completed moves elsewhere, signed new contracts at their existing clubs or showed a marked decline in form. Robin Koch had been in the 'Best XI' for many months before joining Leeds from Freiburg. Orta had been tracking him for years on end. 'There aren't many players you sign who you haven't been watching for a while,' Orta said.[2]

Orta and Middlesbrough had a delicate relationship and so, for a while, did Orta and Leeds. It was not that the ownership at either club doubted him. Though his final months at Middlesbrough were clouded by claims of his interfering in the dressing room and criticism of errors made in the transfer market (the club were relegated from the Premier League a few weeks before he left), he was adamant that Middlesbrough's chairman, Steve Gibson, wanted him to extend his contract for another three seasons. Orta would talk of 'assuming the mistakes we made' at Middlesbrough, of taking the blame for the deals that backfired, but he objected to the insinuation that recruitment was straightforward or an exact science. When we met at Elland Road, he outlined the various analytical packages he relied on: Wyscout, Analytics FC, InStat, StatsBomb, Transfer Room – software designed to help and streamline the process of scouting. There was nothing unusual about it – every big club relied on data alongside more traditional recruitment methods and some were employing dedicated data scientists – but the enormity of it was striking.

In Orta's first year at Leeds, the club's signings ran into double figures with very modest results. Their strategy was to bring in a high number of recruits but keep a lid on spending by limiting individual fees to around £3m and the highest weekly wage to £15,000 (within twelve months, they had changed tack and were paying around twice as much a week to Patrick Bamford). Mateusz Klich proved a find from FC Twente, albeit after a false start, and Gjanni Alioski stuck in England for the duration of a four-year contract but many of the signings came and went without making enough of a splash and Orta's standing suffered as a result. Radrizzani was aware of scepticism about him after the 2017–18 season ended with Leeds 13th in the Championship, no better than the club's support were used to. Money had been wasted but Radrizzani refused to be swayed.

'Everybody can make mistakes in my organisation, including me,' he said at the start of his second season as owner. 'Unless it's Victor's desire to leave, I have no doubt about him. I trust him. We didn't make wrong decisions in terms of picking bad players. Maybe we picked players who at the moment cannot be part of this project. The pressure is very high because we cannot wait ten years [for promotion].'

Those comments indicated a shift in mindset and at the point where Radrizzani made them, Bielsa was already in the building. Orta had inspired that appointment and encouraged by Bielsa choosing to work with a large core of the squad he inherited, Leeds' transfer policy switched from casting the net far and wide to devoting larger sums of money to a smaller group of recruits. Bamford and Barry Douglas were the only permanent deals done in the summer of 2018. Owing to Ronaldo Vieira's £7m sale to Sampdoria, the net spend was negligible. It was, Radrizzani admitted, a 'more rational summer than the last one' and the rethink paid off.[3] Bielsa was the missing piece below a hierarchy who had the right credentials and good ideas but lacked a head coach capable of pulling the threads together. Bielsa was the wand.

Radrizzani's takeover of Leeds went through in May 2017, within weeks of the 2016–17 season finishing. His profile had grown during six months as co-owner alongside Massimo Cellino but, to much of the sport, he was an unfamiliar face and a new arrival in European football. A public relations graduate from the IULM University in Milan, information about Radrizzani was relatively scarce. Reports in Italy named him as an advisor in a Chinese buy-out of Inter Milan in 2016, completed by the Suning Group, but his interest was in TV sports rights. He began making money through them in the Far East after leaving university and joining the new-media firm Media Partners, putting together contracts to take Serie A coverage to Thailand and Japan. In 2004 he co-founded MP & Silva, a company which specialised in broadcast rights deals. MP & Silva thrived for many years but Radrizzani stepped away from it in 2016 after it attracted Chinese investment. From there MP & Silva declined at a rapid rate, running into financial difficulties and losing a spate of contracts. Its Singapore branch entered provisional liquidation in 2018.[4] Companies

House registered a court order for the winding up of MP & Silva's UK operation the following July. In 2019, Bloomberg reported that the company's Chinese owner planned to sue Radrizzani and MP & Silva's other founder, Riccardo Silva, over losses made since its buy-out. Radrizzani had turned his mind to other ventures by then, acquiring Leeds from Cellino for £45m, establishing the investment group Aser and forming an online broadcast company called Eleven Sports. Eleven Sports acquired TV rights for different sports in numerous countries, although a bid to break the UK market and compete with outlets like Sky and BT Sport ran aground rapidly. Radrizzani said the thought of buying Leeds had arisen after a chance conversation at a lunch where Kenny Dalglish, the former Liverpool manager, was present. Dalglish told him that of all the affordable clubs left in England, Leeds were the one with most potential. Despite negotiations hitting a few hurdles, Radrizzani and Cellino were able to shake hands on a price.

Radrizzani's personal wealth was estimated to be in the hundreds of millions but football club ownership was new territory for him; more unpredictable, more difficult to get right and a world away from the sale of broadcast rights. With Cellino gone, he set about establishing a new executive structure at Elland Road, built around a director of football. One of his associates was Ivan Bravo, a former Real Madrid director and the head of Qatar's Aspire Academy. Bravo knew of Orta and told Radrizzani that in spite of muttering at Middlesbrough, Orta would be perfect for the director of football's role. Orta was knowledgeable and had cut his teeth at a high level, working under renowned transfer guru Ramón Rodriguez Verdejo, or Monchi, at Sevilla. Leeds had no extensive scouting network to speak of but Orta could establish one rapidly and Bravo was able to sound him out by phone before any other club made him an offer. Gaby Ruiz, the man who created the video game *PC Fútbol*, Spain's version of *Football Manager*, before crossing into recruitment, was given the task of heading up Leeds' European transfer work. Orta had contacts in the Far East and South America and built a team of six full-time and twelve part-time scouts, giving Leeds much more reach. He had seen first-hand how dramatically the transfer market was changing. When he first began attending South America's Under-20 Championship – a showcase of the best talent on the continent – Orta was one of around only twenty scouts who bothered making the trip. These days more than 300 would turn up, all of them as alert as each other. There were very few secrets any more and when Leeds agreed a £1.5m fee with FC Twente for Klich, the midfielder was on the verge of signing for Middlesbrough. With odd exceptions, any scout worth their salt could dig up the same targets.

The director of football model was commonplace across Europe, a continental structure which many countries embraced. In England, it was still viewed with suspicion and seen by some as a layer of management which impinged on a club's manager himself. Orta found the resistance to it confusing. Football had evolved and running a club was a task for many hands. To him it made no sense for someone like Bielsa to be asked to deal with contracts, transfer negotiations or more peripheral matters. Bielsa had input into most of it and, in the case of transfers, the final say. Orta would put names to him, like Sheffield United's Billy Sharp and Brighton's Glenn Murray in the January window of 2019, but give up on them without arguing if Bielsa said no. Irrespective of the fact that Sharp and Murray were proven goalscorers in the Championship, they matched a different style to Bielsa's so the conversation went no further. Bielsa badgered Radrizzani on WhatsApp throughout the summer in 2019, asking again and again if Leeds were any closer to signing winger Helder Costa from Wolverhampton Wanderers. When a deal appealed to him, Bielsa would fixate on it but Orta tried to defer responsibility away from Bielsa as much as the Argentinian would allow. Orta's team did the legwork by compiling the clips and data Bielsa needed to make a proper assessment of any players Leeds were proposing to buy. Talks over contract extensions fell to Orta and chief executive Angus Kinnear.

I once asked Orta to explain why a director of football was so pivotal from his perspective (something of a rhetorical question). 'These days I think every head coach would want one,' he replied. 'There is too much to think about without one.' What mattered most was that a director of football and a head coach were on the same wavelength. Bielsa and Orta could argue furiously, over issues big and small, and on occasions they would argue to the extent that some who overheard them wondered if they would ever speak to each other again. But the dust always settled and nothing ever festered. For all those heated exchanges, they shared mutual respect. Orta saw the training ground as Bielsa's space so he had no office there and tried to limit his visits to one a fortnight. A valuable piece of advice given to Orta by Monchi at Sevilla was to avoid enquiring about team selection or giving an opinion on it without being asked by the head coach first. The extent to which Leeds got their set-up right was evidenced by the fact that by late 2020, Bielsa's tenure there was the longest of his career in club management. No other board had been able to satisfy him so well.

Kinnear was a different animal to Orta. Orta was flamboyant and awash with Latin temperament, a man who went to great efforts to manage the morale of the general staff at Elland Road. One of the floors in the stadium's East Stand had been designed like a football pitch, with a green carpet and whitewash on it. Orta created the 'halfway-line game' where employees tried to roll a ball as close to halfway as possible. The winner was given a £100 voucher for one of two Spanish restaurants which Orta frequented in Leeds, Ibérica and Fazenda. When the staff got too good at it, he launched a pub quiz instead. But when his fiery temperament showed itself, there were consequences. Orta was fined £2000 and given a one-match stadium ban by the Football Association in 2020 for comments made to referee Darren England in the tunnel during a 3-2 win over Millwall. In jest, someone at Leeds produced a hoodie for him with the FA's Twitter announcement about his punishment on the front of it. On the weekend of Leeds' promotion, he took a pair of binoculars to their penultimate game at Derby County, making a mockery of the 'Spygate' controversy. Between that and their squad setting off flares after full-time, Leeds were fined £20,000 for 'failing to ensure players and/or officials conducted themselves in an orderly fashion'. Orta's impassioned behaviour in the directors' box also attracted attention, including disapproving looks from rival executives when Leeds lost 4-1 at Crystal Palace in November 2020. Midway through the second half of a 2-1 defeat to Everton two months later, he was seen arguing with some of Everton's substitutes after a contentious refereeing decision and stewards were forced to intervene away at Wolves, asking Orta to sit down before he fell over a balcony. Eventually, it was suggested to Orta by some of his own colleagues that he think about reining himself in.

With Kinnear, Radrizzani found a capable administrator with prior experience of prominent, front-office positions at Arsenal and West Ham United. Kinnear's background was in sports marketing and he found a route into professional football after working for Coca-Cola and Procter & Gamble. He was at Arsenal during the club's move from Highbury to the Emirates Stadium and held the position of managing director at West Ham when they made the far less popular decision to relocate from Upton Park to the London Stadium. Leeds had an existing chief executive, Ben Mansford, when Radrizzani became majority shareholder but a settlement was reached with Mansford and Kinnear replaced him as soon as the takeover went through. A Luton Town fan, Kinnear was seen as a voice of reason and a rational presence in the boardroom, 'the boring Anglo-Saxon', to use his own words.[5] 'Victor tries to spend money, I try to save it and make it,' he said. It was his job to ask Radrizzani for cash in the lengthy period where Radrizzani put up £1.5m a month to meet costs and ensure that the wage bill at Leeds was covered. It was Kinnear who put together a wage deferral agreement with the club's squad and coaching staff as soon as Covid-19 hit. It was Kinnear who talked Radrizzani down when the Italian's attempt to change the club's crest in 2018 met with untold opposition and ridicule, much of it from the club's own support. Radrizzani liked the new badge and wanted to stick with it but he was abroad in the Far East and Kinnear, on the ground in Leeds, witnessed the strength of feeling and saw no alternative to abandoning the design completely. It was Kinnear who talked Tottenham into allowing Leeds to buy a new top layer for their pitch when it strayed towards the point of becoming unplayable midway through the Premier League season. And it was Kinnear to whom the baton invariably passed whenever Bielsa began enquiring about things like the Cycle to Work initiative.

His longer-term focus, though, revolved around the infrastructure projects Leeds were sitting on. The club had earmarked a patch of land, over the M621 motorway behind Elland Road, as a viable site for a new training ground. Once occupied by a secondary school, the land was derelict and the local council was happy to allow Leeds to acquire it. Kinnear had an artist's impression of a state-of-the-art facility on his laptop, showing a long building dividing pitches for the first team from those set aside for the club's oldest academy age groups. The estimated cost came in at £25m. A community sports hub on the potholed car park behind Elland Road's West Stand was further forward in the pipeline, a project which would provide indoor and outdoor pitches alongside a pharmacy and a GP's surgery. Leeds aimed to have spades in the ground for the hub by August 2020, though the coronavirus prevented work beginning on time. The club wanted to use it for their younger academy squads. But bigger again were their aspirations for increasing Elland Road's capacity and as the 2020-21 season wore on, a decision was taken to mothball the training ground scheme and focus attention on the stadium. When Kinnear travelled to Leeds' 3-0 defeat at Tottenham, he noted the fact that matchday revenue at Tottenham's modern ground was five times higher than takings at Elland Road.[6] He was intent on pushing forward sketches for rebuilding the North and West Stands when the campaign finished, even though Radrizzani knew that funding the building work would not be cheap.[7]

Radrizzani took the view that Leeds would only move forward in a sustainable way if they married a strong performance on the pitch with concerted improvements off it. As he said, his first season as chairman had not been as rational as it should have been. Aside from the transfers that failed, he went through no fewer than three managers in year one, starting with Garry Monk who resigned within days of Radrizzani completing his takeover. Thomas Christiansen and Paul Heckingbottom only served to convince the board at Leeds that punting on unproven coaches was asking for trouble. Christiansen, a Dane who was best known for top-scoring in the German Bundesliga with Vfl Bochum, had a limited amount of experience. In some respects he was the sort of manager Cellino liked: responsible for training and picking the team each weekend but compliant and happy to have no real influence over transfers. Heckingbottom was regarded as a talented coach but having tried to assert himself on his first day by banning the players from wearing snoods and other winter garments, he stamped no discernible style on performances. Up in the boardroom, the penny dropped about the importance of finding a manager with authority, gravitas and exceptional talent.

Bielsa and Radrizzani were not as close as Bielsa and Orta but Bielsa admired Radrizzani's willingness to see the bigger picture. It was estimated that between his original buy-out and further funds put forward, via loans or equity purchases, Radrizzani had sunk around £100m into Leeds by the time they were promoted. He tried to be careful with his cash, saying he owed it to his family and his son in particular not to burn too much of it on football, but many of the costs were unavoidable. Bielsa worried about financial objectives sucking the soul out of football but in the case of Radrizzani, he saw positive investment.

'The owner of Leeds is someone who's put the interest of the club ahead of his own commercial and financial interests,' Bielsa said. 'From what I observe, he has invested a lot of money in a lot of things that could have been ignored. In the foundation phase he made important changes and on infrastructure he has made important contributions. Those investments are not for the short term. They're for the long term and how you envisage the club to be in the future. If you invest and you want immediate returns, it's artificial. To have a solid process you need investment, patience, tolerance – and of course generosity. Then you can reap the benefits.'

There was a risk of Leeds' success being seen as Bielsa's success alone. His impact was too decisive and profound for anyone to doubt that without him, the club would not have evolved as dramatically as they had. But there were footballers around him who pushed themselves to higher levels of excellence; footballers who did everything he asked, like the academy midfielder Robbie Gotts trimming his weight to nine-and-a-half stone and brushing his teeth to stop himself eating at night, all for the sake of adhering to Bielsa's rules.[8] There was a board above him who held it together and a chairman who, while possessing an ego and an impulsive streak, had the money to fund two years of Bielsa in the Championship and oversaw the club's reawakening (a contrast with the exhausting neurosis of Cellino whose WhatsApp status for years read 'Battery about to die'). There was a director of football who, by establishing a close partnership with Bielsa, formed half of the most important axis at Leeds. The transfers that clicked, like Ben White's loan from Brighton, were perfectly judged. Those that did not, like the ill-fated deal for Jean-Kévin Augustin from RB Leipzig, came at a substantial cost. But Orta's argument was that football was inherently volatile. There were factors, like human nature, which dictated how successful a new signing would be.

After starting out as a sports journalist, Orta got his break in football at Rayo Valladolid, in Spain's second division. At other points in his career he had spent time with Elche and Zenit St Petersburg. It was a path he dreamed of in the days when he risked the wrath of his mother by skipping school to go hunting for players' autographs. One of Orta's favourite stories is of him sneaking off to the airport in Madrid as Juventus flew in for a European tie against Real Madrid. 'When I got home, my mother started asking me how school was. So I said, "Perfect." She asked me lots more questions too. So I say, "why do you ask?" And she says, "Victor, because I watched you on TV. The neighbour knocked on the door and said you were there with the cameras, getting autographs."

She didn't take it too badly because she knew it was my passion.'

All the passion and ideas in the world did not stop football being a sport which was highly strategic but prone to uncontrollable events. As Jürgen Klopp's assistant at Liverpool, Peter Krawietz, put it, 'football is chess but with dice.'[9] Within the industry, it was easy to find people who spoke highly of Orta. Agents considered him to be professional and prepared. Other clubs discussed hiring him themselves. There was tentative contact from Manchester United, although Orta always told himself that he would never go to another English club. Roma made enquiries about him before naming Thiago Pinto as their new sporting director in November 2020. One of the outsiders in the 2021 presidential election at Barcelona was understood to be keen on courting him if the vote went his way. But Orta felt the same as Radrizzani. Ideally, they would see Leeds back into European competition. When that happened, perhaps they would look for another project elsewhere.

The year in which Leeds won promotion was the longest of anyone's life. Bielsa was unable to return to Argentina (not that he did very often anyway) and from the start of his second close-season to the end of his third summer transfer window, the best part of eighteen months passed without a break. Orta fantasised about disappearing to Whitby or the Lake District when his work for the Premier League was done (in the end, he and his family found time for a holiday in Cyprus).[10]

'Somewhere quiet,' he joked. But never for long.

15.

APRIL/MAY

The scale of Leeds United's expenditure in their promotion year is laid bare when their accounts are published by Companies House over the Easter weekend in early April. The figures cover the 2019–20 period and stretch to thirteen months to include the end of a Covid-delayed season. What they reveal is more nuanced than the plain numbers in black and white but even allowing for mitigating factors the deficit is huge: an operating loss of £64m and an overall loss of £62m. Their administrative expenses have soared above £100m and their wage bill (even without promotion-related bonuses of £20m paid to players and staff) is 107 per cent of their total income. Leeds, with Andrea Radrizzani as chairman, have been very good at generating revenue and their turnover of £54m is massive by the standards of the Championship. Merchandising income of £15m is also far beyond the earning power of most sides in the division and their new kit deal with Adidas means it has risen again in the Premier League.

The losses underline how essential promotion in Marcelo Bielsa's second season was. It was no coincidence that while Leeds were in the thick of the run-in, he made enquiries about the average wage of a coach in the Championship. Had they fallen short and stayed in the EFL, he could not have retained his job without taking a pay cut. Where Kalvin Phillips was concerned, the midfielder and Leeds reached an understanding when he signed a new five-year contract in 2019 that he would give it one more season at Elland Road and then leave if the club were still in the Championship. He was a Leeds boy but he had ambition too and there was only so long the club could ask him to stick around outside the Premier League. More pertinently, he was an easy route to a big transfer fee. Other difficult decisions would have been necessary too, to avoid a breach of the EFL's Profit and Sustainability model, a set of rules designed to control debts amassed by Championship teams. In short, the model created for Bielsa in years one and two had a certain lifespan below the Premier League. A reset of sorts would have been unavoidable.

Reaching the Premier League, however, created a completely different financial landscape. The club's 'cash in hand and at the bank' at the end of the 2018–19 accounting period was less than £500,000. On 31 July 2020, they had £31m tucked away – the first block of TV revenue earned through promotion. And by April 2021, results under Bielsa mean that Leeds can count on Premier League income for a second season. Barring a sequence of highly improbable twists, they are already safe before they host Sheffield United (managerless after parting company with Chris Wilder) on 3 April but a 2-1 victory takes them up to 42 points, a mile away from trouble. Forty points was the bottom-line target Leeds set for themselves at the start of the season. The club budgeted for 17th position and are certain of finishing much higher, earning an extra £3m per place in the process. Bielsa goes full strength against Sheffield United, resisting the temptation to experiment or bring through more of the Under-23s who are cruising towards promotion in their own division. He is asked if he might mix his team up with survival effectively secured but insists he will pick his line-ups on merit. 'There's still a lot to play for and a lot to show,' Bielsa says. 'The objectives are always linked to imposing yourself on the next game. There's no position in the table that exempts you from making an effort.'

With the pressure off in a competitive sense, Leeds have increased the incentives for their squad by introducing a new win-bonus structure, encouraging them to push for a top-half finish, but after the victory over Sheffield United there is a buoyant mood among the club's directors. Forty points is a symbolic milestone and they can think seriously about pressing ahead with the expansion of Elland Road. Financial backing for the rebuilding of the West and North Stands is in the process of being arranged. Bielsa's own demeanour gives the impression that relegation is no longer anything to worry about.

Even so, he turns up the dial in the week that follows. There is a more relaxed, more amenable glow around him but Leeds have Manchester City next and City's form is mesmerising. Since they and Leeds drew 1-1 at Elland Road in October, Pep Guardiola's squad have won 36 of their 43 games. They have lost only twice. Guardiola is attempting to claim a quadruple of trophies – the Premier League, which is virtually sewn up, the FA Cup, the League Cup and the Champions League – and Bielsa's admiration for him is as strong as ever. 'Teams who have the capacity to do things that are unexpected make the game full of surprises,' Bielsa says. 'When I classify Guardiola's team and style as magical, I am not calling him a magician. What I'm saying is that his team creates so many surprising attacks and from the outside, it looks as though the manager is doing something magical. It's impossible to detect how he manages this and there's nothing nicer for a spectator than something they do not expect. When you know exactly what's going to happen, this creates boredom.'

He prepares for the game at the Etihad Stadium by running his players through video analysis every day, more than he would in a typical week. Their training sessions start later, running into the afternoon. Murderball is extreme even by Bielsa's standards, stretching to almost three hours, and he works hard on reminding his squad how to swap markers out of possession and cope with excessive pressure (a drill that will help in a big way at the Etihad). The attention to detail suggests he has Guardiola's scalp on his mind and in a season where Bielsa has squeezed every last drop from his team, a victory over a leading Premier League club is one of the few things they are missing. As it stands, Leicester City are the only side in the top seven that Leeds have beaten. Most of their points have been accrued against sides lower down the table, the sides more at risk of relegation. 'It's our objective to modify this,' Bielsa says. 'A lot of teams in similar positions to us have managed to beat those in the top positions. It's possible but we haven't managed to achieve it enough.' He has the bit between his teeth.

Guardiola admits that the meeting with Leeds has fallen at a bad time. His players, as rich in ability as they are, are halfway through a Champions League quarter-final tie with Borussia Dortmund and will fly to Germany for the second leg a few days after Bielsa takes his squad to the Etihad. Guardiola makes seven changes and rests Kevin De Bruyne. Phil Foden and Iker Gündoğan are on the bench and Guardiola does not want to use them but the game takes two twists at the end of the first half. First, Stuart Dallas opens the scoring with a shot off a post, just at the point where City seem to have Leeds where they want them. Three minutes later, the video assistant referee (VAR) upgrades a yellow card shown to Liam Cooper for a knee-high tackle on Gabriel Jesus to a red and Leeds lose their captain. Bielsa gathers his players in the dressing room at half-time and tells them to remember their sessions in the build-up. He instructs them to avoid engaging Guardiola's centre-backs until they come a certain distance over halfway. Let them bring the ball out, Bielsa says, and make their lives difficult by sticking tightly to the players who are looking to receive it; by 'marking the receptors when they are close to the box'. City defender John Stones sees so much possession that his carries cover almost 700 metres. A mere 9 per cent of the second half takes place in City's final third.

Guardiola's side amass 29 efforts on goal and equalise through Ferran Torres in the 76th minute but Bielsa's defensive model forces City to pass laterally and stops them driving forward at pace. Normal time is up when City switch off and Leeds cut through them in a flash as Gjanni Alioski's weighted pass sends Dallas running in behind Stones. Ederson tries to close him down but Dallas keeps his composure and slots a shot under the goalkeeper. It is Leeds' second effort of the afternoon and to the disbelief of everyone, it settles the game. Bielsa has a first win as a head coach against Guardiola and tactically he has produced a masterclass, cleverly negating City's attacks but retaining enough pace in his team to ensure that Leeds could still pose a threat. On account of City's possession and dominance, Bielsa says a home win would have been fair. 'But the reason why I think we deserved to win was because of the belief of the players, that they could do it,' he says. City, unsurprisingly, are the first team to outrun Leeds over 90 minutes all season but only by a couple of hundred metres. Bielsa laughs when he is asked how much Leeds trained for situations where they were heavily on the back foot or totally defensive, self-deprecating about his influence. 'Nada,' he says. 'Never. Nothing that happened today is down to me.' People who followed his training programme all week disagree.

Dallas, over time, has become the epitome of a Bielsa player, selflessly adaptable without complaint and a footballer whom Bielsa likes to describe as 'generous'. Dallas – once a carpenter and a part-time winger in Northern Ireland – is collectively minded and has a way of consistently bettering himself. Bielsa gravitates towards players who are multifunctional and in tune with the bigger picture. Dallas can defend, attack and, at this juncture, is reinventing himself as a central midfielder whom even Mateusz Klich cannot shift from Bielsa's line-up. Leeds are planning to offer him a new contract, taking him well into his thirties, and he has matured impressively from the days when his agent, David Hartley, spotted him in the Northern Irish leagues and decided to take a chance on a kid who was 'as pale as a sheet of paper and as skinny as a rake.'[1] Bielsa compares him to Javier Zanetti, an icon of Argentina and Inter Milan. 'He's a novelty,' Bielsa says. 'The role Dallas has is the role Klich normally has. Klich was usually the best player there. Dallas has shown different ways of playing in this position.' A few weeks later he will pick up Leeds' player of the year award.

Bielsa's continuing impact on the club and his players only strengthens Leeds' resolve to extend his contract. He denies reports from Argentina that he is on the verge of agreeing a new two-year deal – 'this information is not real,' Bielsa says. 'I ignore the origin of it' – but the portents are good. By mid-April he is looking for a new house, something more homely than his bedsit in Wetherby (and more hospitable for the times when his wife comes to visit). He is chirpy and jovial with the press, visibly content. Leeds, as ever, are ready to talk as soon as he gives the green light to engage.

On 19 April his side host Liverpool, a Monday-night game which is slightly lost in the mayhem of the twenty-four hours that precede it. The day before, twelve of Europe's biggest clubs – six from the Premier League, Liverpool included – announce plans for a new European Super League (ESL), an invitational competition

that will rival UEFA's Champions League and ensure annual qualification for a group of fifteen elite teams. It also promises huge
amounts of money for those involved and is an outright challenge
to the existing structure of the game.

The backlash is severe, not least from the other fourteen Premier
League sides who are in danger of being left behind. At face value,
the ESL concept is self-serving and the antithesis of competitive
football. Leeds are not invited to join the project and an official
there quips about 'serving gruel' to Liverpool's directors on the
night of the match at Elland Road. As it is, none of their senior
officials turns up and chief executive Billy Hogan is conspicuous
by his absence. A 1-1 draw ensues as Sadio Mané opens the scoring and Diego Llorente equalises late in the game but there is no
real focus on the nuts and bolts of the match itself. Leeds supporters gather outside the ground to protest against the ESL plan.
Liverpool supporters travel from Merseyside to join them. A plane
flies overhead with a banner reading 'Say No To Super League'
and Leeds produce T-shirts for their players to wear, bearing the
slogan 'Earn It – Football is For the Fans' (a message approved
by the Premier League beforehand). Jürgen Klopp is incensed by
Leeds offering some of the T-shirts to his squad, describing the
gesture as a 'real joke'. Victor Orta gets in on the act by holding
one up in the directors' box for the cameras to see.

After full-time Bielsa is quizzed on the ESL plan and says a
power-grab like it was inevitable, for the simple reason that football has never imposed regulations to actively limit the strength
and selfishness of the biggest clubs. 'The [authorities] could have
anticipated these excesses and avoided them,' he says. 'What happened was inevitable. It happens in all walks of life. Some teams
are bigger than others but they should be conscious of the fact that
we need each other. The real owners of clubs are the ones who love

the badge. Without them, football will disappear. This is going to generate a huge polemic so let's see who talks up in defence of the fans.' Klopp, whose players were jeered as they arrived at Elland Road and during a pre-match walk in Leeds city centre, is on edge and exposed by questions he cannot easily answer. No one above him at Anfield has said anything publicly and he had no warning about the ESL before the news broke. He hits out at pundits and columnists who are criticising Liverpool but when pushed, he agrees that the ESL 'is not a great idea'. James Milner, his captain on the night, goes further. 'I can only say my own opinion – I don't like it and I hope it doesn't happen, for the same reasons as everyone else,' Milner says.[2] Within forty-eight hours, all six of the English clubs involved in the ESL have caved in to criticism and backed out.

In comparison to the controversy, the concurrent success of Leeds' Under-23s is a smaller but more satisfying story. Midway through 2020, the club's academy was awarded category one status, promoting their development team into Premier League 2's second tier. Despite a step up in the quality of the opposition, they have blitzed the division with a style of play in-keeping with Bielsa's and unlike much of what is seen at academy level. Bielsa's tactics have filtered down through the age categories, a deliberate attempt to promote the same principles of pressing, man-to-man marking and interplay. His efforts to make the first team and Under-23s work as a homogeneous group have, in the words of Leeds' academy manager Adam Underwood, left the production line in 'the best health it's ever been in'.

The Under-23s coach, Mark Jackson, stepped smoothly into the shoes of his predecessor Carlos Corberán and he has a touch of Bielsa's work ethic about him. On the night in April when the Under-23s seal the title at Aston Villa, Jackson sits up until 4 a.m.

with a cup of tea, analysing the game. He and Bielsa agreed that it would be Bielsa's prerogative to strengthen the Under-23s with first-team players who needed minutes but Jackson was given the authority to pick the rest of the line-up and coach them without interference. Weight targets, pre- and post-match analysis, leadership groups in the dressing room – all of the ideas and principles applied at first-team level are matched by the Under-23s. Recruitment of players like Joe Gelhardt from Wigan and Cody Drameh from Fulham has enhanced the strength of the development side too. Bielsa was on hand with messages of support on the few occasions when Jackson's team lost and by the time they are crowned champions, they are 12 points clear. 'This isn't me being big-headed about the boys but nearly every team have come off after playing us and said it's the hardest game they've had,' says Jackson, a member of the academy staff at Leeds since 2015. 'This manager, his detail and his attention to it is phenomenal. I've seen a massive increase in analysis. I thought it was detailed when I first came here but it was nothing like this.' On the morning after their title win, Bielsa's senior players line up on the indoor pitch at Thorp Arch to give Jackson's squad a guard of honour.[3]

The theory, which works well in practice, is that Bielsa insisting on joined-up coaching between different age groups means he can confidently call on academy players in the knowledge that they train as the first team does. If he needs to blood them, they ought to be prepared. He is not being frivolous with debuts from the academy this season but he has given more than ten in his three years as head coach and players at that level offer solutions to selection issues. In November 2018, Bielsa lost both of his goalkeepers, Bailey Peacock-Farrell and Jamal Blackman, to injury before a game at home to Bristol City. The EFL granted dispensation for Leeds to find cover by making an emergency signing and the club presented a handful of options to Bielsa but he rejected them all, saying he would rather use Will Huffer from the academy. Huffer, an England international at Under-17 and Under-18 level, had never played for Leeds. He had never made a first-team appearance for anyone. But, Bielsa told the club, he trains with my squad regularly, he knows how we play and I trust him more than an experienced keeper coming in cold. After spending the forty-eight hours before the match in something of a daze, Huffer started and Leeds won 2-0. 'People asked me if I was excited but I didn't know what to think,' Huffer said. 'My dad could tell I was a bit odd. On the Thursday beforehand, the two of us went to a pub to play chess and he absolutely destroyed me because I couldn't concentrate.'[4] Bielsa took the pressure off in the dressing room by telling the rest of his team that the responsibility was on them; that whatever happened, the blame would not lie with Huffer. 'He knows exactly what he needs in any situation,' Huffer said.

Before the Premier League season started, April had the potential to be a tense month for Leeds but the stakes are minimal by the end of it and a 0-0 draw at home to Manchester United on 25 April completes a haul of 12 points from a six-game sequence in which Bielsa's side have played both Manchester clubs, Liverpool and Chelsea. As unspectacular as the stalemate with Manchester United is, there are glaring contrasts between this result and Leeds' 6-2 thrashing at Old Trafford in December. For one thing, Leeds are growing more measured, more stable defensively and less inclined to be reckless. Raphinha is injured and Bielsa's team fail to fire in an attacking sense but Kalvin Phillips marshals Bruno Fernandes and Bielsa is sensible in realising towards the end that a point is worth protecting. Ole Gunnar Solskjær sends on Paul Pogba with 14 minutes to go and Bielsa reacts 60 seconds later by replacing Tyler Roberts with Robin Koch, a central defender for an attacking midfielder. Koch slots in front of the back four and is there for one purpose: to prevent space from opening up and to make a nuisance of himself in the precise areas where Pogba tries to pick passes. It gives the impression that Bielsa is adapting and learning, just as his team are. Since Arsenal away in February, they have conceded at a rate of less than a goal a match and, helped by the easing of defensive absentees, tightened up. Concessions from set-pieces, a handicap previously, are reducing. Bielsa can see the players evolving and growing, and there is a sense of the squad moderating their performances and managing the game in front of them by striking a better balance between aggressive attacking and disciplined structure. Bielsa might be 65 but he is new to the Premier League, and it seems that he is learning alongside them. 'Throughout this [season] the players have made errors and have learned how to correct them,' Bielsa says. 'In the same way, they have learned to avoid the errors that are avoidable. I have the feeling that there has been a growth in their maturity; in their experience of managing these games. The capacity of our players to go up against these very good players has increased.'

Bielsa is in with a shout of the Premier League's manager of the month award for April but loses out to Newcastle United's Steve Bruce. Klopp takes the award for May after a late surge from his Liverpool team. By May, Leeds' results hold diminishing significance beyond the slim chance of Bielsa's squad qualifying for the Europa League. They lose 2-0 at Brighton but overrun Tottenham and Burnley and turn the screw on Southampton during the second half of a 2-0 win at St Mary's. Rodrigo comes good with four goals in the final four matches, including one in a 3-1 victory over West Bromwich Albion on the season's last day, but having worried that intermittent appearances in his first year in England would threaten his place in Spain's squad for the delayed 2020

European Championship, his burst of form comes too late to earn him a call-up.

Leeds are able to accommodate 8,000 fans for the meeting with West Brom, the first crowd seen at Elland Road for fourteen months. It is an emotional moment at the end of an emotional week. A few days earlier, the club announce that Pablo Hernández and Gaetano Berardi will leave when the season ends, Berardi after 144 league appearances and Hernández after 167. Bielsa describes them as 'two excellent professionals, very influential and very decisive' and decides to start them against West Brom. He says he would have liked to have retained them but both players are ready to go; Hernández despite having twelve months left on his contract. The year has been frustrating for the midfielder and Bielsa accepts as much but the results speak for themselves. Leeds finish ninth with 59 points, the second-highest total by a newly promoted Premier League team in a quarter of a century. Far from their batteries running flat, they complete the term with the tireless vigour of a side who are plugged into the mains. 'I can't ignore that Pablo didn't have the minutes he would have wanted,' Bielsa says. 'He would have deserved them and I can't ignore that I'm responsible. I take on that responsibility. Pablo with his behaviour and Berardi with his, they left their mark not just on the pitch.' Bielsa has a habit of avoiding interaction with his players when he substitutes them, staring straight ahead as they trail off behind him, but there is an affectionate hug between him and Hernández when the Spaniard leaves the field 20 minutes before the end of the win over West Brom. Between the dug-out and the pitch, this was the pivotal connection in the Championship, the partnership that defined so much. Bielsa said Hernández would improve him as a coach. And perhaps Hernández has.

Behind the scenes Orta is preparing himself for the start of the transfer market and trying to resolve the matter of Alioski's future. The full-back has played well during the run-in and a contract offer is still being dangled in front of him but Alioski tells Leeds that the clash with West Brom will be his final game. He intends to become a free agent. Then, the next day, he appears at a club function at the Dakota hotel in central Leeds, seemingly in two minds again. He and Orta speak privately and Orta feels suddenly confident that Alioski might about-turn and agree to an extension, despite the higher wage on offer at Galatasaray.

More pressing for Leeds is Bielsa's own deal and the club's desire to renew it. Leeds never like to be presumptuous but they sense his desire to stay. There has been dialogue between him and Orta about prospective signings and the positions which need strengthening, and if Bielsa has a shelf-life at Elland Road, he is yet to reach the end of it. He continues to push for upgrades to infrastructure, like the installation of a pitch at the training ground which will replicate exactly the specifications of the new surface which is about to be laid at Elland Road, and he refuses to think about job opportunities elsewhere. Leeds have been playing in a consistent way and pursuing consistent tactics since day one under him but his team do not look stale. He has a knack of keeping them vibrant. When promotion got away from Bielsa at the first time of asking, there was the slight fear at Elland Road that they might have missed the boat; that they had missed the best chance he would give them. Then Leeds travelled to Ashton Gate on the first weekend of the 2019–20 season and played Bristol City off the pitch, producing a performance which was familiar in its structure but incredibly fresh. The same has been true in the Premier League: Bielsaball, as everyone knows it, but no bland predictability. Three years with him as manager have been an era in themselves, a period which makes Leeds' grim decline seem evermore distant and almost immaterial. No one enjoyed their stint in the EFL but the sensation of promotion under Bielsa was more intense because of it; the sensation of the high ramped up by the severity of the lows.

His players remember how it was before. Liam Cooper, who joined Leeds four years before Bielsa, experienced times when they were too accustomed to, or familiar with, under-achievement. 'As a club, as an organisation, mediocre was how it was,' Cooper said.[5] 'The fanbase almost expected it.' Luke Ayling watched Bielsa 'raise the bar', not just at Elland Road but across the Championship too. 'When I speak to people who are still playing, I feel like they're changing what they do by seeing this at a distance,' Ayling said. 'They haven't got [Bielsa] barking at them but they listen to what me and others say about him and they're interested. I'd imagine other players are looking at him, and a lot of gaffers too.'[6] The squad were desperate for him to stay after their play-off defeat in 2019. The players met for a pint after that game and although they joked about how much easier life could be (one had a list of food he planned to eat in the close season, starting with fish and chips), they clung to the hope that Bielsa would extend his deal. But if he didn't, they would have been grateful for the experience of working with him anyway. 'All of us would still have been in a much better place,' Cooper said. 'But to think of him not managing this team or us training as hard as we do . . . it's very hard to imagine. You go into games and you're flying. It's amazing.'

Leeds consisted of all the facets Bielsa needed. They were a club where he felt at home and a club with real but sensible ambition, a project rather than an underfunded fantasy. They had a squad who realised straight away that Bielsa stepping into the Championship was an elite coach dropping to a level he should not be stooping to. They were excited by him and, therefore, less likely to grow tired of him. And in the stands, he had supporters with an intrinsic desire to learn about him, understand him and fall for him. He was what they had been looking for. And in many ways, the reverse was also true. Bielsa educated the public and restored their equilibrium, without asking them to sacrifice their passion. It was possible to be patient, understanding and still inspired. Ricardo Lunari had it right. In the end you would love Bielsa or you would hate him. 'But,' Lunari told me, 'what he never does is leave you feeling indifferent.'

16.

BIELSA

Most of the information you glean about Marcelo Bielsa comes from other people; the people who know him or the people who have seen the machine whirring at close range. You get a glimpse into his mind whenever he speaks but, consciously or subconsciously, a barrier protects most of what is in it. It is twenty-five years since he granted a detailed one-on-one interview and almost everything he says publicly is managed within the structure of a press conference. Some in Argentina believe he might have helped with a book published about him in 2004, *Lo Suficientemente Loco* (Crazy Enough), but no one is sure. A short time before he took over at Leeds United, and while he was out of work, the *Guardian* explored the possibility of paying him to write tactical columns about the 2018 World Cup but the approach from Leeds turned his attention elsewhere. One of the reasons why Bielsa is so intriguing is because you never quite see the entire tapestry. And because Bielsa does his best not to show it.

Over months and years you piece together as much of the puzzle as possible using insight from elsewhere. Bit by bit, his players create a mental image of training and the aspects of football around which Bielsa's tactics revolve: third-man runs, the compression of space out of possession, and ceaseless movement at the centre of everything. The rudimentary English used by him on the touchline (suddenly audible in empty stadiums after

Covid-19 struck) stresses the importance of energy and repetition: 'move!', 'again!' and deep cries of 'no!' when patterns of play which should be second nature disintegrate. Bit by bit, his players create a mental image of the pressure of coping with the extremities of Bielsa's regime.

In early 2021 I spoke with Robbie Gotts, an academy midfielder whom Leeds had sent on loan to Salford City in League Two. Gotts is a naturally powerful runner but small in size and slight to look at. He was ten-and-a-half stone when Bielsa became head coach and received instructions to bring his weight closer to nine stone (a precise drop from 65kg to 61kg). His only way of doing it was to cut out all snacks, be militant with his diet and avoid eating anything after his evening meal. His assumption was that a lower intake and a body with barely an ounce of fat on it would impact on his energy levels, leaving the tank emptier than it should have been. Yet in no time, Bielsa's squad were fitter and running further than they had been before, blessed with improved stamina. It was almost counter-intuitive.

'The biggest thing I got from it all was learning how to push your body when you think you've got nothing left,' Gotts said. 'You're exhausted and you feel like you're done but he taught you how to find that bit extra, the bit you didn't believe was there. It was amazing. A lot of that's in your head, or so it seemed to me. So while I definitely got physically fitter, I got mentally fitter too. It made me push on.'[1]

Gotts and others would be sent to the exercise bikes if they failed to hit their target weight in the morning but what started as a steep physical challenge became an accepted part of the routine. Bielsa would pull up someone like Kalvin Phillips for being the equivalent of a bottle of water too heavy. Then, in his next breath, he would tell Phillips that he would happily let him marry his daughters. Patrick Bamford liked to joke that Phillips was 'teacher's pet' at Thorp Arch, the player Bielsa appeared most fond of.[2]

Gotts' observations brought to mind Fabian Costello, the former Newell's Old Boys youth-team striker who had spoken to me about Bielsa three months earlier. Connecting their stories made you realise that Bielsa had been pushing the limits in the same way for decades. When Bielsa appeared one morning to tell the Newell's team Costello was part of that he would be coaching them in the season ahead, the boys were sceptical. In that era, the early 1980s, the archetypal coach in Argentina was advanced in years, as close to the age of your grandfather as your father. They looked at Bielsa, in his late twenties, with dubious eyes. They wondered if he was up to it. Bielsa had no profile to speak of at Newell's. He had played a handful of times for their first team but his career was fleeting and in order to find out a little about him, Costello contacted his godfather, Alberto Carrasco, who had been a teammate of Bielsa's briefly. Carrasco described Bielsa as 'strict and responsible' and something of a thinker.[3] Even so, the kids took some convincing.

From day one, Bielsa was divergent. As other Newell's youth teams kicked balls around casually, he introduced his own to the ideas that were in his head. None of his boys had heard of lactic acid but he taught them about the effect of it and sent them on long, sapping runs in the heat, improving their fitness and showing them how muscles fatigued and then recovered. He put them through hard warm-ups before each game, explaining that by building up lactic acid and flushing it out of their bodies, they would feel stronger when the match got going. 'Lactic acid, blah, blah, blah,' Costello said. 'You hear it but it doesn't make sense. None of us could see what he meant – until the match started. Then you felt strong, you felt good and you felt like you could run so much further. So you see, he knows. And now, so do you.'

Bielsa set up sessions called 'handball perfection' to work on his players' positioning (the rationale being that the ease of passing the ball by hand meant the boys did not need to worry about or concentrate on controlling it) and he would stick broomsticks in the ground as a primitive form of mannequins, intended to help his squad understand tactics and rotation. Other kids looked on and laughed at first, delighted to be avoiding his arduous sessions. Bielsa cut a bizarre figure, attacking poles with a hammer dug out the back of his old Citroën, but he told his own players to stick to the programme, irrespective of whether it felt as if everyone else was having more fun. Follow my instructions, he promised, and we'll finish top of the league this season. And they did.

Costello is in no doubt that Bielsa was unusual if not unique. Every day with him was an education, a brush with a new brand of coaching. From time-to-time people ask me what I would try to elicit from Bielsa if he ever agreed to a one-on-one interview (which he hasn't and he won't). It's a good question. Bielsa has a hell of an autobiography in him if he ever chooses to compile it. He possesses the definitive story. But in a one-off interview, there is a risk of disappearing down a rabbit hole. By focusing on everything you could only ever scratch the surface. This is a man who has coached in Argentina, Mexico, Chile, Spain, France, Italy (in a manner of speaking) and England. He has had twenty-one years in club football and ten in international management, without getting into his short career as a central defender or his days growing up in Rosario. Where to start and where to finish? How much time would you need?

Bielsa's younger years interested me more than anything else. Those were what shaped him and brought him into the sport. The Bielsas were an academic family, some of whom pursued professions like politics and architecture. At the point where the coronavirus started spreading in early 2020, Bielsa's brother, Rafael, had just been appointed as the Argentine government's ambassador to Chile. Why did Bielsa shun those career paths? Why did he not gravitate more towards the academic world? And when it came to football, how did he generate his ideas? The understanding of lactic acid, the games of 'handball perfection', the broomsticks in the pitch – where did it all come from so long before the explosion of performance analysis and statistical data? Why, as Costello says, did Bielsa appear to be so different?

These were the questions I wanted Bielsa to pick through. These were the questions I thought would get closest to explaining his evolution as a coach. So in February 2021, I wrote to him and asked them. And at the end of his press conference before Leeds' game against Sheffield United at the start of April, he answered.

*

Earlier that day, Bielsa had been reading a newspaper article about the coaching career of Raúl, the Real Madrid icon and one of the faces of European football in the 1990s and 2000s. Like so many players, Raúl was reinventing himself as a manager and had been given the responsibility of handling Real's Under-19s. Bielsa was interested in him generally but some of Raúl's comments in the piece struck a relevant chord with him. How, Raúl asked, do you go about training players to the nth degree without stripping them of their personality and imagination? How do you nurture highly tuned athletes without going too far and creating robots? How does a manager hit the sweet spot?

Bielsa admitted to thinking about this a lot. He was a stickler for drill work and the intricacy of patterns and technique and it would be wrong to pretend otherwise but one of the traits of a good professional footballer was emotion or instinct. There was something to be said, Bielsa argued, for kids playing and playing until their feet were sore, or playing until it got dark and their parents came looking for them. There was something to be said for football being magical and fun, rather than a world of data and precision. In Rosario, where he grew up, the sport was king. It was all that he and his friends were bothered about. That was where it began for Bielsa, the part of his life which sucked him in and pulled him away from the professional paths his family tended to follow. This is how he remembered his childhood:

> The origin of something is always very difficult to single out but the evidence for me that football was a passion was very clear, throughout my childhood and teenage years. Like all the kids and teenagers, I had this link to football around my studies. When I had free time, all of it was dedicated to playing. In my city and my country, to play football during that time was one of the best things a child could do. It became the only thing to do. There was no recreational activity that could compete with football.
>
> In order to have a career in something other than football – to be able to develop something political – my ability was not the necessary one. I was more interested in myself than the rest of the people. That's to say, I didn't have enough intelligence to try and be a university student nor the generosity you require to help out other people. Public jobs demand this.

Bielsa got a taste of a career as a footballer but only briefly and he was retired by his mid-twenties. It was said that injury contributed to that decision but Bielsa insisted the reality was more prosaic: as a player, he did not have enough talent. Inherently, his ability was insufficient. He was in that huge group of men who hoped the door might open for them but lacked the critical percentage needed to sustain themselves at a high level. As he talked about it, he sounded philosophical. The dream was gone but fewer chances to play the game meant more time to think about it, study it and decode it. If, as he said, he lacked the intelligence to slog through a university degree, pondering the ins and outs of football was no effort at all. He could dwell on it indefinitely. That was the only way in which Bielsa saw himself as singular. When it came to his methods, he did not want anyone to class him as special, let alone unique. But his levels of concentration? They were extreme:

No, no, I never felt any different to the others. The only difference would be that I had a very marked love for the game. I could spend more time than the average person thinking about football, practising football, talking about football. And even if I'm against obsessiveness because I think obsessions only cause harm – adding and subtracting everything – football never tires me.

When I tried to be a professional football player, I rapidly found out that it wasn't possible. I didn't have sufficient ability to do this. And as I couldn't shine by playing, I started to think about football. I tried to interpret it, to distinguish and understand the secrets of the game. I dedicated time to studying it and I put in many years of concrete practice. I also had the luck to be able to spend ten years alongside the master who was Jorge Griffa.

Griffa, now 86, was Bielsa's guiding light, a legendary figure at Newell's Old Boys and the brains behind the extensive scheme of youth recruitment created by the club in the 1980s. Bielsa assisted him in scouting kids and they travelled all over Argentina together, prior to Bielsa becoming manager of Newell's in 1990. Griffa is the person whom Bielsa discusses with most reverence, the person to whom he appears to owe the greatest debt. When Bielsa donated around £2m to help improve Newell's training facilities in 2018, he insisted that the new building be named after Griffa. Griffa taught Bielsa to understand footballers: not only about the ways in which they succeeded or failed but the reasons why they succeeded or failed:

[Griffa] gave me an unconditional love for the game, an interest in the material responses of players and a keen eye for everything that was happening in the game. And also a desire to talk about football by commenting profoundly on it. He saw what was happening in whichever moment he watched football – in a training session, in a trial for a player or in an international game on the television. I had an extraordinary opportunity with him. I was alongside Griffa throughout ten years, accompanying him in the observation of ten thousand players. These were ten thousand young players who arrived at Newell's with the hope of making it. To see how he chose them was to learn about football players. Of course, a coach should have this gift – to know about players – but even if that seems like something very easy, you have to know who plays well and who doesn't. And then you have to know why they play well and why they don't. You can only learn this through ten thousand examples alongside a master. That was how it happened to me. Those who involve themselves in an activity more than the resources they have should allow, it is only possible through the opportunities they have. I had the opportunity to listen to someone wise ten thousand times about football. The only thing I added to this was having the patience and the time to take this on board, to take in all of those messages. Jorge Griffa was able to create this club in the moment when Argentinian football was at its best.

Before he worked hand-in-hand with Griffa, Bielsa's brain was already ticking over. He thought a lot about the tactical structure of football but he was just as interested in the way a player's body worked. Were there advantages to be gained from training differently or applying new thinking to fitness routines? Could something like lactic acid be good for an athlete if it was managed in the right way? And when it came to tactics, could more comprehensive systems allow a team to excel? Could repetition and structural discipline take a team to a different level (as it did with the youth side Costello featured in)? Bielsa did not say exactly where these thoughts came from or if he picked them up from elsewhere, but Costello was adamant about one thing: in Argentina at the time, none of the boys had ever been told to do what Bielsa asked of them. It felt fresh and innovative, even if Bielsa does not consider himself a trendsetter:

I focused on different things while I was learning about the game. I was particularly interested in the physiology of exercise. I was interested in seeing how the body could physically evolve in a sporting sense. In football, players produce spontaneous reactions which come from them individually. The more talent they have, the more they will be able to produce these moments. That's the ideal thing, of course – that a player comes across a problem and solves it in his own way. The best players manage to do this. Then there's an intermediate level of players who have very good technical resources but can't produce the responses generated by instinct so easily. They have the chance to learn how to resolve a lot of actions in a game. This is a very difficult task because you have to try and avoid players memorising things. The memory has a limit but a game has unlimited scenarios. If a player tries to memorise everything, he would take on board a lot less than is required. It's not good. This is the process of forming these intermediate players. The best players, they don't need it. And the worst ones, even with this help they won't be able to convert themselves into professional players. It's that middle class of players who permit a coach to intervene with them.

Today I was reading an article about the development of Raúl's coaching career. He was talking about this exact same thing: avoiding impeding a player from using all his resources and helping him to learn how to use them without creating an automated player. This is a great challenge for football at the moment. It's not that there is less talent available but in my opinion the talent is less stimulated. Before, you would play football for ten hours between the ages of eight and fifteen. Now we don't do this. So the methods I'm talking about here carry a significant risk. The risk is that you roboticise the players.

With that and a little nod of his head, Bielsa was gone; up out of his seat and back to his office, the nerve centre of Thorp Arch which Leeds kitted out with a kitchenette and enough room to sleep if he wanted to. A shelving unit along one wall is packed with an eclectic mix of objects: ornaments, awards, fanzines, shoe boxes, a basketball and a water bottle from the touchline at Arsenal. Nobody sees what happens there, save for the tight circle of staff who buzz in and out whenever he calls for them. He likes the sanctuary and the privacy, and the freedom to graft in peace. Some of his comments gave the impression of a man who was occupied by inner struggles. There were aspects of modern football which grated on him, clearly, yet at 65 the sport appeared to be energising him more than ever. He was a godfather of highly technical coaching yet the threat of declining individuality concerned him. He earned handsomely from management yet seemed to spend very little of his money on himself. Little windows into his life exposed part of the picture but you were always left wondering and guessing. Bielsa seemed to be treading the fine line between genius and insanity and somehow keeping his balance; a madman until his ideas triumphed.

*

What, then, does football do for him? What is the ultimate pay-off? In seeking an answer, I could only think back to remarks he made on the eve of his first competitive game at Leeds. 'Even if people think we work for money, football is a search for strong emotions,' Bielsa said. 'What you remember about football is emotion and sometimes we learn this reality late. To work for emotion, you want money first. But after you have money, emotion is much more important.' Emotion was what he sought when he packed his cases and flew out of Buenos Aires for England. The job at Elland Road would make a rich man richer but the search was for beauty. And in Leeds, he found it.

ACKNOWLEDGEMENTS

This is not the first Leeds United book I've written. The last one, published in 2008, was supposed to mark the end of the circus at Elland Road, a line in the sand after a spate of turmoil. Since then, as crisis followed crisis and the club defied already-low standards of performance and competence, I got used to being told that I should write about Leeds again, as an author rather than a journalist. Write another book.

The problem was the timeline had no natural end. Or not until 2018 when Marcelo Bielsa began delivering what no one else seemed capable of. There was chapter after chapter in Leeds' wilderness years but nothing close to deliverance or redemption. Finally, Bielsa was a story. Bielsa was a phenomenon.

Even so, I took some persuading when Shyam Kumar and The Orion Publishing Group approached me with an offer to publish the tale of Bielsa at Elland Road. You know how it is: work, kids and not much spare time. In footballing terms, my heart said yes but my head said no so I'm very grateful to Shyam for talking me round with his ideas, his flexibility and his confidence that we could make the book work. Tom Noble, Orion's campaigns director, was also involved in positive discussions at the start and I should thank my colleague at *The Athletic*, Adam Jones, for putting me in touch with Shyam in the first place. It was that introduction which got us talking.

The Athletic's editor-in-chief Alex Kay-Jelski and general manager Aki Mandhar were both extremely supportive of the project and for that I owe them my thanks. They have both been extremely supportive in other ways too (as has Charlie Scott, my ever-patient editor and point of contact each morning). I was lucky that the freedom and scope we are given at *The Athletic* had already allowed me to delve properly into Bielsa's background and his work at Leeds. I know I'm not the only person who feels very fortunate to have had the chance to join the company when it launched in the UK in 2019.

I found very quickly that Shyam had unlimited patience and an unflappable character, even when I emailed him to say that I'd been told to prepare for surgery on a brain tumour. It's been a pleasure to work with him and his help has been constant. Alex Layt, Orion's publicity manager, and Storytec's Kat Rose-Martin were also great at dealing with the prospect of me disappearing for weeks of treatment and recuperation. I'm much obliged to Orion's audio manager, Paul Stark, too. We'd started so we were going to finish, one way or the other. And we have.

A big thank you also goes to Victor Orta for providing the foreword for this book and to Leeds' head of communications, James Mooney, for making it happen. I wanted Victor's voice at the very start of the story because to all intents and purposes, Bielsa was his choice. Bielsa was his idea and the gamble he recommended, in a summer where Leeds were at another crossroads. I find it hard to imagine that in the next twenty years, anyone at the club will make a call quite like it. And I know for a fact that Leeds will never have a head coach quite like Bielsa.

To Bielsa, I'm indebted for the wealth of stories there are to tell about him (even if he would not have intended that all of them be told). One of the unique things about him is the sheer number of people he fascinates. In his time at Leeds I've made friends with people I'm yet to meet in person, purely on the basis that they are so interested in him. Jamie Ralph, a long-time supporter of Newell's Old Boys, has been a priceless resource, filling in blanks about Bielsa's coaching career in Argentina and putting me in touch with people who played for Bielsa like Ricardo Lunari and Fabian Costello. I keep joking with Jamie about the number of pints I owe him. By the time Covid-19 calms down, I'll need to buy him a brewery.

The same appreciation goes to the journalists I work with week-by-week: Adam Pope, Jonny Buchan, Graham Smyth, Joe Urqhuart, Beren Cross. All of them have become very good friends in what can be quite a lonely industry if you're not careful.

This book, though, is for my wife Fiona and our girls, Isla and Niamh, even though none of them is actually interested in football (Niamh, to her credit, likes to sing about Bielsa so perhaps there's hope). You cannot be a full-time football writer and devote enough time to your family. The two things are basically incompatible. But we make it work somehow and year after year I build up a debt which I'll repay eventually. Like people say to me, one day I'll need to grow up and get a real job.

SOURCES

Introduction

1 Joël Domenighetti, 'Marcelo Bielsa-Lille, explication ce vendredi aux prud'hommes', *L'Équipe*, 12 February 2021.
2 'A New World', *Take Us Home: Leeds United*, Season 2, Episode 2, Amazon Prime, 2020.

Chapter 1 – September

1 Phil Hay, 'Marcelo Bielsa: the inside story of a Leeds love affair that made dreams come true', *The Athletic*, 17 July 2020.
2 David Trueba, 'Guardiola El hijo del "paleta"', *El País*, 22 August 2010.
3 Phil Hay, 'Promotion clearly not "a formality" for Leeds – even if they remain unscathed', *The Athletic*, 21 June 2020.
4 'Luke Ayling shapes up in order to help Leeds United avoid repeat show at Millwall', *Yorkshire Evening Post*, 12 September 2018.
5 Phil Hay, '"Players have to care about data" – how Leeds use real-time stats in training', *The Athletic*, 4 September 2020.

Chapter 2 – The Appointment

1 Leeds United matchday programme, 22 July 2020, p.11.
2 Phil Hay, 'Victor Orta interview: Bielsa's contract, Leeds' recruitment . . . and Whitby', *The Athletic*, 5 August 2020.
3 Phil Hay, 'Exclusive Massimo Cellino interview', part two, *Yorkshire Evening Post*, 12 April 2014.
4 'Leeds United takeover completed', Leeds United.com. 13 May 2017.
5 Phil Hay, 'What links Bielsa and Bale? And why is Simeone unlikely to move to the Premier League? Step inside the world of football linguistics', *The Athletic*, 31 October 2019.

AND IT WAS BEAUTIFUL

6   *Que Golazo* podcast, 8 January 2021.
7   Murad Ahmed, 'Leeds owner hopes Premier League return will turn it into a £1bn club', *Financial Times*, 11 September 2020.
8   Phil Hay, 'The cult of Marcelo Bielsa and Leeds United – a romantic match made in heaven', *Yorkshire Evening Post*, 15 June 2018.

Chapter 3 – October

1   Daniele Longo, 'L'agente Bara a CM: "I retroscena su Morata alla Juve, la verità su Brozovic e l'interesse di Napoli e Roma per Nacho: vi dico tutto"', Calciomercato.com, 27 September 2020.
2   Dermot Corrigan, 'Bielsa plays down Llorente row', ESPN, 4 October 2012.
3   Leeds CEO Angus Kinnear on 'Take Us Home', *The Tifo Football Podcast*, 29 September 2020.
4   Phil Hay, Adam Crafton et al., 'Inside a failed deal: What now for Leeds and the confident, coveted Cuisance?', *The Athletic*, 1 October 2020.
5   Josep Guardiola, 'Sentirlo', *El País*, 2 March 2007.
6   Phil Hay and Sam Lee, 'Guardiola and Bielsa, the love story', *The Athletic*, 2 October 2020.
7   Sid Lowe, 'Athletic Bilbao make a splash to peg back Barcelona in thriller', *Guardian*, 7 November 2011.
8   Phil Hay, '"Players have to care about data" – how Leeds use real-time stats in training', *The Athletic*, 4 September 2020.
9   'Midfielder Phillips is lynchpin [sic] of the Bielsa revolution', *Yorkshire Evening Post*, 17 August 2018.
10 Phil Hay, 'Marcelo Bielsa: the inside story of a Leeds love affair that made dreams come true', *The Athletic*, 17 July 2020.
11 Francisco Fernández Funes, 'Andrea Radrizzani, el patrón de Bielsa en Leeds: "Todo lo que dice Marcelo tiene sentido"', *La Nacion*, 16 October 2020.

Chapter 4 – The Revolution

1   Verónica Gómez, 'Urban Surrealism by Martin Ron', *Hedonist Magazine*, 26 February 2015.
2   Phil Hay, '"A football revolution" – Bielsa is making Leeds compulsive viewing in Argentina', *The Athletic*, 11 August 2020.
3   Piotr Zelazny, 'Mateusz Klich: Instagram piłkarski to dziś faktycznie targowisko próżności i wybieg mody', *Newonce Sport*, 20 February 2020.

4   Phil Hay, 'In Bielsa, Leeds have a coach tailor-made for the rarest of pro-motion shootouts', *The Athletic*, 22 April 2020.

5   *The Official Leeds United Podcast*, 31 December 2020.

6   'Bueno, Bueno, Bueno', *FourFourTwo*, Issue 299, May 2019.

7   Cristian Grosso, 'Basile: Bielsa es lo más marketinero que he visto en mi vida', *La Nación*, 23 August 2018.

8   Fox Sports, 11 November 2017.

9   Phil Hay, '"A football revolution"', 11 August 2020.

10 'Su reino unido', *El Ciudadano*, p.1, 18 July 2020.

11 Pol Ballus, 'Marcelo Bielsa and Pep Guardiola: rivals, boffins and blood brothers', *The Times*, 3 October 2020.

Chapter 5 – November

1   David Hytner, 'Perfectionist Marcelo Bielsa brings radical approach to Leeds United', *Guardian*, 4 August 2018.

2   Sam Wallace, 'Man Utd and Liverpool driving "Project Big Picture" – football's biggest shake-up in a generation', *Daily Telegraph*, 11 October 2020.

3   Philip Buckingham, Matt Slater et al., 'Explained: "Project Big Picture is dead" – so what happens now?' *The Athletic*, 14 October 2020.

4   Phil Hay, '"When Plan A is sat here, ready to sign, how can you have a Plan B?" Victor Orta on life as Leeds' director of football', *The Athletic*, 4 August 2019.

5   Phil Hay, 'Alioski in talks over new Leeds deal and now he's heading to the Euros', *The Athletic*, 21 November 2020.

6   'Sem ver "rosto", Marcelo Bielsa pede para Leeds atacar sempre, não importa o adversário, revela Raphinha', ESPN Brazil, 5 December 2020.

7   Rafael Reis, 'Vivi racismo em todos os países onde joguei, diz brasileiro líder na França', UOL, 23 September 2020.

8   Joe Mewis, 'Marcelo Bielsa describes the typically meticulous 14-point training plan he uses to get his strikers scoring', *LeedsLive*, 2 October 2018.

9   Jorge Valdano, 'Adiós a Diego y adiós a Maradona', *El País*, 25 November 2020.

10 Michael Cox 'The Bielsa paradox: How can someone so influential also be so unique?', *The Athletic*, 24 November 2020.

Chapter 6 – The Demise

1 Brian Cathcart, 'Money to burn', *Guardian*, 7 March 2004.
2 Peter Ridsdale, *United We Fall*, Pan Macmillan, 2008, p. 229.
3 Phil Hay, 'The doomed and the damned? Leeds and Wolves are clubs transformed', *The Athletic*, 19 October 2020.
4 Rob Preece, 'Ex-Leeds United director Simon Morris jailed over business blackmail plot', *Yorkshire Post*, 25 October 2011.
5 Phil Hay, 'The Leeds hero who became Judas – why did Alan Smith move to Manchester United?', *The Athletic*, 12 May 2020.
6 'Stars fight for cash', *The Mirror*, 20 May 2007.
7 Nick Harris, 'Directors sell Elland Road and clear own liabilities', *Independent*, 13 November 2004.
8 David Anderson, 'Bates: "If you want to go up then pay up"', *Mirror*, 6 August 2005.
9 Phil Hay, 'How Dennis Wise turned tide at Elland Road', *Yorkshire Evening Post*, 26 October 2007.
10 Simon Yaffe, 'Matt Kilgallon: "Dennis Wise didn't take a shine to anyone at Leeds United"', *Planet Football*, 27 May 2020.
11 Phil Hay, 'Derry's verdict on Wise', *Yorkshire Evening Post*, 23 January 2008.
12 David Conn, 'Why did Leeds sell to Ken Bates, who claims he has no money to invest?', *Guardian*, 3 May 2011.
13 Rob Conlon, 'Simon Grayson: "Ken Bates didn't have ambition to get Leeds Utd promoted"', *Planet Football*, 9 January 2019.
14 Neil Warnock, *The Gaffer: The Trials and Tribulations of a Football Manager*, Hachette UK, 2013, p. 350.
15 Amitai Winehouse, 'The madman who made Leeds a laughing stock', *Daily Mail*, 21 March 2019.
16 'Do the cleaning, Cellino told Leeds United No2 Nigel Gibbs – now he wins £330k damages', *Yorkshire Post*, 4 May 2016.
17 '"It's me that failed, it's me that made bad decisions" – Steve Morison on his contentious time at Leeds', *The Athletic*, 9 September 2019.
18 Phil Hay, 'When Massimo Cellino tried to ban Sky from Elland Road', *The Athletic*, 6 November 2020.
19 Phil Hay, 'After 15 managers and five owners at Leeds – is football's biggest comeback on?' *The Athletic*, 14 July 2020.
20 'I'm here to work for the good of the Whites – Carbone', *Yorkshire Evening Post*, 17 May 2014.
21 'Leeds United in Myanmar: Andrea Radrizzani "never reconsidered" controversial trip', *BBC Sport*, 10 May 2018.

SOURCES

Chapter 7 – December

1 'Fans return to football: Chelsea Supporters Trust angry over ticket prices', BBC Sport, 28 November 2020.
2 Leeds United matchday programme, 19 October 2020.
3 "'I'm not dwelling on it" – Lampard on history with Bielsa and renewing an old rivalry', Chelsea official website, 4 December 2020.
4 Robin Bairner, '"Scandalous" that Bielsa has been nominated for The Best FIFA Coach award – Villas-Boas', Goal.com, 27 November 2020.
5 Phil Hay, 'Explaining Leeds' weakness at corners and the risk Bielsa feels is worth taking', *The Athletic*, 8 December 2020.
6 Leeds United v Newcastle United, Amazon Prime, 16 December 2020.
7 Kalvin Phillips, 'My game in my words', *The Athletic*, 21 July 2020.
8 Phil Hay, 'How Hernández helped to rescue the club he loves – and why he'll surely play for them one day', *The Athletic*, 5 September 2019.
9 Phil Hay, 'Hernández: "Leeds is home now. To play in the Premier League is a present at 35"', *The Athletic*, 17 September 2020.
10 Mark Ogden, 'Sir Alex Ferguson reveals baying mob outside Leeds hotel ahead of Manchester United's Carling Cup tie was like a scene from Zulu', *Daily Telegraph*, 23 September 2011.
11 Stuart James, 'Manchester United's Sir Alex Ferguson admits to "disappointing year"', *Guardian*, 15 March 2012
12 Manchester United v Leeds United, BBC Sport, 20 December 2020.
13 *The Official Leeds Utd Podcast*, 24 December 2020.

Chapter 8 – Murderball

1 Phil Hay, '"As hard as it is, I miss it": Bielsa drill that makes Championship look gentle', *The Athletic*, 9 June 2020.
2 *Studs Up* podcast, 26 February 2021.
3 Phil Hay, '"He broke the rules inside our heads": Bielsa the "Professor" at Newell's', *The Athletic*, 10 December 2020.
4 *Take Us Home: Leeds United*. Season 2, Episode 1, Amazon Prime, September 2020.
5 'Kalvin Phillips analyses his game: "Every time I get the ball, I look for Pablo"', *The Athletic*, 21 July 2020.
6 Chris Taylor, 'Argentina build on Bielsa's total success', *Guardian*, 8 December 2001.
7 Phil Hay, 'Hernández: "Leeds is home now. To play in the Premier League is a present at 35"', *The Athletic*, 17 September 2020.

8   Ander Herrera, *The Big Interview* podcast with Graham Hunter, 14 May 2018.

9   Brian Homewood, 'Riquelme solves Maradona's biggest dilemma', Reuters, 11 March 2009.

Chapter 9 – January

1   FIFA.com, *2020 FIFA Global Transfer Market Report*, 18 January 2021, p. 30.

2   *Financial Times* Business of Football Summit, 18 February 2021.

3   Phil Hay and Jack Pitt-Brooke, 'Leeds' fresh £300k Elland Road pitch will allow Bielsa-ball to flourish', *The Athletic*, 22 January 2021.

4   Phil Hay, 'One door opens for Diego Llorente, but another slams in £18m signing's face', *The Athletic*, 26 January 2021.

5   Sky Sports, 31 January 2021.

Chapter 10 – Analysis

1   Phil Hay and Sam Lee, 'Guardiola and Bielsa, the love story', *The Athletic*, 2 October 2020.

2   'Full transcript of every word Marcelo Bielsa said in Leeds United spygate conference', *Yorkshire Evening Post*, 16 January 2019.

3   Phil Hay, 'Revealed: Don Revie's dossiers', *The Athletic*, 27 May 2020.

4   Phil Hay, 'Leeds want to resume matches but will lobby for promotion if they are called off', *The Athletic*, 1 May 2020.

5   Jason Burt, 'How Marcelo Bielsa's "Murderball" training sessions are turning hard-grafting Leeds United into European hopefuls', *Telegraph*, 2 November 2020.

6   Luke Ayling, post-match interview, YouTube, Leeds United Official, 8 February 2020.

7   Phil Hay, 'Ayling exclusive: "Look at standard of Championship. Bielsa's raised the bar"', *The Athletic*, 16 June 2020.

8   'We definitely have more momentum than Leeds right now … they couldn't pick a worse place to play Tuesday night.' Brentfordfc.com, 10 February 2020.

9   John Percy, 'Derby County "spied on" during training in countdown to trip to Leeds United', *Telegraph*, 10 January 2019.

10 Neil Goulding, 'Leeds Utd players see funny side of Spygate after they catch surveillance mission', *Mirror*, 19 January 2019.

11 'Spygate', *Take Us Home: Leeds United*, Season 1, Episode 3, Amazon Prime, 2019.

12 Phil Hay, 'Marcelo Bielsa reveals he personally paid Leeds United's hefty fine following Spygate', *Yorkshire Evening Post*, 3 May 2019.

13 Phil Hay and Ryan Conway, 'The Leeds–Derby Spygate story: a cultural war and tussle of football ethics', *The Athletic*, 17 March 2020.

14 RMC Sport, 5 February 2019.

15 The Phil Hay Show, *The Athletic* podcasts, 13 November 2020.

16 Stuart James, 'Bamford exclusive: "My style of play, the way I run means I've always had doubters"', *The Athletic*, 19 November 2020.

17 '"We cannot buy players and never sell players." Leeds United owner Radrizzani defends Vieira exit', *Yorkshire Evening Post*, 4 August 2018.

18 Kalvin Phillips, 'My game in my words', *The Athletic*, 21 July 2020.

19 Piłka Nożna, 'Mateusz Klich: W Utrechcie mnie chcieli', *Sportowe Fakty*, 19 February 2019.

20 Phil Hay, 'A late bloomer with "fast feet and a fast brain": Klich's path from Poland to becoming Bielsa's lynchpin [sic]', *The Athletic*, 5 February 2020.

21 Phil Hay, 'Liam Cooper exclusive: "Before Bielsa, we accepted being mediocre. The fanbase expected it. We won't let it go back to being like that"', *The Athletic*, 25 December 2019.

22 'Marseille accuse Bielsa of holding club to ransom', AFP, via Yahoo Sports, 9 August 2015.

23 Florian Plettenberg, 'So kurios wurde Koch überzeugt', *SPORT1*, 2 October 2020.

Chapter 11 – February

1 'Luke Ayling: You can't afford to go two goals down', Leeds United Official Website, 4 February 2021.

2 Phil Hay, 'Lampard's thighs, Pirlo's precision, scoring tips from Villa . . . but Harrison's mother is the biggest star of his career', *The Athletic*, 24 September 2019.

3 Tim Spiers, 'Growing list of hindrances leave Nuno's Wolves searching for identity', *The Athletic*, 13 January 2021.

4 Federico Cristofanelli, 'Viaje a la intimidad de Bielsa: la desconocida historia de amor con su esposa y el sostén emocional que le dan sus hijas para rendir como entrenador', Infobae.com, 1 March 2021.

5 CBS Sports, 20 February 2021.

Chapter 12 – Right-hand men

1 Phil Hay, 'Explained: Who are the men behind Bielsa?', *The Athletic*, 23 September 2019.

2   Richard Cawley, 'Millwall boss Harris: Leeds United's celebrations were a disgrace', *South London Press*, 17 September 2018.

3   Phil Hay, 'Marcelo Bielsa: the inside story of a Leeds love affair that made dreams come true', *The Athletic*, 17 July 2020.

4   Hernán Laurino, 'Diego Flores, de dirigir en la Liga Cordobesa a trabajar con Bielsa en el Leeds', *La Voz*, 26 September 2018.

5   Phil Hay, 'Explained: "Who are the men behind Bielsa?"', *The Athletic*, 23 September 2019.

6   Vincent Garcia, 'Jan Van Winckel: "Bielsa avait toujours raison"', *L'Équipe*, 14 March 2016.

7   Cynthia Serna, 'Marcos Abad: "Con Bielsa aprendes a no utilizar el 'no se puede'"', *Panenka*, 6 August 2020.

8   'Seizing the Day: Carlos Corberán', *The Coaches' Voice*, 2020, https://www.coachesvoice.com/carlos-corberan-huddersfield-leeds-marcelo-bielsa/

9   Phil Hay, 'Living the dream with Leeds United and Marcelo Bielsa', *Yorkshire Evening Post*, 28 March 2019.

10 Phil Hay, 'Romario Vieira: "I can't lie. If I'd known Ronaldo would leave, I'd have stayed"', *The Athletic*, 18 January 2021.

11 Stuart Rayner, 'Harry Toffolo enjoying a new education with Carlos Corberán', *Yorkshire Post*, 30 October 2020.

Chapter 13 – March

1   Phil Hay, 'Ayling exclusive: "Look at standard of Championship. Bielsa's raised the bar"', *The Athletic*, 16 June 2020.

2   West Bromwich Albion v Leeds United, Amazon Prime, 29 December 2020.

3   Phil Hay, 'Twenty years on from Istanbul: the night when football became murder for Leeds', *The Athletic*, 2 April 2020.

4   Stuart James, 'Bamford exclusive: My style of play, the way I run means I've always had doubters', *The Athletic*, 19 November 2020.

5   Oliver Holt, '"One coach said he was impressed by how hard I worked – since my dad was a billionaire!": Leeds striker Patrick Bamford, whose father is actually an architect from Newark, on fighting prejudice that he's too posh to be a proper footballer', *Mail On Sunday*, 13 February 2021.

Chapter 14 – The Hierarchy

1   Phil Hay, '"When Plan A is sat here, ready to sign, how can you have a Plan B?" Victor Orta on life as Leeds' director of football', *The Athletic*, 4 August 2019.

2 Phil Hay and Raphael Honigstein, 'Robin Koch's journey from flunking in gym class to joining Bielsa's Leeds', *The Athletic*, 25 November 2020.

3 'Leeds United chairman Andrea Radrizzani on Bielsa, transfers and the season ahead', *Yorkshire Evening Post*, 4 August 2018.

4 Mohamed Shamir Mohamed Osman, 'MP & Silva's Singapore office in provisional liquidation following London HQ's insolvency', *The Straits Times*, 29 December 2018.

5 *Take Us Home: Leeds United*. Season 1, Episode 1, Amazon Prime, August 2019.

6 Leeds United matchday programme.

7 Phil Hay, 'Explained: What 49ers investment means for Leeds and Radrizzani', *The Athletic*, 25 January 2021.

8 Phil Hay, 'Robbie Gotts: Eating less, running more, Bielsa's stats and blisters vs Arsenal', *The Athletic*, 15 March 2021.

9 Christoph Biermann, *Football Hackers: The Science and Art of a Football Revolution*, Blink Publishing, 2019, p. 45.

10 Phil Hay, 'Victor Orta interview: Bielsa's contract, Leeds' recruitment . . . and Whitby', *The Athletic*, 5 August 2020.

Chapter 15 – April/May

1 Phil Hay, 'Bielsa's new deals show he believes Dallas and the core of this squad can cut it in the Premier League', *The Athletic*, 15 September 2019.

2 Sky Sports, 20 April 2021.

3 Phil Hay, 'Leeds U23 coach Mark Jackson: 4am analysis and getting guard of honour from Bielsa's first team', *The Athletic*, 21 April 2021.

4 Phil Hay, '"I just want to play football": Will Huffer on his Leeds release and injury hell', *The Athletic*, 28 October 2020.

5 Phil Hay, 'Liam Cooper exclusive: "Before Bielsa, we accepted being mediocre. The fanbase expected it. We won't let it go back to being like that"', *The Athletic*, 26 December 2019.

6 Phil Hay, 'Ayling exclusive: "Look at standard of Championship. Bielsa's raised the bar"', *The Athletic*, 17 June 2020.

Chapter 16 – Bielsa

1 Phil Hay, 'Robbie Gotts: Eating less, running more, Bielsa's stats and blisters vs Arsenal', *The Athletic*, 15 March 2001.

2 *The Official Leeds United Podcast*, 28 January 2021.

3 Phil Hay, '"He broke the rules inside our heads": Bielsa the "Professor" at Newell's', *The Athletic*, 10 December 2020.

PICTURE CREDITS

First Plate Section
1. Bielsa in a selfie at Elland Road, 7 March 2020. (Getty Images)
2. Bielsa on his bucket during the home game against Birmingham, 2018. (Getty Images)
3. Bielsa's famous touchline crouch, away at Forest. (Getty Images)
4. Bielsa hugging his assistant Pablo Quiroga. (Getty Images)
5. Scarves at Elland Road. (Getty Images)
6. Banner flown over Elland Road on Good Friday 2019. (Getty Images)
7. Cameras all around Bielsa at Brentford. (Getty Images)
8. Bielsa orders Leeds and Pontus Jansson to let Villa score. (Getty Images)
9. Bielsa and Lampard in the 2019 Championship play-offs. (Getty Images)
10. A dejected Stuart Dallas as Derby celebrate victory in the play-off semi-final. (Getty Images)
11. Andrea Radrizzani, Angus Kinnear and Victor Orta. (Getty Images)
12. A scramble for photos as Bielsa gets off the coach. (Getty Images)
13. Supporters massed around Bielsa outside the Elland Road West Stand. (Getty Images)
14. A rare yellow card for Bielsa against West Brom. (Getty Images)
15. Luke Ayling euphoric after an injury time win at Aston Villa. (Getty Images)
16. The scoreboard from Forest away, 2020. (Getty Images)
17. A signal box painted in Bielsa's honour in Leeds. (Getty Images)
18. Bielsa and staff celebrate the winning goal at Middlesbrough in February 2020. (Getty Images)
19. Luke Ayling on the volley against Huddersfield. (Getty Images)
20. Bielsa takes the knee before a 3-0 win against Fulham. (Getty Images)
21. Crowdies used to fill empty seats at Elland Road. (Getty Images)

22. Swansea away, 2020. (Getty Images)
23. Pablo Hernández sprints away after scoring the winner at Swansea. (Getty Images)

Second Plate Section
1. The city of Leeds marks promotion by naming a street after Bielsa. (Getty Images)
2. Bielsa with his players as Leeds lift the Championship title. (Getty Images)
3. A packed Elland Road on the night that Leeds are crowned champions. (Getty Images)
4. Fans gather to celebrate in the centre of Leeds. (Getty Images)
5. A mural of Bielsa. 'Marching on Together': 2020. (Getty Images/'Bielsa the Redeemer' mural designed & painted by Nicolas Dixon with assistance from Andy McVeigh)
6. A second mural of Bielsa on a building in Hyde Park, Leeds. (Getty Images/painted by @tankpetrol)
7. Bielsa on socially distanced media duties. (Getty Images)
8. Bielsa and Klopp. (Getty Images)
9. Casting a keen eye over Leeds under-23s. (Getty Images)
10. At home to Fulham. Empty stadiums due to Covid-19. (Getty Images)
11. Patrick Bamford completes a hat-trick at Aston Villa. (Getty Images)
12. Bielsa arriving at Crystal Palace. (Getty Images)
13. Raphinha finds the top corner against West Brom. (Getty Images)
14. A beaming Bielsa after Leeds' incredible win at Manchester City, April 2021. (Getty Images)
15. Leeds signal their opposition to the European Super League. (Getty Images)
16. An affectionate hug between Bielsa and Hernández. (Getty Images)